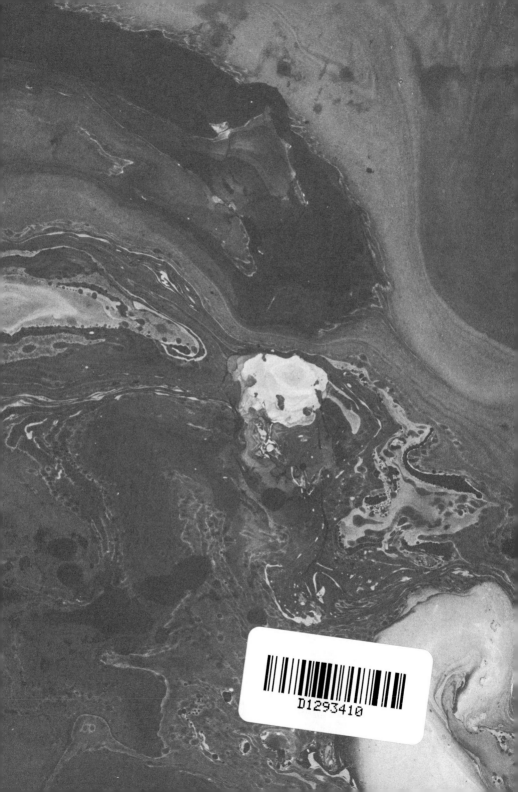

D1293410

ip 175⁰
(1982)

Bky - 8⁵⁰

The Edwardian Theatre

Drama and Theatre Studies

GENERAL EDITOR: KENNETH RICHARDS
ADVISORY EDITOR: HUGH HUNT

Also in this series:

Theatre in the Age of Kean
JOSEPH DONOHUE

British Theatre, 1950–70
ARNOLD P. HINCHLIFFE

The Scandinavian Theatre:
A Short History
F. J. AND L.-L. MARKER

Theatre in Ireland
MICHEÁL Ó HAODHA

Theatre in the Age of Garrick
CECIL PRICE

The Theatre of Goethe and Schiller
JOHN PRUDHOE

A Short History of
Scene Design in Great Britain
SYBIL ROSENFELD

J. C. TREWIN

The Edwardian Theatre

Basil Blackwell · Oxford

© Basil Blackwell 1976

All rights reserved. No part of this publication –
may be reproduced, stored in a retrieval system,
or transmitted, in any form or by any means,
electronic, mechanical, photocopying,
recording or otherwise, without the prior
permission of Basil Blackwell & Mott Limited

ISBN 0 631 14870 1

Set in Tiffany and Photon Baskerville
Printed and bound in Great Britain
by The Camelot Press Ltd, Southampton

Contents

Plates

For Wendy
Always

Acknowledgements

For permission to quote from various plays, poems, and books, I am most grateful to:

Mrs John Drinkwater for lines by John Drinkwater;

The Trustees of the Hardy Estate and Macmillan of London and Basingstoke for an extract from *The Dynasts*;

Mrs George Bambridge and Macmillan of London and Basingstoke for a passage from Rudyard Kipling;

The Society of Authors, as the literary representative of the Estate of John Masefield, for quotations from Dr Masefield's works;

Samuel French, Ltd., as the Trustees of the Pinero Estate, for quotations from Sir Arthur Pinero;

The Society of Authors, on behalf of the Bernard Shaw Estate, for the extracts from *Man and Superman* and *Misalliance*; and

M. B. Yeats, Miss Anne Yeats, and Macmillan of London and Basingstoke, for a passage from W. B. Yeats.

To Miss Jennifer Aylmer, MBE, Miss Jean Scott Rogers, and Mr George F. Nash, much gratitude for their help with the illustrations which come from the Theatre Museum (formerly the Enthoven Collection) at the Victoria and Albert Museum, and from the British Theatre Museum collection at Leighton House.

J.C.T.

Author's Note

This survey of the 'Edwardian' theatre takes in the last eighteen months of Queen Victoria's reign and, later, the early Georgian period to the outbreak of the first world war. The annexation, I think, is forgivable. To confine events within the limits of King Edward VII's reign would be arbitrary; the beginning of the century and the great convulsion of mid-1914 are more reasonable historic points. The stage at the first date was moving into the running conflict between the theatrical and the intellectual, romantic and anti-romantic; and after the second date it was—with so much else—never the same again.

We are apt to concentrate on Shaw at the Court and the efflorescence of the new drama. But the Edwardian period—call it that for convenience—was the last surge of the Theatre Theatrical. Some time ago one of the most consistent veteran playgoers I have met said that, with so much to see in the years before 1914, he did not fully realise the impact of Shaw, Granville Barker, and their fellow-innovators until the period was almost over. I have tried now to hold the balance (occasionally to report the effect on later audiences of some of the plays discussed). A few of my opinions, let me confess, have changed with experience.

Here, then, are the rooms of the house and their residents. I am grateful for much help: from my wife, a drama critic quietly wise; and from the works of Professor Allardyce Nicoll, Mr George Rowell, and others who are cited in the Notes. To Professor Arthur Colby Sprague (though he is not responsible for any of the opinions expressed) I owe a great debt, and to Miss Mary Richards the gift of an invaluable pack of programmes. Finally, all gratitude to the Editors of this series and to Mr J. K. D. Feather, of Basil Blackwell, for their kind tolerance.

J. C. T.

CHAPTER ONE

About the House

I

'I like a book with a plot in it,' says Johnny Tarleton, that Philistine young man of the period, to his father in Bernard Shaw's *Misalliance*.[1] 'You like a book with nothing in it but some idea that the chap that writes it keeps worrying like a cat chasing its own tail. I can stand a little of it, just as I can stand watching the cat for two minutes, say, when I've nothing better to do. But a man soon gets fed up with that sort of thing.'

Johnny, on 'a book with a plot', might well be speaking for the plays of the Theatre Theatrical—the institution, officially unrecognised, that in Britain during the first years of the twentieth century was embroiled with the Theatre of Ideas: opponents used the phrase ironically. (The cat is immaterial in spite of its echo from a play Johnny could reasonably have enjoyed, Sir Daniel Ridgeley saying in Pinero's *His House In Order*: 'A cat, *yes*. I like to watch a cat occasionally'.)[2] We look back now on the contention of the Edwardian stage, a war that only the most persuaded playgoer knew was being fought. *Misalliance*, a briskly capricious debate written in 1909 by a dramatist who considered plot to be the curse of the serious drama[3] (though he had no objection to an aeroplane with a

Polish acrobat crashing into a Hindhead greenhouse), was acted early in 1910, an hour when conflict was at its most resolute. At the time the play, in Charles Frohman's fated Repertory Theatre season, did not do much for its cause: it comes up better now.

Remembering the period, Ivor Brown said twenty years later[4] that Edwardian playgoing—he would not have included events at Hindhead—had become 'as homelike as a wet Sunday, with the family fractious. It was a glorious change for serious young people whose appetite for drab delights had been cockered up by the Shavian slamming of the romantic theatre.' But not everyone was so grave. Johnny Tarleton would have applauded the newly successful dramatist who said to a silly interviewer—herself a period piece—during the first act of *Lady Epping's Lawsuit* (1908), by Hubert Henry Davies:[5]

No one seems to think a play is serious unless it's about unpleasant people. However, if you'll give me time, I'll show you some most objectionable specimens of both sexes and prove that all our English principles are wrong. I don't want people to think I have no ideas.

The gentle actor-dramatist, H. V. Esmond, husband of the actress, Eva Moore, described in *Eliza Comes to Stay* (1913) the climax of an intellectual drama:[6]

The man says: 'Misery, misery—that's all our lives have led to!' and then his wife says: 'My God, and we've tried so hard!' And he says: 'We *have* tried, Mary,' and she says 'Is this the end?' and he says 'I wonder'—and the curtain comes down very slowly.

That, by no means Shavian, was the kind of scene loved then by the glummer intellectual; naturally the Theatre of Ideas was attacked at its most vulnerable point by writers whose own often excellent ideas were frankly commercial, and who felt that, unfairly, they were under-valued. Between them and the Royal Court Theatre, heart of the stage rebellion, lay what Mrs Browning, in another context, called 'the pale spectrum of the salt'.[7]

At the turn of the century the Theatre of Ideas had not concentrated its forces. Certainly the Theatre Theatrical continued to rule the London stage and its provincial dependencies; a theatre 'resplendent and majestic and enlarged' (the line is from Henry Arthur Jones's sole and desperate venture in the verse drama, *The Tempter*, 1893).[8] In London it was still the actor-managers' high holiday, the meridian of paternalism. Expert actors, generous managers, they gave to their public in all forms of theatre, from the tragical-historical to the plummiest musical comedy, precisely what they felt the hour required: Herbert Beerbohm Tree (knighted 1909) in the splendour of Her [His] Majesty's; George Alexander (knighted 1911) in the courtesy and decorum of the St James's ('the cathedral'[9]), replaced now by a dull office block with a few stage friezes on its balconies; Charles Wyndham (knighted 1902), who had gone from the Criterion to a new house named after him in Charing Cross Road; Cyril Maude at the Haymarket; Seymour Hicks, with Ellaline Terriss, at the Vaudeville; soon Arthur Bourchier in his long career at the Garrick. Generally, playgoers knew what they might expect at any given theatre, undeniably at Daly's and the Gaiety—both the old house and its successor across the road—where the coloured balloons of musical comedy soared into the Edwardian evening: now and then (usually a popular sensation) a Gaiety or Daly's actress would marry into the peerage. These houses were controlled by George Edwardes of whom another kind of manager, George Alexander, said admiringly to the critic William Archer:[10]

... Nothing but genius. He is a superb organiser and stage-manager. The class of work he does may not greatly interest you and me: but, such as it is, he does it to perfection. I assure you that management to George Edwardes is like croquet to [a] champion player . . . it is not merely a game of skill, but a science.

It was a time of unrepentant make-believe: in the straight theatre a world of upholstered classical drama; of the well-pressed, starched-cuff narratives that had replaced the derivations from Scribe and Sardou; and a brand of Balkan romanticism, with its principalities and powers, that Shaw had once derided in *Arms and the Man* (1894). 'Anthony Hope', unheeding, had created simultaneously the glorious tushery of Ruritania, and its play, adapted by Edward Rose, *The Prisoner of Zenda*, ran at the St James's two years later. It was still a theatre 3 with little that was self-consciously 'relevant', one that worked in primary colours and—in spite of Shaw as theorist and practitioner—preferred to lurk round the edges of a problem. It had not felt too uncomfortably the tingle of tactless polemics; excessive sentiments about politics or religion. Periodically, an icy north-easter, calculated to stir the Vikings' blood, drove down upon the stage, but the inner West End was muffled too closely to suffer much. Henrik Ibsen's ideas were taken more conveniently if they were warmed and filtered through the mind of Arthur Wing Pinero, that impressive, sharp-featured figure with the bald dome and the thatch of black eyebrow. It would be a few years yet before the 'congregation' attended at the Court Theatre in Sloane Square, outside the true West End line, for the so-called Thousand Performances. On this same stage, intermittently down the century, every window (a recurrent metaphor) would be opened. In 1900 few playgoers grumbled about draughts; windows were better shut, and they were kept so.

True, critically-minded people were talking of the theatre in 1900, beginning to treat it seriously. Not so long before, and in spite of Matthew Arnold on *The Silver King*, it had been a rogue-and-vagabond of the arts. Victorian classical players strove for it—early there was William Charles Macready; later, Henry Irving—but the contemporary drama was a poor thing until Pinero and Jones helped to redeem it: it could'be said of them as Tennyson did of Macready, 'Thine is it that our Drama did not die / Nor flicker down to brainless pantomime.'[11] In Edwardian London, with the efflorescence of Shaw and the Royal Court adventure of 1904–7, the theatre's prestige would grow. Yet, in considering our period between 1900 and 1914, we must avoid the stock response that the Barker-Vedrenne season was everything that mattered. Richly important though it was to the future of the stage, it had to be at the time a minority excitement; for the mass of Edwardians a fringe benefit. Drawing-room and play-room meant more than the study; the need was for a moderately decorous entertainment at a good address, and managers would shy at the unusual, boys fearing to be conspicuous.

Outside London, in spite of Archer's gloom in his talk with 4 Alexander[12]—

Hopeless vulgarity and blatant imbecility . . . A glance at the posters on the hoardings in any provincial town is enough to make one feel suicidal

—playgoers seemed as a rule to be perfectly content. Scores of touring companies (there could be as many as 250 on the road) took round current or recent West End work, carbon-copied, or else the kind of routine melodrama that so worried Archer. In various grades, Number One to Numbers Three or Four, they contrived to spread over much of the map. Thus, during the autumn and winter of 1899, a minor company in *The Sign of the Cross*, Wilson Barrett's ecstatic Christian-martyr drama, driven home with the force of an itinerant gospeller, had moved, often in one-night stands,[13] through such places as the Music Hall, Barnard Castle; the Corn Exchange, Kelso; the Public Hall, Lockerbie; the Public Hall, Alyth; the Town Halls at Tillicoultry, Aspatria, Egremont, and Millom: altogether seventy-two towns in a tour of seventeen weeks. This had to be in one of the lowest ranks of what southern Cornish people knew, in all varieties of plumage, as the 'pomping folk' ('pomping' meant any kind of acting, or loosely, flamboyant display). In those years there were dozens of unexpected and possibly fruitful dates: at random, the 'fit-ups' at the Temperance Hall, Tredegar; the Corn Hall, Fakenham; Masonic Hall, Spilsby; Druids' Hall, Redruth; and St Andrew's Hall, Stranraer; besides such theatres as the Lyceum, Govan; Hippodrome, Todmorden; and New, Bargoed. Sundays on the railway belonged to the actors, to the caravans of the stage on their golden journeys with the equivalent of printed hangings in enormous bales, certainly a good deal of chintz. Transiently, any platform at a complex junction was a theatre club. If the history of Crewe station were written, much of it could be theatrical. So, too, with Normanton junction. Whitford Kane[14] recalled a Sunday stop at Normanton in the winter of 1901. A friend took him from one train across to a siding where carriages labelled for the Bandmann-Palmer company were waiting; by the time this second train left he had a 'shop' with the plump little tragedienne who played everything from Hamlet to Lady Isabel in *East Lynne*, and who was accustomed to say to any watcher in the wings: 'I am a great actress, am I not?' Who, on such an occasion, could contradict?

Major companies on their course through the big cities, Birmingham, Manchester, Liverpool, Leeds, faithfully reflected the London stage. Many new theatres had been built during the last decades of the nineteenth century; but there were old ones as well. Most of them had a family resemblance; cavernous and tiered, formal in plush and velvet and gilt, with intrusive pillars, heavy framed mirrors, caryatids in profusion, an occasional palm, and pictorial drop-curtains of the battle of Trafalgar, the Grand Canal by moonlight, or this at the Grand, Derby:[15]

The centre medallion represents a scene from *A Midsummer Night's Dream*, and falling away from it is a very charming design in simulated lace curtains, while beneath the medallion are depicted the arms of the borough of Derby—*viz.* a buck couchant within park palings.

The Temperance and Masonic Halls and Corn Exchanges also had a family likeness. Sternly functional, ready for all comers from a shabby fit-up to a public meeting, they could do without brass and gilt, mirrors and plush. Victorian playgoers of one sort and another had known these places, opulent, fraying, or harsh, Theatre Royal or Druids' Hall, during a period artistically as dark as the 'coal-sack' in the Milky Way. The actors were not really at fault. Granted the day's slower tempo, they were fit, basically, to deal with most things, though the ensemble then was less important than the leading man or woman. Round these it would be everyone for himself; the companies were almost defiantly professional. Until the 1890s the plays they fought with, either new or in revival, could be disastrous; the lower levels did not change noticeably until after the first world war. In 1900 the repertory movement, revolving mirror of the stage, was unforeseen. Lesser provincial 'stock' rested on the battling melodramas one might still meet, in the remoter gaffs, as late as the 1920s: *Her Road to Ruin*, *A Woman's Shame*, *The Eve of Her Wedding*, *Guilty Gold*, *The Fatal Wedding*, and—who has heard of Mrs Kimberley?—*A Soldier's Honour*: 'Take his sword and kill me rather than bring disgrace upon my father.' At the foot of all were the strollers, the barnstormers, of the portable theatre. Sir Barry Jackson was delighted to remember the Edwardian company he found in a tent at Bidford-on-Avon. That night the hero said to the Judge with

6

all the intensity he could manage: 'Though you bring in a verdict of hinnocent against me, I shall go to my death guiltless.' The twist of words, said Jackson,[16] 'passed entirely unnoticed, for it was spoken with tremendous conviction. Allowing for that, it is possible to say almost anything to an audience.' Audiences were suitably receptive. The theatre had no competition; it would be some years before the Electric Palaces and the Cinedromes, the Bijou Picture Theatres and even the Bioscopic Tea Rooms, cast their animated shadow.

II

West End details from the late-Victorian ebb look odd today. Nearly twenty of the theatres (and music-halls) of 1900 have disappeared, and two others built before the 1914–18 war. Between 1900 and 1924 there were twelve new West End theatres: names as familiar afterwards as the Apollo, Aldwych, New (Albery), London Coliseum, and Queen's. Productions—the Royal Court group aside—hardly varied in character. Investigators, tracing an underground stream, throw in a colouring powder, fluorescein, to see where the colour emerges. In what we call for convenience the Edwardian stage we can find many of the crimsons and greens of 1900 still vivid in 1914.

Two exhibits, a pack of programmes (provincial and a few from London; 1898–1908), and the matter-of-fact notes of a suburban playgoer (1905), can speak broadly for the period, though, surprisingly, neither of these mentions Arthur Wing Pinero or Henry Arthur Jones.

Within the bulging marbled covers of a school exercise book[17] a Midland playgoer named Phillips, the only clue we have to him, pasted carefully the programmes he had collected through a decade. These are mainly provincial, though they begin in London during the late 1890s when theatre-minded visitors would move first, as a matter of duty, towards the massive, sombre pillars of the Lyceum at the bottom of Wellington Street, Strand. There Sir Henry Irving and Ellen Terry had led the company through years that would become a closely-documented legend. Mr Phillips went to *Madame*   7

Sans·Gêne (Comyns Carr from the French; 1897), but as a rule he stayed within the Birmingham radius. Early in 1900, at the Grand Theatre in Wolverhampton, he saw a company, sent out by Charles Frohman, with *The Christian* (a cast of 18), one of the sentimental-religious melodramas that dripped easily and efficiently from the pen of Hall Caine. A virile actor-manager, Wilson Barrett, who wrote *The Sign of the Cross*, had worked in a comparable mood; but whereas Barrett preferred the kind of rhapsodic Early Christian scene that Bernard Shaw would examine one day in *Androcles and the Lion*, Caine liked to be somewhere, decoratively and soggily, round the Isle of Man. In *The Christian* he had to make do with a prologue ('Love's Cross Roads') at the tilting-ground in the ruins of Peel Castle; Thereafter, labelling his acts as he went, he proceeded to the saloon of the Colosseum, London ('The Chaplet of Flowers'), the clubroom of St Mary Magdalene's Church, Soho ('The Crown of Thorns'), an apartment in the Garden House, Clement's Inn ('The Triumph of Love'), and back to Soho ('Love's Sacrifice'). It was about 'a Christian clergyman of intense earnestness and sincerity' and a beautiful music-hall singer, exposed to temptation and 'endeavouring to keep herself unspotted from the world'. Both feverish and pompous, it was a sustained success and a prized example of what in those days was regarded as superior melodrama; something beyond Mrs Kimberley's reach.

The next programme in the book is *The Only Way*, adapted from *A Tale of Two Cities*. Martin Harvey ('little Jack Harvey', Ellen Terry called him), who had not long discovered the sacrificing Sydney Carton, brought it to one of the two big theatres in Birmingham; a damp melodrama that his admirers would never allow him to forget. Meant for far, far better things, this appealing pictorial actor with a gift of pathos and no marked sense of humour, could be a doubtful judge of a play. (Once in later life, a trifle puzzled, he put on Shaw's *The Devil's Disciple*, the wrong kind of melodrama for an actor-manager;[18] he returned to *The Only Way* and Sydney Carton.) Still, whatever he did, his public remained constant; he could return regularly, twice a year, to the same town. The owner of the programme-book pursued him to London and, at the Royalty Theatre,

8

cream and white and mirrored in Dean Street, Soho, caught the season's last performance (1900) of *Pelléas and Mélisande*, Maurice Maeterlinck's symbolist drama of fate governing love. Here Martin Harvey, thirty-seven then, and uncanny in a wistfulness too often discarded, was Pelléas to the Mélisande, lost in the forest, of Mrs Patrick Campbell, resolutely in management: she was an actress, hypnotic when she wished, whose fame is fogged by eccentric anecdote. Maeterlinck kept a place on the Edwardian stage, even if—the children's fantasy of *The Blue Bird* excepted—critics were apt to review him, in Douglas Jerrold's phrase from another century, as the east wind would review an apple tree. His theatre, in general, is one of bleak, twilit simplicity; of orphan princesses, pale knights, and aged seers, all somnambulistic and slightly deaf. Yet, reasonably acted, he has always held a responsive audience.

The versatile Mr Phillips moved on, in the summer of 1900, to the underground Criterion in Piccadilly Circus: a house, managed by Charles Wyndham and Arthur Bourchier, that with its tiled and sinuous corridors looks much the same today. The piece was R. C. Carton's comedy, *Lady Huntworth's Experiment*; its second act in a country vicarage kitchen. There Lady Huntworth masqueraded as a cook; a fusion of two worlds, upstairs and down, that Edwardians, with their rigidly defined class system, found irresistibly daring and such a veteran as Sir Squire Bancroft deeply saddening. At the Criterion the masquerader was the dramatist's wife, known always as Miss Compton, a large, drawling, but incisively-timed comedienne. Dion Boucicault staged the play: a producer's name—they are directors now—was seldom noted. A. E. Matthews (who died in 1960, aged ninety), and who in those years, he said, was usually a 'dishonourable Honourable',[19] acted a country curate. Prices at the Criterion, like those of other London theatres, would stay firm for many years: Stalls, 10s 6d.; Dress Circle, 7s.; back row (bonnets allowed), 4s.; Family Circle, 4s.; pit, 2s. 6d.; gallery, 1s. 'Bonnet' was a euphemism for the obliterating matinee hat—so-called because it was not worn at night—a horror of Edwardian afternoon playgoing. It inspired a parody of Austin Dobson:[20]

9

Wicker-skin, intricate, slight,
  'Glowing like gardens at Kew,
Flowers in a riot of white,
  Rose-pink, mauve, yellow and blue;
  Mark all the dainty *frou-frou!*
Fixture as wide as a mat,
  Size that would well cover two!—
This is the Matinee Hat!

While in London our playgoer went on to the red damask of the Avenue (later reconstructed as the Playhouse), for *A Message From Mars*. Charles Hawtrey, who put it on, was out of the cast at the time, a bad miss; E. W. Tarver, stage manager and prompter and a ready professional, appeared as the rich selfish young man, a variant of Scrooge, whom a dream regenerated. The author was Richard Ganthony, an American; after preliminary reshapings, his piece ran from November 1899 into 1901 and Hawtrey often revived it. The central figure, falling asleep by the fire, was visited by a Messenger—Max Beerbohm said 'the man from Maskelyne and Cook's'[21]—who, banished from Mars, could return only after he had reformed the most selfish person on earth. Hence an elevating second act; the Scrooge-figure in the extremes of hunger, cold, and penury, and enlarging his social conscience every few minutes. A very moral piece; Edwardians liked to be elevated.

For a while Mr Phillips stayed in Birmingham. Thither during 1901 Herbert Beerbohm Tree brought his recent productions. *Twelfth Night* had the Elizabethan·Illyrian garden, the broad steps, the topiary, and the expanse of grass terraces that *Punch* called 'swardy', all copied by Hawes Craven from a picture in *Country Life*. Tree was spanieled by four minor Malvolios, images of their master, who stiffened to attention when he spoke. Maria, Olivia's gentlewoman, became the 'waiting maid to Olivia': Edwardian rules of degree must be observed. The second play was Stephen Phillips's verse tragedy of *Herod*, with its great bronze staircase. Up this Tree as the King, oblivious of his Queen Mariamne's death, moved slowly at the end of the second act; as he went he recited the roll of his new-granted territories:[22]

Hippo, Samaria, and Gadara,
And high-walled Joppa, and Anthedon shore,
And Gaza unto these, and Straton's towers.
SERVANT (*aside to Gadias*): O, Sir, the queen is dead!
GADIAS (*aside to Herod's mother, sister, and brother*): The queen is dead!
HEROD: Mariamne, hear you this? Mariamne, see you?
  Repeating the words and going up steps.
Hippo, Samaria, and Gadara,
And high-walled Joppa, and Anthedon shore,
  As he moves up.
And Gaza unto these, and Straton's towers!

It was a dream for any actor of the Theatre Theatrical. On the same Birmingham stage in the autumn of 1901, two incorrigible romantics in their prime, Fred Terry, who was thirty-seven, and his wife Julia Neilson, who was thirty-two, acted Charles II and Nell Gwyn in a coy and involved flutter, *Sweet Nell of Old Drury*: the name is eloquent. Like *The Only Way*, this would be a cult; for thirty years or so it lingered relentlessly in the Terry-Neilson programme. They were expert animators of the empty romantic flourish, and an audience delighted by full-scale sets and a cast of twenty, never minded waiting for thirty minutes, in all, between the acts. Yet the next week at the same theatre must have been more exciting. Johnston Forbes-Robertson—the hyphen was creeping into his name—arrived as Hamlet, prince of courtesy, his most complete Shakespearian portrait and except, as recordings show us now, for occasional trouble with the vowel 'o', mellifluously spoken.

Next, a long gap of two years during which we can wonder what happened to Mr Phillips. He resumed playgoing in Birmingham with a double bill; they were currently popular, and a 'curtain-raiser' was not infallibly trivial. Mrs Patrick Campbell had chosen Lady Bancroft's *A Dream*, followed, more substantially, by W. L. Courtney's version of the *Undine* legend: Undine, niece of the King of the Water People, was a changeling in the home of a Rhineland fisherman. Courtney was a respected London drama critic; his play left little mark on the records. Mr Phillips may have enjoyed himself more at an English treatment of a German comedy, *Old Heidelberg* in which George Alexander, of the St James's, toured in person: some of the 11 actor-managers held it to be their duty. Over forty, he could look agreeably like the young Hereditary Prince of Sachsen-Karlsburg in a Ruritanian idyll. Twenty years on, the gentle sentiment of a love affair between Prince and innkeeper's daughter would be overlaid by the clangour and the wildly waving beer-mugs of an American musical version:[23] Alexander might not have been amused.

Next, Wilson Barrett ('and entire London company of 100') reached the Midlands in the revived melodrama, *Claudian*, as subtle as the panes of coloured glass in a villa window; humanity re-entered, in the spring of 1904, with Mary Moore, Lady Wyndham, in a 'flying matinee' of Hubert Henry Davies's *Mrs Gorringe's Necklace*, most Pinerotic of his comedies; and Phillips went on to Shrewsbury to catch 'Mr F. R. Benson and his Dramatic Company' at a matinee of the Oresteian Trilogy of Aeschylus. Described in various places as an Austrian Trilogy, an Australian Tragedy, and an Acetylene Trinity,[24] it was an impressive production with its flame-quivering altar, purple and saffron hangings, and some good speaking, though Mrs Benson's voice never had the timbre for Clytemnestra. Frank Benson had a special feeling for the *Agamemnon*: nearly a quarter of a century earlier, in June 1880, he had himself played Clytemnestra at a celebrated Oxford performance in Balliol Hall.[25]

That autumn of 1904 Sir Henry Irving brought *Becket* to Birmingham. It was the year before his death: he was still, in his winter, frail and majestic, the tragedian who had been the crown of the English stage. In that extraordinary muffled-bright voice, striking like lightning through mist, he could carry such daunting lines as:[26]

> Seal? If a seraph shouted from the sun
> And bade me seal against the rights of the Church
> I would anathematise him. I will not seal.

It took an actor to carry the word 'anathematise'. At Birmingham the touring company was in the sumptuous Irving manner: a cast of twenty-seven, as well as an assemblage of Knights, Monks, Heralds, Soldiers, and Retainers. Martin Harvey, who was either Mr Phillips's favourite actor or the one

12

most often about—he got through a prodigious amount of work, with every trapping of a leading man—was in Birmingham at the same time; and he and his old Chief stayed at the same hotel. Harvey's programme began with the inevitable renunciatory heroics of *The Only Way*, went on to a piece called *A Cigarette Maker's Romance*—amiable fustian again; he was moving as a courtly fantastic—and ended with *The Exile* by Lloyd Osbourne and Austin Strong, Robert Louis Stevenson's stepsons. This presented an idealised and talkative Napoleon during a single day in his last years at Longwood. Thinly devised, with the expected characters, Montholon, Gourgaud, Las Cases, Bertrand, and so on, it failed in London and slid out of the English repertory almost at once. Few remembered it three decades later during the success of another play on the same theme, the R. C. Sherriff-Jeanne de Casalis *St Helena*.[27]

On to 1905: another company from His Majesty's, but without Beerbohm Tree. In *The Tempest* G. W. Anson was the Caliban Tree had sentimentalised. At the final curtain, so he said in his printed notes, 'The ship is seen on the horizon, Caliban stretching his arms towards it in mute despair. The night falls, and Caliban is left on the lonely rock. He is a King once more.' William Haviland, of the original cast, was Prospero; the company travelled Telbin's set of the Yellow Sands; sea-nymphs peered round the rocks and Ariel (Iris Hoey) flitted across the pools. Forward again: untiringly, *The Only Way*, the Conciergerie, Mimi, and The Vengeance; a special matinee of *Othello* (Lewis Waller, H. B. Irving's Iago, Henry Ainley as Cassio); and, once more (March 1906), Martin Harvey, now as Hamlet. Irving had discussed it with him when they met at the Birmingham hotel for pre-theatre coffee on an autumn night in 1904:[28] 'Going to play Hamlet, eh? Quite right not to delay too long. You must be young when you play Hamlet for the first time': Harvey then was forty-one, Irving sixty-six. The production, eleventh-century and carefully archaeological, had had no luck in London at an hour (1905) when Hamlets multiplied and Harvey had to withdraw his after a fortnight of 'beggarly receipts', a nightly average of £28.

Soon afterwards, Phillips in London tried the showcase of the Theatre of Ideas, the Barker-Vedrenne season at the Royal 13

Court. It was largely, one suspects, because in her stage jubilee year a loved actress,

> Britain's pride,
> The genius of her stage personified,
> Queenlike, pathetic, tragic, tender, merry—
> O rare, O sweet, O wondrous Ellen Terry—[29]

was playing Lady Cicely in Shaw's *Captain Brassbound's Conversion*: the governing charmer who was 'a titled Candida with a castle in the middle of Morocco'.[30] She was not very happy—'an absence of sureness in her acting sometimes spoilt its effect', said Desmond MacCarthy—[31] but this seems to have been so with most of her post-Lyceum work.

During the same visit Phillips returned sharply to the Theatre Theatrical: to *Raffles, the Amateur Cracksman* (1906), an adaptation by Eugene W. Presbrey and E. W. Hornung of Hornung's novel about the cricketer-crook, A. J. Raffles. Gerald du Maurier created him for the stage, bringing to a poor play his personal quality, 'making of Raffles', said his daughter Daphne,[32] 'someone highly strung, nervous, and finely drawn, yet fearless and full of a rather desperate indifference'. Here Phillips seems to have been unlucky again; du Maurier's understudy, Vernon Steel, was appearing at the Comedy Theatre in a part round which the entire fabric was built: among the earliest of a succession of crook melodramas. Du Maurier himself would act in *Arsène Lupin* (1909) and *Alias Jimmy Valentine* (1910). Phillips, unbeaten, continued his London season with another visit to the Court, finding Henry Ainley and Louis Calvert as the five-shilling dentist and the waiter in the not especially testing *You Never Can Tell*; hearing Oscar Asche, Lily Brayton, and a cast mainly Bensonian, disposing of the burst of iambics in Comyns Carr's *Tristram and Iseult* at what was then the Royal Adelphi; and finally returning to Ellen Terry, now as Hermione in *The Winter's Tale* at His Majesty's; Charles Warner as Leontes. There she did add to the Queen's racked dignity her own sense of a perpetual spring; it was fifty years since she had acted the child Mamillius for Charles Kean at the Princess's and tripped over her go-cart.

14   Back at length to Birmingham until the sudden end of the

programme-book: to H. B. Irving (April 1907) recreating with his curious originality some of his father's renowned parts, Lesurques and Dubosc, merchant and cut-throat, in the mistaken identities of *The Lyons Mail*; Mathias, guilty burgomaster of *The Bells*; and the doomed Charles I in W. G. Wills's Cavalier play that has some richly Victorian lines in the King's farewell to Henrietta Maria:[33]

> I fear me I may sometimes fade from thee,
> That when thy heart expelleth grey-stoled grief
> I live no longer in thy memory:
> Oh, keep my place in it for ever green,
> All hung with the immortelles of thy love.

Mrs Patrick Campbell that autumn was strenuously Magda in a version of Sudermann's *Heimat*, challenge to old-fashioned morality. Martin Harvey, too, was on his rounds—as Reresby, the 'Rat', in an English Civil War melodrama, *The Breed of the Treshams*, by two American women, Mrs Evelyn Greenleaf Sutherland and Miss Beulah Marie Dix, writing as 'John Rutherford'. Reresby, Martin Harvey said,[34] was more than a 'romantic abstraction': he carried his actor away and became 'like a Callot drawing, with the raffish habits of the stable and guardroom. . . . The authors were shocked.'

Presently, and less deplorably, *You Never Can Tell*, advertised as 'The Intensely Amusing Play . . . The Pleasant Play', came in a Vedrenne-Barker touring company (William the Waiter, J. D. Beveridge); the all-but-thousand performances at the Court had ended. A companion comedy was *John Bull's Other Island*, here with William Poel, the Shakespearian zealot, in one of the few modern parts that suited him, Keegan, poet, priest, and visionary. Henry Tonks painted this Keegan in the sunshine, gently smiling, hat in hand, the mountains behind; the picture hangs today in the National Portrait Gallery. Next, with a smothered rumble, Hall Caine's lugubrious Drury Lane drama, *The Bondman* (cast of thirty-two); two scenes in the Isle of Man and two in Sicily at a period, 'the middle of the nineteenth century when the maritime relations of the two islands were closer than they are now'. Quotation:[35]

15

JASON: God give me that man into my hands! He has taken everything I had in the world. He has stolen all the love and tenderness out of my life! He has made me a thing to pity and to spurn. Curse him! Damn him! Let him not escape me any longer—let me meet him face to face!

> *The stage is empty. All is quiet and peaceful. Sun setting, pigeons cooing, birds singing, lambs bleating, and a line of cows coming across the fields. The church bell is pealing merrily in the distance.*

Last, without rural atmospherics, another visit (1908) from the H. B. Irving company: *The Lyons Mail, Charles the First, Hamlet,* and a new four-act tragedy in unrhymed verse, *Cesare Borgia* by Justin Huntly McCarthy, that allowed Irving to 'exploit his sinister vein',[36] but was not acted in London.

The roughly-pasted book keeps the mingled chime of the Edwardian theatre: its battering melodrama, decorated Shakespeare, verse tragedy, dizzily romantic 'costume' drama, misty symbolism, drawing-room comedy, moral fantasy, the new crook drama, and the Theatre of Ideas; all the players, too, for whom we can use the astronomical term 'acronychal', a rising of stars at nightfall. Two important gaps: no Pinero and no musical comedy. We must assume that Mr Phillips, who did not bother about such trivia as *Woman and Wine, The New Housemaid,* and *The Woman Pays,* was equally not a devotee of the period's swirling nonsense:

> By the shore of the Mediterranean
> So blue, blue, blue,
> They twang their guitars and light their cigars,
> They do, do, do,
> And kiss you and talk in the starlight,
> With a coo, coo, coo . . .[37]

The programme-book ends sadly. Clipped to it is a leaflet from a Wolverhampton picture-house in the middle of the first world war. News of a 'four-reel Vitagraph drama', *A Prince in a Pawnshop,* is some distance from the Irvings, Alexander, Ellen Terry, and Tree.

III

After this, the casual notes[38] of an anonymous London suburban 'pittite', not a regular first-nighter, all from the year 1905 when the Edwardian theatre was in full stately progress (the dates are seldom premières):

18 January: *The Taming of the Shrew* (Shakespeare): Adelphi. Souvenir night. I consider myself lucky to have survived this night, and no souvenir will be needed to recall the struggle. I felt decidedly tamed for a week afterwards; never thought the ponderous Oscar Asche could be so brisk.

Asche, an Australian of Scandinavian descent, born in 1871, was a massive figure with a rumbling bass-baritone voice. Trained with Frank Benson, he was loyal to his beginnings; former Bensonians, led by Lily Brayton, his wife, composed the Adelphi cast in a long season with Otho Stuart as joint manager. It had some reward in the Press, not enough in the box-office except for the 'breathless, knockabout, rampageous *Shrew*, played on broadly farcical lines'.[39] Asche's memory today is overlaid by the fame of his 'musical tale of the East', *Chu-Chin-Chow* (he wrote the libretto) which is out of our period. He meant more than that to the Theatre Theatrical as an actor of immense, undisciplined power. A showman and an unrestrained gambler in whatever he undertook, he left twenty pounds at his death.

The notes continue:

20 February: *The Walls of Jericho* (Alfred Sutro): Garrick Theatre. Enjoyed this very smart piece.

9 March: *Peter Pan* (J. M. Barrie): Duke of York's. Mr Barrie writes for the children in a delightful way. Though not one myself, I felt I was that afternoon. Must see it again.

5 April: *Alice Sit-by-the-Fire* (J. M. Barrie): Duke of York's. Return of Ellen Terry to the London stage after long absence. The play, though by Barrie, was a second consideration to me.

The writer might have been puzzled by Barrie's mockery of the day's conventional stage plotting, as in this speech by one of 17 the girls in the first act.[40] 'She was most foolish, especially in the *crêpe de chine*, but *we* know that she only went to the man's chambers to get back her letters.'

After *Henry V* and a souvenir picture of Lewis Waller, the romantic actor whose admirers formed a lucklessly-named K.O.W. (Keen on Waller) club; *The Scarlet Pimpernel* in its fresh April, with Fred Terry and Julia Neilson defying the French Revolution; and Sydney Fairbrother singing nasally 'I want a ban like Robeo' in a musical comedy, *The Talk of the Town*, the diarist reached *The Catch of the Season* (Vaudeville), also a musical comedy, and the return of Ellaline Terriss, Mrs Seymour Hicks, who had been ill. It was the evening of 1 May:

At the end she stood alone on the stage, looking very happy, and flowers all round her. About forty bouquets were thrown at her feet, then a larger basket, and lastly a sunshade composed of tiny pink rosebuds was handed up to her. By this time we could see tears were in her eyes. . . . After this a rose-pink curtain was lowered with the words, 'Thank you', in white roses, and, as Ellaline came in front to acknowledge the continued cheers, the roses lit up with electricity.

Then Irving's farewell in *Becket* (Drury Lane; Irving, theatrically, was the Abbey and the Tower), R. C. Carton's *Mr Hopkinson*, and a play called *Everybody's Street*. Suddenly, on 7 June:

Candida (Bernard Shaw): Court. Georgie and self felt rather curious to sample this author's work. It was quite out of the ordinary and rather difficult to describe. There is hardly any plot, yet it remained very interesting, and we liked it. Granville Barker very good as a young man [Marchbanks, the poet] with strange ideas and a bit of a puzzle.

Encouraged, the pair tried again:

20 June: *You Never Can Tell* (Bernard Shaw): Court. Our first taste of this author's work was so much to our liking that we look forward to seeing this again. Were much interested and amused. Granville Barker looked quite fetching as a dentist.

The charms of Shaw and Granville Barker had not entirely conquered. These playgoers went four times to Hall Caine's *The Prodigal Son* (Drury Lane). On the first day, 7 September:

I met the girls at door 11 a.m. We took short walks to pass the time. . . .
The play realised all expectations; about a dozen calls after each
curtain, and when we left at 12.15 the audience was still applauding.

The hero, surprisingly, was George Alexander of the St James's,
the first time in fifteen years that he had acted under any other
management: he was paid £250 a week, the total sum to be not
less than £3,500.[41] When he returned to his own theatre in 1906
it was to play Hilary Jesson, one of the triumphs of his career, in
Pinero's *His House in Order*.

Another excitement for the diarist was a new theatre, the
marble-cold Scala—never warmed into lasting success—in
Charlotte Street behind Tottenham Court Road. The play, John
Davidson's romantic drama from the French, *For the Crown*:

A disappointment awaited us in the announcement that Forbes
Robertson was not in the cast, and it was on his account that we wished
to see the piece. Henry Ainley proved himself a worthy successor in a
fine part in a fine play, but rather sad. . . . After the performance we
had a walk round and much enjoyed the most beautiful of new
theatres.

A little later, to *Lights Out* (Waldorf, which became the Strand),
presented by Maundy Gregory, notorious two decades later in
the sale of honours: 'First time I had been in this house. Found it
a very handsome one indeed; our theatres have become
palaces.' Finally, at the tail of the year, the diarist just caught
Shaw's *Man and Superman*, out at Sloane Square:

30 December: Court. One can hardly call this a play, for there was
small amount of acting, but a deal of talking. Georgie and self have
become interested in G.B.S.'s work for the reason that they are so
different from other plays; quite a line of their own.

IV

That, briefly, was the palace-haunting life of average South
London playgoers: pittites who would wait regularly in the
queue for two or three hours on three evenings a week; who
were bred to a stage of magnetic personalities—Waller acted
invariably to an audience of iron filings—roses lit up with   19

electricity, souvenir nights, picture-postcard queens (Marie Studholme), the elaborate charade-stuff of the theatre, the kind of piece about which Barrie's Ginevra says ecstatically to her sister:[42] 'Real plays are always about a lady and two men; and, alas, only one of them is her husband. That is Life, you know. It is called the odd, odd triangle.' Even so, probing timidly into waters outside the West End, or like explorers in the untamed fen country by lantern-light, these playgoers found Shaw with 'a line of his own' at the Court, and Granville Barker 'fetching'. I doubt whether they would have joined the Court 'congregation' permanently to the exclusion of more central pleasures. Indeed, not many devoted to the ruling Theatre Theatrical, to Tree, Alexander, and Waller, would have done so, though the Court was naturally high heaven for earnest seekers for truth, accustomed since the century began to find the intellectual drama only on special occasions, Stage Society productions, single matinees. This minority would have agreed with the lament by A. B. Walkley, of *The Times*—a writer who steadily annoyed the romantic Martin Harvey—that, while the French theatre during the last half of the nineteenth century had treated every social and ethical question of importance, in England all, or nearly all, of these questions had been rigidly excluded.[43] (Walkley, like other English drama critics of varying quality, was firmly Gallic-minded.)

It was true that hardly anything in the late nineteenth-century theatre had lingered. William Archer, as a young writer not long down from Edinburgh, chose in 1882, for his essays in *English Dramatists of Today*, such names as James Albery, F. W. Broughton, Bronson Howard, Paul Merritt, Robert Reece, S. Theyre Smith, F. C. Burnand (who edited *Punch*), Herman C. Merivale, George R. Sims, W. G. Wills of *A Royal Divorce* (though this, a collaboration, would come later), and Henry J. Byron, the punster. Archer deferred until 1923 his strongest attack on what he called 'the mid-Victorian imbecilities'[44] of the burlesques which established Byron; the punning verse which—except in pantomime—had faded from the stage by the Edwardian period. This kind of thing: the speaker is the lackey, Dandino, in *Cinderalla: or, The Lover, the Lackey, and the Little Glass Slipper* (1860):

As I have made my bed, so must I lie.
Continuing *bed* metaphor, sir,—I
When quite a child, the blackest draught would drain,
And took my *pill—oh!* on *account o' pain!*
And as my youthful feathers all unfurled
Seemed formed to make a *bold stir* in the world,
Little dreamt I I should appear a valet as,
For I seemed born to reign in royal *palliasse*;
But suddenly the future seemed to frown;
Fortune gave me a *quilt*, and *I'd a down*.

'Is it not appalling to think' (said Archer), 'that two generations of our immediate forefathers crowded to the theatre to hear and applaud drivel like this?'

One or two better names in *English Dramatists of Today*: Arthur Wing Pinero ('You'll have to include young Pinero,' Sydney Grundy had said to Archer as if it were a rather original and debatable idea); Henry Arthur Jones; Sydney Grundy himself whose name, I think, somehow fitted him; W. S. Gilbert, unmatched librettist—he had not yet done his best work—and mediocre dramatist; and Alfred Tennyson, probably startled to meet himself in this company, assuming that anyone ever drew his attention to it. No Shaw yet. As dramatist and drama critic he was in the future, the flash and outbreak of a fiery brain. Very few of Archer's men of the present were men of the future. By 1900 who was left that mattered? Inevitably, Pinero and Jones; Gilbert in his decline; Grundy, tetchily second-rate. By that time all the fuss about Ibsen had flared and smouldered. In spite of Shaw and *The Quintessence of Ibsenism*, the 'bleak Norwegian' (Jones speaking) had not noticeably aerated the hothouse of the West End stage, though today, with hindsight, we know his indirect influence. Playgoers in general were satisfied, if indeed they ever thought of it in this way, with Ibsenite criticism of life through drama in one of Pinero's commercial variants. Jones, Pinero's rival and senior by nearly four years—the names still run off the pen together—took his cue less readily. True, he once made, and was later embarrassed by, an odd gloss on *A Doll's House* called *Breaking a Butterfly* (1884), in which Nora repented; Walkley held also that Jones's confession-dramas were prompted by *Pillars of Society*. But one cannot think of this   21 scratchily endearing dramatist who, sometimes, could be as irascible as Gilbert or Grundy, without recalling his preface to *The Tempter*[45] in which he said: 'Mr William Archer has laboured long and gallantly in the cause of the lobworm-symbolic drama.' In a verse prologue to the play Jones urged his hearers to 'shun the crude present with vain problems rife, / Nor join the bleak Norwegian's barren quest'. A good fourteen years later the Irish dramatist, John Millington Synge, was saying:[46]

The drama is made serious—in the French sense of the word—not by the degree in which it is taken up with problems that are serious in themselves, but by the degree in which it gives the nourishment, not very easy to define, on which our imaginations live. We should not go to the theatre as we go to a chemist's or a dram-shop, but as we go to a dinner where the food we need is taken with pleasure and excitement. This was nearly always so in Spain and England and France when the drama was at its richest—the infancy and decay of the drama tend to be didactic—but in these days the playhouse is too often stocked with the drugs of many ready problems, or with the absinthe and vermouth of the last musical comedy.

(The final phrase must have puzzled George Edwardes; poor *San Toy*; unhappy *Toreador*.)

A few years before Synge wrote, the insulated English theatre was in a transitional period. It had Pinero and Jones to see it into the new century, Jones always a few paces behind, and both of them absorbed, as a rule, by the sins of society, the woman with a past, the 'odd, odd triangle', and the stern laws of Edwardian life and behaviour. A few competent men were ready with the competent play, few hints of any theme or moral: R. C. Carton, whose wit (in the situation) and steady industry would leave the barest dint on the shifting sands of the theatre; Robert Marshall, C. Haddon Chambers, and Sydney Grundy (ever dazzled by Scribe), who was always about to create a sensation, but who never did. Mock-Ruritanians and random romantics were all over the place. The poet's stage belonged temporarily to a former Bensonian actor, Stephen Phillips, described—and by Archer, astonishingly—as 'the elder Dumas speaking with the voice of Milton'. (That was among the more tepid praise.) A forty-year-old Scot, J. M. Barrie, had an independent air, though nobody could do much with *The Wedding Guest* in which he tried to be modish: never his line. An ominous sound of drum-and-trumpet in the near distance meant the approach of the Irishman and former critic, Bernard Shaw ('nothing exasperates me more than to be Georged in print').[47] Though he had not yet expressed it in so many words, he regarded the theatre as[48] 'a factory of thought, a prompter of conscience, an elucidator of social conduct, an armoury against despair and dullness and a temple of the Ascent of Man'. Few turn-of-the-century dramatists would have confessed to the first and last of these, especially the last.

Pinero never accepted any argument from his companies; they were there to speak his lines, and that was that; Shaw, at the Court, abetted by Granville Barker, would know precisely what he wanted. But the Edwardian period opened with the actor-managers in control. Though his day was waning, Henry Irving, knighted in 1895, had been for years the stage's undisputed head: an extraordinary original, however compact of visual and vocal mannerism (Macbeth's 'To tram-mele up-p the cunsequence'). As a boy he lived for seven or eight years in remote West Cornwall with an aunt and uncle; I have often thought that the haunted nature of his playing, its extra dimension, could well have derived from the influences of Halsetown, bleakly behind St Ives. During the spring of 1901 he had ended his glorious Lyceum career: nothing could make him look or sound like Coriolanus, that pillar of fire on a plinth of marble, or get his partner of many years, Ellen Terry, to suggest the fibre of Volumnia Victrix. Too soon there would be the extreme weariness of the last *Becket* night at Bradford in the autumn of 1905, the collapse in the hall of his hotel, and the passage of the coffin through Westminster Abbey under its thickly-woven pall of laurel. His principal successors at the head of the theatre were Tree, Alexander, and Forbes-Robertson. It was a period for Decorated Shakespeare, for the extra-illustration, the grangerising, of the Folio. Herbert Beerbohm Tree, an often bizarre chameleon-actor, better when away from the classics, filled the stage of his 'beautiful theatre' (Her/His Majesty's in Haymarket) with the most elaborate pictorial display: gleaming Alma-Tadema marbles, spreading terraces, umbrageous woods, pageants and tableaux, wave-beaten ships, 23 practicable gondolas, the grandiose and the spacious. If he had needed Crummles's pump and two tubs, they would have been the most expensive in memory. Still, all his work was directed to the ample 'pleasure and excitement' of the Theatre Theatrical. Puritans detested Tree; but, looking back, we can see that at His Majesty's the Edwardian West End did have a sumptuous 'repertory' stage, never officially recognised in that chilling term.

George Alexander (born George Alexander Gibb Samson), the mould of form and a business man as generous as he was alert, conducted the St James's for twenty-seven years. Fashionable society drama, fashionable costume plays were made all the more so by their admittance to his theatre. Only one person disturbed him: Mrs Patrick Campbell. According to Hesketh Pearson, when Shaw offered him *Pygmalion*, Alexander—who genuinely admired the play—answered: 'Go on for another play with Mrs Campbell I will *not*. I'd rather die.'[49] Johnston Forbes-Robertson, with a voice that reminded Shaw of the chalumeau register of a clarionet, was a nobly dignified Shakespearian given to using cut and bowdlerised texts, as most of his colleagues did. None would have called him an infallible judge of contemporary drama: Jerome K. Jerome's *The Passing of the Third Floor Back*, ridiculed by Max Beerbohm, scorned now, but not entirely worthless, would be his *Only Way* or *Sweet Nell*; the public would not allow him to drop it. While these and other actor-managers, the constellation of the stage, moved nightly in their accustomed courses, playgoers were contented enough. Respecting their profession, the benevolent dictators saw that their admirers did. There was no wanton cheapening. They strove to preserve the mystery of the stage, something that now is under-valued. To an Edwardian curtain-rise and curtain-fall meant much.

Before long, as the Theatre of Ideas prospered, the dramatists asserted themselves strongly. Shaw, whose record of production had been complicated and largely hole-and-corner (Independent Theatre Society; Stage Society, and so forth) would move into the fierce light of the Vedrenne-Barker season of 1904–7: 701 performances of eleven of his plays; another 288 performances shared by sixteen writers. Harley Granville

Barker, also out of step with convention, would prove to be imperious, intellectually exhilarating, and intense. Soon few would be surprised to find a play sharpened to what another man, John Galsworthy, in the theatre a humanitarian equilibrist, called 'a spire of meaning,' a term that had not occurred to the Marshalls, Cartons, and Grundys, or to the provincial authors of *For Her Husband's Sake* (characters including Lieutenant Seymour, R N, Abraham K. Silas, and Alphonse de Pom-Pom), and *The Power of the King* (King of Vallombrosa, Fritz Tarlheim, Lady Florina, Crown Prince Oscar): not, I think, aggressively outcrops of the Theatre of Ideas.

V

A dramatist of a later era, Sean O'Casey, wrote in another context:[50] 'This is a wonderful house, so it is! It's an honour to be workin' in it.' Once self-indulgently, I built and furnished a 'wonderful house', a castle in the air fashioned entirely from books on the neighbouring shelves. Thus outside was a garden planned by Sir Francis Bacon, with 'the double white violet, the wallflower . . . flower-de-luce and lilies of all natures'; within, a dining-room from Sir Pitt Crawley's mansion in Great Gaunt Street, a library from *The Picture of Dorian Grey*, a drawing-room from Lady Sneerwell's in the famous Bancroft production of *The School for Scandal* (1874), bedrooms from *Jane Eyre* and *Cymbeline*, and so cheerfully forward.

That was just amiable fantasy; but it is possible to see the Edwardian theatre in and round a single house, though its features are more coherent: drawing-room and principal bedrooms designed, according to the rules of the game, for Pinero, Jones, and their followers; dining-room (usually off-stage) at the service of all; study with a conference-table for Shaw and Barker; a kitchen diversely peopled; a music-room for the poets' drama ('This odorous amorous isle of violets / That leans all leaves into the glassy deep / With brooding music over noontide moss');[51] a play-room—absinthe and vermouth for Synge on a side table—and a maze of linking passages. Here   25

is the house; first we might go to its drawing-room, announced
by the severest of starched parlourmaids.

Notes

All references are to books published in London unless otherwise stated.

1. *Misalliance.* The Bodley Head Bernard Shaw, Vol. IV (1972), p. 170.
2. *His House in Order* (1906), Act IV, p. 192.
3. '. . . and indeed of serious literature of any kind'. Foreword to *Cymbeline Refinished: A Variation on Shakespear's Ending.* The Bodley Head Bernard Shaw, Vol. VII (1974), p. 182.
4. *The Week-End Calendar* (1932), p. 27.
5. *The Plays of Hubert Henry Davies*, Vol. I (1921), p. 153.
6. Quoted by Allardyce Nicoll in *English Drama, 1900–1930*, p. 329.
7. *Lady Geraldine's Courtship.*
8. *The Tempter* (published 1898), p. 108.
9. Owen Nares: *Myself and Some Others* (1925), p. 119.
10. William Archer: *Real Conversations* (1904). p. 199.
11. *Macready's Reminiscences and Selections from his Diaries and Letters*, ed. by Sir Frederick Pollock, Vol. II (1875), p. 388. This ode by Tennyson, then Poet Laureate, on Macready's farewell, was read by John Forster at the London dinner to Macready in the Hall of Commerce, 1 March 1851. Robert Eddison read the ode before Macready's coffin in the vaults of Kensal Green cemetery when the Society for Theatre Research (on 27 April 1973) marked the 100th anniversary of the actor's death.
12. *Real Conversations*, p. 207.
13. H. F. Maltby: *Ring Up the Curtain* (1950), pp. 46–8.
14. Whitford Kane: *Are We All Met?* (1931), p. 64.
15. *The Era*, 11 August 1900; quoted by Ernest Reynolds in *Modern English Drama* (1949), p. 190.
16. Barry Jackson: 'Barnstorming Days' in *Studies in English Theatre History* (1952: Society for Theatre Research).
17. Given to the author by Miss Mary Richards, of Birmingham.
18. Maurice Willson Disher: *The Last Romantic* (1948), p. 248.
19. A. E. Matthews: *Matty* (1952), p. 106.
20. By 'Roode Knight' in *Parodies and Imitations*, edited by J. A. Stanley Adam and Bernard C. White (1912), p. 335.
21. *Saturday Review*, 25 November 1899; reprinted in *More Theatres* (1969), p. 213.
22. *Herod: A Tragedy* (1901), p. 97. (See also Errata slip, p. 9.)
23. *The Student Prince*, New York, 1924; London, 1926.
24. J. C. Trewin: *Benson and the Bensonians* (1960), p. 143.
25. *Ibid.*, pp. 7–11.

26. Alfred Lord Tennyson: *Becket*, Act 1, Scene 3 (in *Dramas*, 1928 edition, p. 244). Henry Irving's acting edition, Act I, Scene 4.
27. London, 1936.
28. *The Autobiography of Sir John Martin-Harvey* (1933), p. 295.
29. Louis N. Parker. Spoken by Tree at His Majesty's, 1906.
30. George Rowell: *The Victorian Theatre* (Oxford, 1956), p. 132.
31. Desmond MacCarthy: *The Court Theatre: 1904–1907* (1907), p. 90.
32. Daphne du Maurier: *Gerald: A Portrait* (1934), p. 115.
33. *Charles the First*, Act IV.
34. *The Autobiography of Sir John Martin-Harvey* (1933), p. 293.
35. *The Bondman*, play (1906), p. 105.
36. Laurence Irving: *The Precarious Crust* (1971), p. 145.
37. Lyric by Fred E. Weatherly from *The Earl and the Girl* (1903); book by Seymour Hicks; music by Ivan Caryll.
38. Lent by Mrs K. Clark.
39. Hesketh Pearson: *The Last Actor-Managers* (1950), p. 66.
40. *Alice Sit-by-the-Fire*, Act 1. *The Plays of J. M. Barrie* (1928), p. 601.
41. A. E. W. Mason: *Sir George Alexander and the St James's Theatre* (1935), p. 169.
42. *Alice Sit-by-the-Fire*, Act 1, Scene 1. *The Plays of J. M. Barrie* (1928), p. 601.
43. A. B. Walkley: *Drama and Life* (1907), p. 28.
44. William Archer: *The Old Drama and the New* (1923), p. 275.
45. *The Tempter*: produced 1893, published 1898.
46. J. M. Synge: Preface to the revised *Tinker's Wedding* (1907) in *Plays, Poems, and Prose*, Everyman edition (1941), p. 33.
47. Letter to Ernest Rhys, 3.4.31. Quoted in Rhys's *Letters from Limbo* (1936), p. 165.
48. 'The Author's Apology' in *Dramatic Opinions and Essays* (1907).
49. Hesketh Pearson: *The Last Actor-Managers* (1950), p. 26.
50. Sean O'Casey: *Purple Dust* in Collected Plays, Vol. III (1951), p. 61.
51. Stephen Phillips: *Ulysses* (1902), p. 56.

CHAPTER TWO

The Drawing-Room

I

The early Edwardian theatre was primarily a drawing-room, located as often as not in Belgravia, though it might be, daringly—this was midway through the reign—at Mr Filmer Jesson's place, Overbury Towers, on the outskirts of a town in the Midlands. Matters in it were organised principally for the benefit of stalls and dress circle, even if pit and gallery and that half-world of the upper circle were allowed to watch. The usherettes, at a time of stern distinctions, would have hated to be told that they looked, as they did, like parlourmaids of whom there would certainly be one or more on the stage. It was a time of ritual for which a wistful remembrancer, W. Macqueen Pope,[1] who never ceased to mourn the Edwardians, would use the shorthand of 'shirtfronts and sables'. In aspect, a West End theatre (the St James's and Criterion were perfect examples) kept the drawing-room manner; audiences and actors knew their places. Dramatists wrote to pattern. On lighter occasions the play would be a formal exercise, a passing anecdote that merely interrupted general conversation. But at most times it was a pleasant *soirée*; and a writer who chose another setting—a country-house garden, maybe, or a lawn by the

28

river—would still attempt more or less what Shaw did in *You Never Can Tell*: there, tongue in cheek, the needs of the commercial stage in mind—though he discovered that West End managers blankly misunderstood him—he indulged a public fancy for 'fun, music, and even an exhibition of eating and drinking by people with an expensive air attended by an if-possible-comic waiter'.[2] (I once met the inspired misprint, 'comic writer'). Shaw was bold enough to choose for first act the seaside surgery of a 'five-shilling dentist', but this was merely caprice. The approved drawing-rooms were various enough (we can begin with one still inside the old century):

Lady Rosamund's drawing-room, Cadogan Gardens, a very elegant apartment, furnished in good taste. . . . Large low window forming an alcove up stage right. (Henry Arthur Jones: *The Liars*, 1897.)

The Jacksons' drawing-room at Chedleigh, a handsome room, suggests opulence rather than taste. Not vulgar, but not distinguished. Too full of furniture, pictures, knick-knacks, chair-covers, plants in pots. Too full of everything. (St John Hankin: *The Return of the Prodigal*: 1905.)

The drawing-room at Epping House. Two large french windows at the back which being open show an extensive view of lawns, flower gardens, and trees. The furniture and hangings are of rich pale green brocade. (Hubert Henry Davies: *Lady Epping's Lawsuit*. 1908.)

Mrs Moxon's drawing-room. It is a pleasant room in a substantial country house. The furniture is good but not new, and rather early Victorian in style. (Davies: *Captain Drew on Leave*, 1905.)

Mrs Dallas-Bower's drawing-room at Crediton Court, Kensington. . . . The furniture is in excellent taste of a commonplace sort. On the walls are autotypes after old Italian masters. There is good china in the cabinets. It is the kind of drawing-room which every woman of the upper middle class has in London. It is agreeable to the eye, unoriginal, artistic, and inexpensive. (W. Somerset Maugham: *Smith*, 1909.)

A drawing-room, decorated and furnished in the French style. (A. W. Pinero: *Mid-Channel*, 1909.)

The drawing-room at Oldwick Rectory, comfortably, conventionally furnished, with a door in the middle of the back. On the left is the fireplace; on the right are windows looking on to a short drive which leads to the front door. In the middle of the foreground are a tea-table and an easy chair; to the left of these, and near the fireplace, a sofa and other chairs; to the right a settee, chairs, and

29

against the wall a mahogany escritoire. At the back is a cabinet full of china heirlooms, and a table with photograph albums and a small silver casket. Photographs in frames are to be found wherever it is possible to stand them. The pictures on the walls prove the inmates of the Rectory blameless of artistic perception. (Rudolf Besier: *Don*, 1910.)

One of the drawing-room's inhabitants on more serious evenings was the woman with a past. These could have formed a club with a line from Pinero's Paula Tanqueray as motto: 'The future is only the past again, entered through another gate.' The drawing-room was also the place for the intricate fibbing, the sequence of cross-questions and crooked answers that occupied many of the day's frisks on the rim of the Divorce Court: nothing to do with social problems but good, bland Society theatre when the dramatist knew his business and, according to the Edwardian code, his place.

No one knew his work better than Arthur Wing Pinero (1855–1934), master of the *scène à faire*. A solicitor's son of Portuguese-Jewish ancestry (the name was originally Pinheiro), he had been a mediocre actor with Henry Irving, but established himself in the theatre as a dramatist able to manipulate the most swiftly inventive farces (those at the Court during the 1880s), sentimental comedy in the line of *Sweet Lavender* or, far better, *Trelawny of the 'Wells'*, and the tactfully watered Ibsen—not that he would acknowledge this—of the drawing-room dramas. Though he attacked the late Victorian and Edwardian double standard of morality—a woman allowed nothing of a man's freedom—it could be testing for any woman to be born into a Pinero drawing-room. Few of them, when in the toils, could have echoed lines he wrote—a collector's prize, for he was no poet—in Clement Scott's magazine, *The Theatre*, during 1884:[3]

> A woman has one happy day in her life,
> It trips in her teens or it lags in her age,
> It glides in a calm or it stumbles in strife,
> But oh! there is bliss in that sanctified page! . . .

By the turn of the century he had become an autocrat, watching relentlessly over the production of his plays from their printed texts. He could frighten even Alexander at the St

James's. Each act, in its sanctified pages, would be sent to the printer as soon as it was finished, and the actors were not permitted to stray for a comma's space. With Pinero it was an author's theatre; anyone who ventured on a triple laugh where only 'Ha! ha!' was marked, had to be firmly rebuked: rehearsals of *A Wife With a Smile*—see later— must have been agonising. As a man, Pinero starts to life in a talk with his friend William Archer early in the century.[4] 'You English dramatists as a body,' Archer said, 'have of late years concentrated your attention rather too exclusively on one corner of life: the Hyde Park Corner.' Pinero retaliated that his people in *The Benefit of the Doubt* were surely as suburban as even Archer could desire.

Archer: Suburban, perhaps, but they all lived at the rate of five thousand a year. You did not take us out of the eternal drawing-room. And if there was no duke in the play, there were a knight and a bishop.
Pinero: Well, would you have me play chess with nothing but pawns?
Archer: No, but I think you overwork your castles.
Pinero: . . . I think you would find, if you tried to write drama, not only that wealth and leisure are more productive of dramatic complications than poverty and hard work, but that if you want to get a certain order of ideas expressed or questions discussed, you must go pretty well up in the social scale. I assure you I have often tried to keep my characters down, as it were, and found I could not. I would feel, 'No, no, this won't do in this environment.' My characters would force me, in spite of myself, to lift them up in the world. You must take into account the inarticulateness, the inexpressiveness, of the English lower-middle and lower classes—their reluctance to analyse, to generalise, to give vivid utterance either to their thoughts or their emotions.

Pinero's outlook here reminds me sharply of a veteran actor, an Edwardian out of time;[5] for several seasons in the 1920s he was among the lights of a repertory theatre in the south-west of England. It was his destiny, as well as his desire, to play Dukes. If, thriftily, the dramatist had not provided one—and, even in the Edwardian plays still at that hour a staple of the repertory, there could be gaps—he would descend to an Earl, possibly to the near-disaster of a baronet. A week came when the director, who had a wry humour, cast him for Sam Bilson, the coffee-shop owner of *The Likes of Her*, Charles McEvoy's play from as late as 1923. Bilson is a stage Cockney in the vein, if without the phonetic intricacies, of Shaw's Burgess and Felix Drinkwater. We had seldom known anything sadder than our Duke in the toils of 'The bigger the clard the bigger the lining. . . . Walk art wiv me. Try me company a bit. Come to 'Ampstead wiv me on Bank 'oliday.' To observe him lifting the aspirates with both hands and struggling to drop them, was a sight that held us in sympathetic silence. Presently, to acute relief, he was raised again to the peerage, first as Chesterton's Duke in *Magic*, then as Lord Rockingham in *Under Two Flags*; audiences who had trembled for him settled down. I am sure Pinero would have understood.

In that conversation for the *Pall Mall Magazine*, Pinero had other things to say to Archer.[6] Thus (the critic had praised the versatility of The German dramatists):

. . . Chiefly, you forget that German audiences don't mind being bored, and ours do. Our people demand a certain sparkle and brightness in their plays that the Germans entirely dispense with.

Archer: You mean that we want 'smart' society, in two senses?

Pinero: Yes—is not that so?

Archer: Only, I believe, because no one has as yet had the art to present other strata of society (except in melodrama) strongly, interestingly.

Pinero: Perhaps, perhaps. But I don't think you realise the difficulty of dealing on the English stage with any special environment, other than what is vaguely known as society. A serious political play is impossible; we take our politics so tragically in real life that we can only make a farce of them in the theatre. A military play you might have, or a sporting play—but these, after all, would only be a particular brand of the society play. . . .

Again:

Is it not the fact that, from the Greeks onwards, the dramatist has always drawn his inspiration, or at any rate borrowed his method of expression, from the lives of people of exalted rank? Nothing of considerable merit, but low comedy, has ever come from the study of low life. Shakespeare, even in comedy, deals far more largely in dukes and duchesses than any dramatist of today. *The Merry Wives of Windsor*, if I remember rightly, is the only exception to this rule, and certainly not his happiest inspiration. As for tragedy, there is nothing that can be properly so esteemed in low life; because there is no height from which a common person may fall, consequently no irony of circumstances, no refinement of suffering. What have you to say to that?

Archer had a good deal to say. His last words were: 'The peasant's tragedy may be just as affecting as the peer's . . . Jude the Obscure moves us, in his obscurity, a good deal more than all the kings and princesses of Ruritania in all their insignia of state.' But Pinero would have none of it:

Fiction is one thing, the stage another. It was all very well for Turgeniev in fiction, to call a Russian peasant *The King Lear of the Steppes*. But the King Lear of the stage is Shakespeare's—the King of Britain—the man who stands on such a pinnacle that his fall from it excites pity and terror. For all our democratic theories, is it not true, as a matter of fact, that we are not greatly stirred by the sorrows of those in humble condition?

It was the full Edwardian voice. A younger man, William Somerset Maugham, put it with more irony in an essay written before his success as a playwright:[7] 'We English are idealists. . . . When a dramatist presents Duchesses to our admiring eyes, we feel in our element; we watch the acts of persons whom we would willingly meet at dinner, and our craving for the ideal is satisfied.' Pinero held to his view, even though in portions of *Letty*, in the depressing comedy of *A Wife Without a Smile*, and in *The Thunderbolt*, he did briefly slide down the scale. Some would include *His House In Order*, but I would not describe Overbury Towers ('the ice-house my brother calls his home' says Hilary Jesson, the *raisonneur*) as a place for 'the sorrows of those in humble condition.' Philosophic though he grew in an old age that saw the ruin of his theories—I have always wondered about that polite meeting with Sean O'Casey in a London club[8]—he might be a little disturbed to know that during the 1970s he was regarded as either a farce-man, creator of those frenzies by gas-light from ninety years before, or as the dramatist of the wistful *Trelawny*, gently evoking the Robertsonian stage. There one of the stock company actresses says to Tom Wrench, who is talking of his plays: 'You know, the speeches were so short and had such

33

ordinary words in them.'[9] Tom retorts:'I strive to make my people talk and behave like live people, don't I?' Pinero did; but his harsher critics refused to believe it: Max Beerbohm said, with some exaggeration, when reviewing *Letty* (1903) that its people spoke 'nothing but the lowest and most piteous kind of journalese'.[10] It is clear that his dialogue, never street-corner demotic, can be tryingly 'over-gowned and over-hatted'—the phrase for the French governess in *His House in Order*—and I have always recognised the truth of an emendation in a radio treatment of *The Gay Lord Quex*. 'I must relieve my heart; it is bursting' came through as 'I *must* speak to you, I must.' There are passages that could have taken iron courage to commit to paper. When Ardale appears at the window to Ellean in the third act of *The Second Mrs Tanqueray*, he exclaims: 'Isn't this fun! A rabbit ran across my foot while I was hiding behind that old yew.' At one of the latest revivals I could have sworn that sweat glistened on Ardale's brow as he spoke the words. It puzzled me that they could have occurred to a dramatist with his sense of the ridiculous in the right place: as in the third act of *The Schoolmistress*: 'It is embarrassing to break a bust in the house of comparative strangers.'

Pinero had important gifts. He was a generous, calculated storyteller. In marshalling a plot, he insisted upon suspense, never letting a play strike twelve in the middle of its first act and thereafter run down. In the 1970s craftsmanship is not a regarded virtue. Pinero, the Edwardian, lived for it and may very well live because of it. Imposed conventions could be tiresome. Generally a play had to be in four acts; most dramatists would climb their peak in the third. A flag planted, they had little to do but come down as quickly as possible. Pinero could suffer like his colleagues; but some of his fourth acts (*His House in Order*, *Mid-Channel*) are fluently resourceful. He approached playwriting with an actor's instinct for the dramatic, and he fortified it by a belief in technique that would not allow a play to droop off (as the Cornish put it) 'in ribbons, like wet weed'.

It may seem forced now, that moment in *The Second Mrs Tanqueray* when Aubrey realises he has a couple of letters to finish, so that Drummle, Jayne, and Misquith can put us safely in

34

the picture. And thirteen years later (1906) there would be the prelude to *His House In Order*, with secretary and journalist making sure in a rapid tic-tac of question-and-answer that we know the detailed background of life with the Jessons:[11]

FORSHAW [journalist]: . . . Do you mind explaining to me about the park—the park that's to be opened tomorrow.
HARDING [secretary]: Jesson Park.
FORSHAW: In memory of his late wife, isn't it?
HARDING: A memorial to the late Mrs Jesson—yes.
FORSHAW: And she was—who was she?
HARDING: A Miss Ridgeley—Miss Annabel Ridgeley, second daughter of Sir Daniel Ridgeley.
FORSHAW (*scribbling with a pencil upon the back of a letter*): Sir Daniel R-i-d-g-e—
HARDING: —l-e-y.
FORSHAW: The large colliery owner?
HARDING: Yes.
FORSHAW: Mr Jesson and Miss Ridgeley were married——? Kind of you to help me if you can.
HARDING: Delighted. Twelve years ago.
FORSHAW: The lady died——?
HARDING: Tomorrow is the third anniversary.
FORSHAW: Wasn't it a very sudden affair?
HARDING: Shocking.
FORSHAW: Carriage accident.
HARDING: Horses bolted . . .

We may smile, yet it is less alarming than those Victorian soliloquies—vanished for ever, with the aside—or the informative exchanges between butler and parlourmaid, telling each other, for no apparent reason, what each knew already. Pinero, writing without benefit of telephone—soon an inevitable prop—saw that his exposition was lucid and reasonably persuasive before he elaborated his play. A parodist, Wendy Monk, caught in a few speeches[12] the Edwardian manner that Pinero could make more readily plausible:

FIRST GUEST: Since Sir Arthur's poor wife died so suddenly in the hunting-field four years ago, Mrs FitzGeorge has been a constant visitor to The Grange.
SECOND GUEST: Mrs FitzGeorge? . . . But is she not the-the-person

who was involved in that unfortunate affair at The Firs in the year of
her late Majesty's diamond jubilee?
FIRST GUEST: Quite. The facts, as you will doubtless remember, were
these . . . [So on for two pages].
Enter Mrs FitzGeorge, followed by Sir Arthur.

Better this than a fragment of chaos uncontrolled.

Pinero did a lot for the dignity of the dramatist. Before his
time (he wrote)[13] there existed an impression that the
manuscript of a play, could it ever be dragged from the
prompter's shelf, would reveal itself as 'a dissolute-looking and
formless thing mercilessly scarred by the managerial blue pencil
and illuminated by those interpolations with which the
desperate actors have helped to lift the poor material into
temporary, unhealthy popularity'. That is the true Pinerotic
tone: he was writing in 1891 after changes in the law of copyright
had aided the dramatist and allowed him to protect and publish
a work without fear of piracy, in the kind of reading edition (not
the mere technical instrument of the acting edition) that would
please a waiting public. Pinero's plays, from *The Times* (1891)
were regularly issued. Later, Shaw, though at this hour he was
not a dramatist for the West End managers, proved, with the aid
of manifold and pictorial stage directions, that he would be 'the
cleanser of our day, / Whose art is both a Preface and a Play.'[14]
When his work did get to wider theatre audiences it had already
a solid band of readers behind it.

II

Pinero, in the new century, had been a dramatist for twenty
years. His first Edwardian play, *Iris* (1901), was not one of his
shapeliest: a triangle-drama that was, in effect, a relentless
portrait of a woman without moral stamina: a young widow
who will lose a fortune if she remarries. It ends with her
degradation, thrust out of doors while her betrayed protector, a
Spanish-Jewish financier, Maldonado, cries in volcanic rage,
'This is your punishment'; when she has gone, he tears the flat to
pieces. Originally, Pinero intended that Maldonado should
strangle the woman—what Stephen Phillips, in another context,

called 'this fell throttle'. Wisely, he changed his mind; but the play, as we have it now, is in no sense a major piece: the dramatist is a technician aloof from his characters. Even if Oscar Asche enjoyed the last tempestuous fury, Fay Davis, we gather, did not act Iris with any special power.

We cannot say much of the too ornately-phrased comedy, or social satire, *Letty* (1903). There Irene Vanbrugh—the Pinero actress of her time—played a girl clerk, Letty Shell, pursued by a sentimental profligate, Neville Letchmere (H. B. Irving), one of a family for which nothing goes right and which cannot shake off its past. 'We're all rotten,' he says; and 'The family record is monotonous reading, old girl!' It is a tautly composed narrative, but Pinero was not listening closely when he wrote it. Letty wants to say, 'We must realise that some women are luckier than others.' Poor Irene Vanbrugh found herself with this:

> To my imperfect intelligence, it seems that the first essential is to be capable of resigning oneself to a scheme of things which ordains that some women shall spend their lives in perpetual fag, while others—our more fortunate sisters, as they are styled—enjoy freedom and luxury galore.

We cannot be surprised that Irene Vanbrugh, remembering Pinero, thought first[15] of 'the sudden absence of all words and apparently almost trivial movements in the tensest and most shattering moments of feeling. . . . These are the moments which must inevitably live with an actress more than any amount of long speeches.'

The next full-length play, Pinero's least important, was *A Wife Without a Smile* (Wyndham's, 1904), baffling now if we do not recognise his fatal condescension when away from the peerage. Most people have taken care to forget the vagary of this all-but-farce. Max Beerbohm did not mind at the time—to regret its diction, as he did, was common form—but some critics were intensely shocked by the presence of a dancing doll, attached to the ceiling, that signalled dubious movements in the bedroom above. It was a silly idea: as Sir George Arthur said,[16] Pinero customarily had 'no use for suggestion. . . . What he had to say he said outright, and this robbed it of any veiled offence.' The piece, cheap though it is, seems comically harmless in a period   37 when (3 July 1974) the critic of *The Times*[17] can describe a comedy in which 'the married couple sit tensely over the teacups while the coital exclamations of Dave and his current girl resound from a room upstairs'. Max was obviously right about the verbal manner. We cannot believe that Archer, usually ready to forgive Pinero most of the way and still praising him (to Sean O'Casey's astonishment) in 1923, was happy about such lines as 'Our engagement followed a particularly superficial knowledge of each other's idiosyncrasies,' or 'The mere contemplation of two images so violently opposed in itself makes for mirth.' The anecdote of a dull riverside week-end at Taplow, a husband who believes passionately in his sense of humour, and a newly-married wife without a smile, is superfluous fooling, thorny now to read because of Pinero's ceaseless notation of laughter, 'Ha, ha! ho! ho! ho!', 'Ha, ha, ha, ha!' 'Ho, ho!' and so all the way, every sound having some particular nuance for the dramatist, if no one else. Phrase-hoarders may like Mrs Lovette's 'I suppose I may have the shandrydan to carry me to the station?'[18] (This meant a light, two-wheeled cart, or old rickety vehicle— probably the second: Mrs Lovette's request is 'withering'.) But it is little enough to remember from a long text.

Everybody was relieved when Pinero reached, in 1906, what would live on as one of his two most famous plays, though I was puzzled in 1974 to learn that a distinguished man of the theatre had never heard of it. This was *His House in Order*, tale of a conflict between the living and the dead. George Alexander, most generous of managers, was sure that *A Wife Without a Smile* had been simply an error. In 1897 he and Pinero, whose association had meant so much to the St James's, had had a dignified difference: it might have led to 'a stately dog-fight',[19] said A. E. W. Mason. For eight years they did not work together. 'To put the case shortly,' Pinero explained, 'there is not room for two autocrats in one small kingdom.' But in 1906 'Alec' and 'Pin' were together again. *A Wife Without a Smile*, worthless though it was, had been the means of reuniting them. The actor believed in the dramatist; Pinero acknowledged it gratefully, and Alexander's confidence grew as he received the earlier acts of *His House In Order*, sent to him as they were completed and printed. Soon all was prepared for those unexampled St James's

38

rehearsals: settings, properties, lighting, ready a fortnight before the opening; Pinero (Irene Vanbrugh remembered)[20] 'walking slowly up and down the stalls, his hands behind his back, his keen hawk-like eyes under the heavy black eyebrows. . . . He had no script in his hand, knowing every word of the play by heart; not one syllable could you alter without his immediate correction.' Pinero as ever had his own house in order. When Filmer Jesson insisted that 'every wheel of the mechanism of my private affairs, however minute, shall be duly oiled and preserved from grit', he spoke in his creator's voice. The play—'I never saw anything so *du théâtre*,' Max Beerbohm wrote to a friend—was a narrative of rebellion; the outbreak of a young second wife, Nina, the second Mrs Jesson, who must endure the patronising distaste of her predecessor's family. Overwhelmed, she hits upon evidence to prove that, after all, the first wife, Annabel Mary, legend of the virtues, was no paragon. Today we may wonder, a little smugly, about this bagful of compromising letters found by a child under the boudoir boards; no one in the St James's Theatre blinked. When Hilary, Nina's brother-in-law and the period's supreme *raisonneur*, gentler than some though still too talkative, urged her to tolerance, Pinero's craft was unwavering. Nina had had the audience with her from her first dishevelled entrance, 'with an air of subjection but with eyes full of rebellion'. It had later to be a grand theatrical moment when, with Irene Vanbrugh's kindling reality, she exclaimed: 'I go to no park tomorrow; as God hears me, I do not', and burst from the Jesson drawing-room.

That drawing-room was 'a vast apartment with panelled walls against which stiff-looking chairs are placed at regular intervals'. Pinero approved of this; he had other reservations. 'The drawing-room,' he told Alexander,[22] 'is perfect.' Not so the library. 'The scene was to have been our touch of the picturesque'—the old part of the building—'and Mr Macquoid has given us a bit of brand-new Shoolbred.' However, it duly survived a run of more than a year: no complaints from the moment when—an example of Pinero's minute instructions—Forshaw, the journalist, is found at curtain-rise, 'seated, gloved, upon the settee'. I wish that the management of the last London revival (1951), in several ways impressive, had realised that Pinero himself must be the final arbiter. In a permanent-set production Overbury Towers lacked its full gloom. The house was not perfectly in order; we lost the visual effects of Filmer's library and the mausoleum of the drawing-room. Moreover, not all of the cast had the period quality, the right weight. Long ago a charming woman picked up a paper with news of the sinking of the *Titanic*. She put it down in horror: 'Another boating accident!' It can be difficult if a modern cast in a Pinero drama falls into boating-accident understatement. Some of the 1951 cast had the true manner; Godfrey Tearle knew what to do with the diplomatist who finds room in his brother's house for both his diplomacy and his gift for the lay sermon.

We have had two excellent short-lived revivals of *The Thunderbolt* (1908) which Pinero entitled, boldly for him, 'An Episode in the History of a Provincial Family' (a family Henry Arthur Jones would have recognised and exaggerated). In the theatre where there's a will there's a way. Pinero's drama, in 'a sitting-room' for once, exposes the cupidity of a pretentious, hypocritical Edwardian group in a small town: the Mortimores of Singlehampton, gathered after the death of their relative, a wealthy brewer. Presumably he would have left everything, £170,000, to his cherished illegitimate daughter Helen, an art student. No will is found. The family, delighted at its luck, offers a small sum that the girl refuses. Suddenly a poor music-teacher's wife (the man was by no means a part for Mr Alexander, said the St James's audience) confesses that she has burned a document that left the estate to Helen. Until then the play, in its story-teller's manner, is compelling: the Theatre Theatrical serenely confident (and with no hope of inclusion in any monograph on the Theatre of Ideas). The last act, as so often, is the trouble, though a treatment by Brian Oulton in 1966 (Peggy Thorpe-Bates as the wife) proved that the play could still be dramatically valid. Max Beerbohm, in 1908, thought the dialogue better than usual, even if the heroine did leave him unpersuaded. (He quoted glumly:[23] 'I refused their help before I was fully acquainted with these, to me, uncongenial relations of father's—I don't include Mr Tad in that expression, of course.')

40

Sadly for Archer, plumbing always for the deeper meaning, Pinero stayed calmly aloof from the new intellectual theatre. Now and then he gave it a friendly nod, no more. In 1909, the year of his knighthood, *Mid-Channel* appeared at the St James's: a chillingly genuine play marred simply by one of the stock figures of the Edwardian stage who is altogether too obtrusive; the part can be acted, but it must put off any modern director. Alexander himself was not in the cast of a drama he continued to admire. Indeed nothing would infallibly have suited him, either the weak and unpleasant husband—entirely plausible in the context—or the *raisonneur*, the part that saddens us now, the man who is the judicial voice of polite society, social convention, more hortatory if less theatrically at the centre than Hilary Jesson had been in *His House in Order*. Alexander's absence aside, everything else at the St James's was amply Pinerotic. The play was written massively, according to plan, as if the Shaw-Barker method had never existed: a precise and truthful emotional statement and a plot tightly controlled. Zoë Blundell, self-centred, drearily married, has not been on the stage for more than two minutes before she says:[24] 'Why is it that more people commit suicide in summer than in winter? . . . You'll see, when I put an end to myself, it will be in the winter-time.' Four acts later, when the curtain drops after the *raisonneur*'s horrified 'She told me once it would be in the *winter* time—!' it is in the glowing sun of a June afternoon. As much as anything, the manner of the suicide shattered the play's chances. Alexander's absence might have been borne; the St James's could not take the horror of that ultimate fall from the top-floor balcony of a block of flats. The height is emphasised in Pinero's note on 'a distant view of the upper part of the Albert Hall and of other lofty buildings'; a girl's, 'Mother, do come and look at the tiny men and women,' and the mother's 'You know I don't care for heights.' At the last a young man, standing in the doorway between bedroom and sitting-room, exclaims: 'I can't make it out, she's not there'.[25] C. M. Lowne, who was on the stage when the words were spoken, told A. E. W. Mason[26] that an audible shudder quivered through the house; only one thing could have happened. It killed the play.

Mid-Channel now is seldom on the stage; but when I saw it last, in 1945, it excited a critical audience in a small London theatre, 41 few of whom, I imagine, had heard of Pinero or knew the circumstances in which he wrote. The grave trouble, as we read the text, is the aggressive *raisonneur*, 'the Honble. Peter Mottram, a spruce, well-preserved man of fifty'. Talking throughout in italics, he begins by explaining to Zoë just why she and her husband Theodore—they have refused to have children—are sick of each other after nearly fourteen years. To weight his homilies, the man is prodigal in analogy and metaphor. He suggests that nothing can be more depressing than the row of trophies on the sideboard.[27] 'So it is with life generally. You scoop in the prizes—and there are the pots on the sideboard to remind you that it ain't the *prizes* that count, but the pushin' and the strugglin' and the cheerin'.' Shortly after this he is telling—and almost one writes tellin'—both Zoë and Theodore about a shoal midway between Folkestone and Boulogne, Le Colbart, or The Ridge, in mid-Channel.[28] Here, during the crossing, he feels 'fidgety, restless, out o' sorts—hatin' myself and hatin' the man who's been sharin' my cabin with me.' The sensation has not lasted long:

> Gradually the beastly motion has died down, and in a quarter-of-an-hour or so I've found myself pacin' the deck again, arm-in-arm with the travellin' companion I've been positively loathin' a few minutes earlier.

THEODORE (*gaping demonstratively*): Very interesting.

PETER: My dear pals, I remember the idea once occurrin' to me—I mentioned it to Charlie Westbrook at the time—there's a resemblance between *that* and marriage.

THEODORE (*shortly*): Ha! Thought that was coming.

ZOË *turns in her chair to listen to Peter.*

PETER: Yes, and marriage, mark you, at its best and brightest. The happiest and luckiest of married couples have got to cross that wretched Ridge. However successful the first half of their journey may be, there's the rough-and-tumble of mid-Channel to negotiate. Some arrive there quicker than others, some later; it depends on wind and tide. But they *get* there; and a bad time it is, and must be—a time when travellin' companions see nothin' but the spots on each other's yellow faces, and when innoomerable kind words and inoomerable kind acts are clean forgotten. But, as I tell you, it's soon over—*well* over, if only Mr Jack and Mrs Jill will understand the situation; if only they'll say to themselves, 'We're on the Ridge;

we're in mid-Channel; in another quarter-of-an-hour the boat'll be steady again—as steady as when we stepped on to the gangway.'

The analogy would be all right if only Pinero had cut it short. Ivor Brown, who respected his technique as much as he lamented his verbosity, used to say that he should have the discipline of writing on the arts within the limits of a war-time newspaper. During the second act of *Mid-Channel* Mottram is back again. This time there is a long passage on the breaking of china, the collection and fitting together of the fragments:[29] 'Go into the homes of three-fifths of the married people you know—*I* know—and you'll find some imposin' specimens of porcelain that won't bear inspectin' very narrowly.' Further: 'Ain't it wiser to repair the broken china, rather than chuck the bits in the dustbin.' Of course, it will never be repaired, but Mottram is doing his duty as wandering moralist. The play is full-scale Pinero. He shared with Henry Arthur Jones a trick of padding his cast with names. Jones's *raisonneur* (acted by Charles Wyndham), in the key speech of *The Liars*, refers to Charles Gray and Lady Rideout, Billy Dover and Polly Atchison, Sir Bonham Dancer, George Nuneham ('George is conducting a tramcar in New York'), and Mrs Sandys: we have not heard of any of these before, but there they are, filling out the speech. So, too, in *Mid-Channel*, we have Zoë's 'tame robins', Harry Estridge, Jim Mallandain, Cossy Rawlings, Gus Hedmont, Bobby Relf; Sir Gerald Duckfield is glanced at, and the Langdales, and the objectionable Claud Lowenstein on his jealous watch in Italy. 'He arrived at Perugia the day you left. . . . He put up at the Brufani too.' Pinero was always the man of the world: 'I saw him about a fortnight ago at the Opera; I was with the Ormerods in their box'; 'We were at Madame Levine's yesterday . . . ordering frocks, and Camille, the skirtmaker, told us you were back.' Alexander was known to chide his players if he saw them in the street looking at all informal; they must never forget their responsibility to the St James's. Pinero never forgot. The diction of *Mid-Channel*, in spite of Archer's praise ('absolutely irreproachable') can be as starched as the men's collars. Speeches unnoticed in performance when spoken by players trained in the mode—they are hard to find now—rise again and   43 again to worry a reader: Mottram's 'Those faulty old Mings are emblematic of the establishment they adorn'; Thedore's 'Stand the naughty boy in the corner; he's earned any amount of humiliation you choose to inflict'; Ethel's 'Surely, if there is one thing which is a girl's own particular business, it is settling preliminaries with her best young man'; and Zoë's 'Ah, Theo, I believe we should have crossed that Ridge safely enough (*Laying her hands upon his heart*), but for our cursed, cursed selfishness——.'

Alexander's St James's has gone, and its style of dialogue with it; and yet *Mid-Channel* continues to be an enduring play of its world, a work to shame later tinkerers in flimsy plywood. Hardly an 'idea' to its name (if Peter Mottram will forgive us), but real feeling, a direct theatrical impulse, a narrative strongly ordered. Platitudes can sometimes be exasperatingly true. It is certainly true that if one does not want to know what happens next, a play is failing. Pinero's story-telling gift defeats mockery; it was something the Edwardians knew about and respected. And when James Agate reviewed the 1922 revival (once more with Irene Vanbrugh), he wrote:[30] '*Mid-Channel* is a good play because we want urgently to know what will be said by Ferris and done by Blundell when the lover opens the door behind which Blundell's wife is concealed. It is a very good play because it makes us debate what the characters would or should have done in real life. And it is a supremely good piece of playwriting because the climax is made to appear not an isolated trick of pretty craftsmanship, but the culminating point in a sequence of inevitable happenings. We do not feel, as in the purely artificial drama, that if the postman had not mislaid the letter the tragedy would not have happened.'

Pinero had only four other plays in our period. Two were at full-length. One was a comedy called *Preserving Mr Panmure* (1911) which—and this is among the exceptions—is not worthy of preservation, though it had a London revival in 1950: a girl named Josepha Quarendon has been kissed and makes a prolonged fuss. The satire of *The 'Mind-the-Paint' Girl* (1912), a piece with a hard, bright varnish, is about the chorus marrying into the aristocracy and 'mixing the breed a bit'. The names roll as usual: 'Look at the two lads who've married Gwennie Harker

and Maudie Trevail—Kinterton and Colenroy; and
Fawcus—Sir Guy Fawcus—Eva Shafto's husband; they haven't
a chin or a forehead between 'em, and their chests are as narrow
as a ten-inch plank.' Amiable but minor, the play ends with a
line spoken by the mother of one of the actresses: 'Think—think
wot a lot o' good you're all doin' to the aristocracy!' Yes; but
this musical-comedy theatre lacked the spirit of Bagnigge Wells
in *Trelawny*. Pinero, I think, showed what he felt about the
swaying of the London theatre when he wrote the short
'domestic episode' of *Playgoers*, his second one-act play at this
time. The other was *The Widow of Wasdale Head*, an anecdote
about what J. T. Grein dismissed as 'a funny ghost with a
Cumberland accent'; Frederick Kerr, who was the ghost and did
not look in the least like one, said that Pinero made one of his
rare mistakes in production.[31] 'I had to make my entrance on to
a darkened stage through the fireplace, and to the accompani-
ment of flickering lights. I was, in short, a very palpable human
being, although my clothes were ineffectively painted with
phosphorus.'

Pinero enjoyed himself far more in *Playgoers*. A mistress,
having engaged and purred over her new servants—cook,
parlourmaid, housemaid, kitchenmaid, useful maid, a full
house—offers them a visit to the theatre:[32] 'What you will see is a
play of ideas, something to stimulate your imaginations and
make you think . . . A slice cut clean out of life in fact.'

THE HOUSEMAID: Sounds 'orribly crool.
THE KITCHENMAID (*awe-struck*): Does that mean that knives is freely
used, mum?
THE MISTRESS: Not necessarily—except by the Censor.
THE COOK: Well, any'ow, girls, it strikes me we're in for a preshus
dull evenin'.

The result is, naturally, a domestic rebellion. We return to
Johnny Tarleton in *Misalliance* three years before:[33] 'If I find that
the author's simply getting at me the whole time, I consider that
he's obtained my money under false pretences. . . I'm a natural
man; and, as such, I don't like being got at. . . . Who and what
is an author that he should be privileged to take liberties that are
not allowed to other men.'   45

III

Where Pinero had eight full-length plays staged during our period, an older man, always a step behind, Henry Arthur Jones (1851–1929), had fourteen acted, though only eleven in London (the other three were done in New York); he also wrote seven that were unacted, as well as various short pieces, produced or unproduced. Combative, forthright, generous, he had a certain sandpaper quality. Pinero, masterful in the theatre, ruled every semi-colon; to have outfaced him would have been like ordering the sun to stand still upon Gibeon. But the testier Jones was not readily welcome at a rehearsal: Tree in 1899 excluded him from *Carnac Sahib*.

Of puritanical farming stock from Buckinghamshire, he had given himself wholly to the stage. He left school at twelve, worked in a draper's shop, became a commercial traveller, and began to write plays; when he was thirty he had an overwhelming success with the melodrama of *The Silver King* (1882), almost wholly his own though the hack writer Henry Herman's name would linger on the title-page. With his nonconformist upbringing he never lost his urge to preach. He was a man of simmering energy, affectionately respected by such people as Shaw and Beerbohm in spite of his readiness to fight at any moment. At heart Jones believed that he could have been a bigger man than he was. To him his life was a lost cause; yet he would not believe that in mid-career he was harming himself by returning over and over to the same themes, the same people. One became conscious—prolific though he was—of a cramped imagination. He lagged behind Pinero because, even if he could write suppler dialogue, he wanted the innate sophistication, the gloss, of his always friendly rival. Somehow he could never fully escape from his emperor of melodramas, put on by Wilson Barrett, applauded by Matthew Arnold, improbably but sincerely, and recalled through the years for a line with several ancestors, 'O God! Put back Thy universe and give me yesterday.'[34]

46   By the turn of the century Jones had progressed from the

sensational to the social, from Black Brake Wharf to the late-Victorian achievement of his two real triumphs, *The Liars* (1897) and *Mrs Dane's Defence* (1900), the first a shimmering tissue of drawing-room comedy, the second a formal drama minutely-pieced. *Mrs Dane*, though he wrote so much else, would be the last of his major plays. Its Mrs Dane of Sunningwater was really Felicia Hindemarsh of Tawhampton, with a troublesome past—inevitably the woman had to suffer—somewhere near the bluer reaches of the Danube. In Gilbert's words from another theatre:[35]

> I once was Some One—and the Was Will Be.
> The Present as we speak becomes the Past,
> The Past repeats itself, and so is Future.

Mrs Dane was fated to love the son of a formerly eminent judge, not a sound plan for a woman with her background, especially if the potential father-in-law at his meridian could have squeezed the truth from a Munchausen in a couple of questions. But if Mrs Dane had not been foolhardy, there would have been no play; the stage would have missed the kind of third-act *coup* ('Woman, you are lying! You are Felicia Hindemarsh!') in which Jones could be redoubtable. As a 'slice of life'—a phrase unknown then—*Mrs Dane* may be vulnerable. I do not believe we should try to discover unintentional subtleties. It is an example of construction, tenoned and mortised, from the bench of an intermittently inspired craftsman. He said once[36] that, having made his design, he wrote the third act—with the scene for Sir Daniel and Mrs Dane—inside four hours. It was a pity that he had to brace on a fourth act; turn-of-the-century rules demanded it, for a Mrs Dane could never go free. Here she is dismissed to Devon. Mr George Rowell has said wittily:[37] 'The final act of a problem play could be relied on to dispatch the awkward characters to the grave or the Colonies, and the others to church, with equal speed and skill.' True, and Devon was as good a place as any other.

Jones, unlike many of his colleagues, wrote in later life a study of his working methods. Over and over, at this hour, he was asking himself why he was no longer a fashionable dramatist—in 1923 the belated London success of his old 47 drama, *The Lie*, did give him some startled joy—and he perpetually revisited his past work, reconsidering and remembering. In 1923 he answered an American questionnaire. The important points, looking back, are these:[38]

Whatever may be the force and insight of your character drawing; whatever may be the loftiness of your ideas and opinions, until you have smelted them into a story, you have got no play that will hold a general audience; and I would particularly impress these points upon a young dramatist. Of course, there is nearly always a temporary reputation and a momentary success to be gained by anyone who is clever enough to discover some new way of boring people in the theatre. . . .

Being addressed to a general average audience [a play] should try to meet them on the common ground of the permanent passions, emotions, follies, vices, and humours of humanity. It should not be written for a clique, or for a coterie of superior persons. Repertory theatres have failed in England because their promoters have mainly produced freakish and eccentric pieces, and have tried to elevate the drama by offering plays that keep the general public out of the theatre.

(We can guess what Barry Jackson at Birmingham, William Armstrong in Liverpool, or even George King in Plymouth, might have said of this.)

I take great pains with my dialogue, and, so far as the necessary conventions of the theatre will allow, I try to make it the exact utterance of the character in that situation. When I write a scene, I hear every word of it spoken. Here, again, the best work is automatic, and the best and truest dialogue is not that which is taken from real life, but that which registers itself upon the inner ear as the veritable utterance of that particular character.

My . . . plays since 1894 have been rehearsed from printed books, and in most of them not a line has been changed since they left my study.

He may not have liked the unofficial Theatre of Ideas; but he had many resolute ideas of his own. He was obsessed, Edwardianly, by the perils and ramifications of lying (Hawtrey's work as an actor further illustrated the Edwardian pre-occupation with this theme). He detested moral hypocrisy. Though he wrote various useful guilty-wife light comedies, his most deeply-felt play was *The Hypocrites* (New York, 1906;

48

London, 1907). In this, frequently revived out of London during the 1920s, a pregnant girl is terrorised into perjury by a provincial family whose son has seduced her. One of the characters observes: 'Civilisation is rotten at the core, especially in a rotten little place like this.' ('Rotten' was a great Edwardian word.) He wrote, too, a steady flow of work now largely overlooked: a good family man himself, his people were usually in compromising circumstances and his heroine in need of a *raisonneur*.

In *The Lackey's Carnival* (1900), an upstairs-and-downstairs contrivance soon forgotten after Barrie's *The Admirable Crichton*, Evelyn Millard threw up her part because she would not speak the words, 'I swear to you by my unborn child'.[39] In the wildly-named *The Princess's Nose* (1902) a wife tries to regain her husband's affection by using a mistress's tricks. *Chance the Idol* (also 1902) is about a woman who takes to the casino in the hope of making enough money to pay her faithless seducer's debts and tempting him to marry her. *Whitewashing Julia* (1903) dramatises a scandal about a young widow in a small cathedral city: had she, or had she not, been married morganatically to a Duke? *The Chevaleer* (1904) has the usual guilty pair, but with a cheapjack showman—a florid character-part hardly under-played by Arthur Bourchier—always at hand. *Joseph Entangled* (1904) was a trivial affair of which Max Beerbohm could say at least, 'In the art of writing realistic comedy of manners, [Jones] is far pre-eminent over our other playwrights . . . There is never a line that has not the true oral ring.'[40] *The Heroic Stubbs* (1906) concerned a romantic Bond Street bootmaker played by James Welch. And *Dolly Reforming Herself* (1908), a comically observant and fluent business, developed into a third-act crescendo of husband-and-wife quarrelling (C. E. Montague called it 'a cyclonic tiff')[11] over Dolly's unpaid dress bills. George Alexander staged *The Ogre* (1911) at the crest of the militant-suffragette outcry; it contained an anti-feminist scene in which the man of the household nailed his riding-breeches above the mantelpiece. The play failed. *Mary Goes First* (1913), which did better, is a corrosive light comedy about middle-class snobbery; it had Marie Tempest in one of her exact and metallic performances, all technique. Several of these pieces are 49 competent, but they have left few marks. *Dolly Reforming Herself* did reappear momentarily in a very good radio revival during 1950. William Archer, writing in 1923, put Jones's principal flaw into one sentence.[42] 'There is no sin in this society,' he wrote, 'that cannot be expiated, no wound that cannot be healed, by Mr Jones's famous panacea for the ills of matrimonial life—a little dinner at the Savoy, to be followed next day by a visit to a Bond Street jeweller's or a fashionable fur-shop.'

One play, *The Divine Gift*, I have not mentioned because, although published (1913), it was never performed. Jones believed it to be among his most important works, next to *Michael and His Lost Angel* (1896) which dramatised a struggle between an ascetic's allegiance to his religion and his passion for Audrie, the lost angel, a part that the maddeningly temperamental Mrs Patrick Campbell refused to play. Time has faded *The Divine Gift*. Its main figure, philosopher and 'sage', confesses, 'I do preach terribly,' and he does; surprisingly in Pinerotic diction that was not, as a rule, a Jones failing. We get such trip-wire lines as 'Confound this universal amorosity that's always confounding everything else in the universe.'[43] There is also, in the last act, an embarrassing young Cornish composer who repeats that his mother used to say to him: 'Now Jan my sonny boy, daun't 'ee be vulish weth thase heere music.'[44] But the preface, dedicated to Professor Gilbert Murray who had unguardedly called Jones old-fashioned, but who accepted the dedication with disarming serenity, counts now more than the play. It spoke for a desperate fighter, a dramatist who knew himself to be beaten, however briskly he disguised it, but who would not allow himself to be pitied. In the preface Jones complained that the realistic drama of modern life had become 'an eavesdropping photographic reporter, taking snapshots and shorthand notes'.[45] Again:

A drama without ideas is empty and sterile, That we all allow. But a drama that sets out to exploit and enforce ideas and opinions is of the nature of a political caucus and ends by grinding out wind.

And further:

The field of the modern drama is strewn with disabled riders who have hastily mounted raw wild colts of ideas, and never get home with them, but lie crippled and groaning while their ideas are aimlessly kicking and stampeding the country.[46]

However he dissembled it, Jones was always a late Victorian; he could not compromise. During the Edwardian period he was something of a permanent shadow, a dramatist whom his admirers hoped anxiously to see again at his strongest, but who had lost the knack of surprising himself or his hearers. Having nothing of Pinero's massive repose, he fell out of general stage fashion and sought irritably to occupy himself with a sequence of rhetorical pamphlets. Except for a stirring Casson-Thorndike production of *The Lie* (1923), a melodrama acted nine years earlier in New York, the 1920s would hear little of him. He died in relative obscurity, loved by his friends but a champion of an outmoded theatre who had seen his world pass. *The Life and Letters of Henry Arthur Jones* (1930), by his daughter Doris, is a loyal and touching memoir with an epigraph from *The Divine Gift*: 'Endurance, not enjoyment, is man's pass-key though this world.'

IV

Jones was a more sympathetic figure than William Somerset Maugham, formerly a doctor (and author of the realistic novel, *Liza of Lambeth*), who found a prescription for the Edwardian popular theatre. It was some time before he was called in; when he was, his brougham seemed to be always at the door. At first his plays accumulated, unwanted, in his desk. There was a false London start with *A Man of Honour*, a grave, unremarkable piece—class distinction again—about a barrister's marriage to a barmaid (written in 1898; revised; Stage Society, 1903; brief West End run, 1904). Silence then until the acceptance of *Lady Frederick* (1907), after which he could use up his scripts, seized at once by managements in waiting. *Lady Frederick*, four years old, got its production by luck when Otho Stuart needed a stopgap for the Royal Court, never out of the news for long. No one had considered the comedy earlier because of its third-act scene in which an 'adventuress with a heart of gold' deliberately disillusions her infatuated young lover. Stage direction: '[Lady   51

Frederick] comes through the curtains. She wears a kimono, her hair is all dishevelled, hanging about her head in a tangled mop. She is not made up and looks haggard and yellow and lined.'[47] This, in fact, would establish the piece. Transferred to four London theatres during more than 400 performances, it has been revived three times, though by now it has begun to fray. In 1908 Maugham was at the heart of fashion. Three of his trifles pleased the half-guinea stalls and had a note of astringency beneath the comic invention. At one point he had four plays running together. The most amusing, *Jack Straw* (1905; produced 1908) was a farce about a waiter masquerading as the Archduke Sebastian of Pomerania, who proves—among general bewilderment—to be the Archduke Sebastian: Charles Hawtrey used to time Straw's evasions as if he were flicking sunlight into his watcher's eyes with a twist of a hand-mirror. (Maugham himself, in several comedies, was good at this harmless legerdemain.) The dullest of the four plays, and the oldest (1899), was *The Explorer*, staged by the idolised Lewis Waller; even under this auspicious star it had to struggle for life.

Maugham's work seldom struggled. *Smith* did not. In this (1909), most likeable of his early works, a young parlourmaid attracts her mistress's brother, home from Rhodesia, because she is simple, candid, and a relief from her social superiors ('I might as well be shocked by the marionettes in a child's theatre'). To them she is just a maidservant, an automaton in a dismally repressive uniform that might have extinguished any actress but Marie Löhr. To him she is an honourable human being. The play get a little doughy as it goes on, but it does confirm, to our pleasure, that Maugham had a heart. In that world, hardly one for Beaumarchais and *Figaro*, it was thought unwise and tasteless to have a servant as the centre of a narrative. That would have been said, undoubtedly, of *The Lackey's Carnival* and *The Admirable Crichton*: to span the abyss between rigidly-defined 'classes' was as dangerous as to leap from the Swaying Spur to the Trembling Stone.[48] 'Pray heaven a professional will never captain England!' Lord Hawke, the cricketer, said once; we cannot imagine what he would have made of *Smith*. In the theatre servants were useful functionaries; if properly dressed and respectful, they could provide a little incidental comedy;

but except in the Theatre of Ideas and the occasional subversiveness of Barrie and Maugham, one had always to be discreetly conscious of the baize door and a voice from *Troilus and Cressida*[49] that spoke across three centuries to the Edwardian audience (Ulysses and Pinero would have had certain things in common):

> The heavens themselves, the planets and this centre,
> Observe degree, priority and place,
> Insisture, course, proportion, season, form,
> Office and custom, in all line of order . . .
> . . . O, when degree is shak'd,
> Which is the ladder of all high designs,
> The enterprise is sick! . . .
> Take but degree away, untune that string,
> And, hark, what discord follows!

Still, in general, Maugham observed degree; after *Smith* there followed a line of 'trim parlourmaids'. One adventure was enough.

It was Maugham's own fault if critics filed him away as a perpetual cynic. I believe that Blenkinsop, in *Mrs Dot* (1904; produced 1908) speaks with the dramatist's personal voice when he says:[50] 'There's nothing the world loves more than a ready-made description which they can hang on to a man, and so save themselves all trouble in future. When I was quite young it occurred to someone that I was a cynic, and since then I've never been able to remark that it was a fine day without being accused of odious cynicism.' The reply to this, 'My dear Mr Blenkinsop, what everyone says is always true; that is one of the foundations of society,' comes straight from the writer who has said elsewhere that epigrams are simple: 'You have only to loop the loop on a commonplace and come down between the lines.'[51] Maugham's last play before the war—there had been others of no special importance—was *The Land of Promise* (London, 1914), a change from the steady heliograph-flash, or the diamond-scratching, of his artificial comedies. Deserting the profitable formulae, it was, like Jones's *The Ogre*, a man's play at a time of feminine assertion: 'There's only one law here and that's the law of the strongest.' Masculine affirmation aside, *The Land of Promise* studies the lot of British settlers in Canada. Its curtain 53 should have stayed down after the third act when the girl whose pride has forced her into matrimony with a strong man in a Manitoban shack, acknowledges that she is beaten:[52]

NORAH: To-morrow. (*A look of shame, fear, anguish, passes over her face, and then, violently, a convulsive shudder runs through her whole body. She puts her hands to her eyes and walks slowly to the door*).

Maugham's richest years in the theatre were to come. But the man himself hardly altered. A. V. Cookman, drama critic of *The Times*, once said of him:[53] 'He has seen no point in writing a play that should not be successful, but. . . he achieved the popularity he was resolved to have without being good-natured, expansive, optimistic, romantic, or soothing. His humour was sardonic, his attitude towards the virtues untrustful, his romanticism that of one who had discovered with a certain wry pleasure that there was precious little in it; and if he gave the public what it liked—a good story—it was what he himself liked. That was why the stories were so good, and why . . . he tired of the theatre when theatregoers seemed no longer to share his taste.'

Now, if some of his Edwardian comedies look haggard and yellow or lined, *Smith*, *Jack Straw*, and *Mrs Dot*, all creditably restored in the 1950s, might bear further revival. But, an urgent reservation (and it applies to the entire Edwardian drama), no director should approach them condescendingly as fragments of period fun. That way disaster lies.

V

Many other dramatists were welcome in the drawing-room. I was lucky enough, no doubt, to see the Edwardian stage in microcosm through the productions of one of the remotest and quietly courageous of British repertory theatres, kept going on rather less than the end of a shoestring. Today it is lost so utterly beneath the street-plan of a rebuilt Plymouth that we can hardly determine where it stood in the lawyers' precinct. Founded in 1915 (just outside our scope) it endured until 1935. When I knew it during the mid-1920s, its programmes were still largely pre-1914. The ironically smiling George S. King, active partner in its management and himself a man of the Edwardian stage, was a curious blend of the aspiring and the commercial. He would not scruple to do *Three Weeks*, *The Sorrows of Satan*, or *Our Flat*; but he preferred that the stage of his doll's house theatre, a tilted and cluttered tea-tray poised on a spiral stair (where a Falstaff, inevitably, stuck half-way), should be given to the work of Shaw—*The Philanderer* to *Heartbreak House*—Pinero, Galsworthy, Barrie, Jones, Maugham, Hankin, and Sutro, as well as the best of the period's lesser men. Shaw, who respected the enterprise, was invariably helpful.[54]

King changed his bill week by week: hard labour for the cast, pleasure for young collectors. He would have agreed with George Saintsbury about 'that basest of limitations, the single appetite for modernity'. So he saw that the Repertory's yellow-and-black posters, benevolent wasps round the town, announced an entire festival of drama. Work rarely paused in that severe little building where the drawing-room, thirty weeks out of the fifty-two, was in old oak, and the sharply-spurred hero of a Ruritanian romance knocked down a range of snow-crested mountains as he entered. Here, in King's programmes, the major names aside, were such plays as *Lady Huntworth's Experiment* (R. C. Carton), vicarage garden, kitchen, library, Captain Dorvaston (late Bengal Cavalry) and the Rev. Audley Pillenger, vicar of Stillford in the parish of Dronesborough; *Mice and Men* (Madeleine Lucette Ryley), Hampstead in 1786, the masquerade ball at Belsize House, a 'scholar, scientist, and philosopher' and a demure orphan; Captain (always the prefix) Robert Marshall's *His Excellency the Governor* in the Government House of the Amandaland Islands, Indian Ocean; C. Haddon Chambers's spirited *Passers-By*, with an independent heroine Galsworthy might have applauded; and Hubert Henry Davies's *Mrs Gorringe's Necklace*: 'David takes a revolver from his pocket, examines it, and goes out into the garden.'[55]

A few years ago, discovering the text of *Mrs Gorringe* (done originally by Charles Wyndham and Mary Moore) in the mixed and cosmopolitan bookcase of a *pensione* on the Fiesole hill, I asked yet again whether a play that ended in suicide could legitimately be termed a comedy. At its prime no one objected, probably because Mrs Gorringe, owner of the stolen necklace 55 and seldom given to consecutive thought, was an entertainment in herself: not in the least like those other matrons of the theatre, a regiment over twenty years or so: Mrs Tanqueray, Mrs Dane, Mrs Warren, Mrs Ebbsmith, Mrs Dot, Mrs Daventry, Mrs Repton. Davies, a gentle, amusing man—like Jones, of stern puritan stock—was a student of feminine psychology. He could not join the halves of *Mrs Gorringe's Necklace*—the serious scenes are pancake-flat—any more than he could manage *Cousin Kate* (1905) which, in the text, never quite knows what it is doing. His subtlest play is *The Mollusc* (1907), a quartet-comedy and one of the first, about a woman's method of domestic dictatorship from an armchair: she is limp and she clings. It is still wise and cheerful. A few lesser parts would help, but in those days thrifty dramatists could keep the theatre alive without the telephone that would be another generation's life-preserver. *Lady Epping's Lawsuit* (1908), plentifully cast—nineteen speaking parts besides 'barristers, solicitors, clerks, pressmen, footmen, and the general public'—rests on its incidentals rather than its tall story: the closing scene is a mere welter of farce.

Davies, though he might have been, was not in the Theatre of Ideas. Similarly, Alfred Sutro, nearer dramatically to Maugham than Davies but without Maugham's cool detachment, never used the stage as a teaching hospital. He liked strong, not particularly silent, men and the style of dialogue expected in society drama: it was a time when you could afford to approach an epigram with some pomp, inspect the terrain, manœuvre into position for the delivery, deliver, accept the applause, and re-charge. Sutro's most adroit union of the elements was in his early play, *The Walls of Jericho* (1904), for Arthur Bourchier, in management at the Garrick, and Violet Vanbrugh. Before it opened, Sydney Valentine, who was in the cast, said gloomily: 'I don't think it stands a dog's chance'; it ran for 423 performances. Its rich Australian sheep-farmer, Jack Frobisher ('Fighting Jack' with 'the eyes of a man used to living in wide spaces') is married to the daughter of a Marquis; at the end he bears her off from Mayfair to Queensland, something we are ready for after his speech at the end of the first act: 'I found myself snared, caught by the heels, trapped! I found that I had 56 grown sensitive to ridicule; and I live in the midst of people who only smile. I found that my will had forsaken me, that I no longer wanted to do things, that I had become a mere doll and a puppet. And now the rebellion in me is dying away. . . .' Not at all. See the end of the fourth act:

ALETHEA: No, no, I will go with you, Jack—I will go with you! and, oh!—I will try!
JACK: Ally! (*He takes her in his arms*).

Thinking of *The Walls of Jericho*, which used to fit into place with the assured snap of a gladstone-bag (it might not do so now), one remembers such a speech as this by Lady Westerby:[56] 'We women cry out at tyranny, but in our hearts we admire the tyrant. They call us complex, we are as elementary as the tide beneath the moon. Govern us, we cry to our husbands—and if you do, we scratch, but our soul is at peace.' The observation, at which Shaw must have chuckled, was Edwardian through and through.

The cast included a Duchess (good at bridge), a Marquis, two Barons, Lady Westerby, Lady Porchester, Lady Lucy Derenham, and Lady Alethea Frobisher. Clearly a play fitted: efficient in its mood and better than most of Sutro's later work; an attack on the 'smart set' which itself enjoyed the experience and ensured that the attack continued for fifteen months. There were other captains of industry, though fewer members of the peerage, in *John Glayde's Honour* (1907) and *The Builder of Bridges* (1908). Possibly Sutro—a man ineradicably charming and sociable—worked with most ease in his one-act plays, skilled miniatures, not the form of 'curtain-raising' sketch that competed against late arrivals in stalls and circle.

Time has been as cruel to several of his contemporaries as to Sutro. Even historically-minded repertory directors (few of them touch the Edwardian shelves) forget Captain Marshall's *The Second In Command* in which Cyril Maude gave his crisp-biscuit quality to Major Christopher Bingham, VC. Yet the play, like other of Marshall's—a farcical romance, *The Duke of Killiecrankie*, for one—is professionally put together. We might suppose now that a wittier dramatist, R. C. Carton (1856–1928) wrote in invisible ink that was warmed into view only on the night of a performance and then faded again. Max Beerbohm, 57

who enjoyed his comedies in moderation, described him[57] as
'the one and never wavering exponent of what may be called
Hymeneal Dramaturgy.' That was because his wife Katherine,
'Miss Compton,' was in nearly all of the plays, few with titles that
have continued to mean anything. Who were *Mr Hopkinson*, or
The Rich Mrs Repton, or *The Eccentric Lord Comberdene?* But Carton,
in his extended anecdotes, had a fertile good humour—he was,
maybe, the William Douglas Home of his period—and his
people, could they have assembled round him, might have
chanted a line from the early *Robin Goodfellow* (1893), 'There is
orange peel on every square of life's pavements.' Normally
Carton could be counted on for reasonable drawing-room
procedure, though *Lady Huntworth's Experiment*, with its three
men stowed away in different cupboards, was scarcely the mould
of form.

That was not the right word for Charles Haddon Chambers
(1860–1921), an Australian, jaunty, easy-going, and lonely.
More fluent in the 1890s, he wrote a dozen plays: the most
permanent is *The Tyranny of Tears* (1899), artificial domestic
comedy, colloquially written, about a wife who could have
shared some useful confidences with the woman in *The Mollusc.*
Chambers, whose sole later piece of note was *Passers-By* (1911;
tramp and cabman as wealthy's man's fortuitous guests on a
winter night), is principally remembered, I suppose, for his
phrase, 'the long arm of coincidence', used by a bushranger-in-
London in *Captain Swift*, as far back as 1888. Like Macduff's 'one
fell swoop' which few actors isolate now, the words are so
rubbed that one hardly hears them. *Captain Swift* had a trick that
the Edwardians would lose: titles for its acts. Thus: (1)
Retrieving a Past Life; (2) Retaliation; (3) Brother Against
Brother; (4) A Sacred Promise. Somerset Maugham said of
Haddon Chambers:[58] 'It exasperated him to have his best play,
The Tyranny of Tears, ascribed to Oscar Wilde . . . I cannot
imagine how such a notion can have been as widely spread as it
certainly was. No one could have had it who had any feeling for
dialogue or any discrimination in humour.' For all that, it is
never less than lively.

Unexpectedly, W. S. Gilbert, of the Savoy operas, enters the
58 Edwardian theatre; only faithful students recollect his one

substantial work of the period. As a legitimate dramatist, except for *Engaged*, which Oscar Wilde must have known when planning *The Importance of Being Earnest*, Gilbert without Sullivan was wry and solitary. When he wrote *The Fairy's Dilemma* (1904), he was sixty-seven; had he been less conspicuous, we might ask whether Bourchier—hospitable though he was to a variety of writers—would have chosen it for the Garrick. Sullivan was missed in a comedy like the skeleton of a protracted Bab Ballad. Granted a few nicely idiotic lines, such as Fairy Rosebud's

> Dance on the sward before these stucco portals
> Which I may say are Mr Justice Whortle's . . .

the piece must have seemed, even in the Edwardian theatre, as out-of-date as a consort of crumhorns and sackbuts. Gilbert's sub-title was 'a domestic pantomime'. Assorted personages, a Colonel, a vicar (of St Parabola), a judge, and the Earl of Harrow's daughter, Lady Angela Wealdstone—a local joke; Gilbert lived at Harrow—are transformed by the muddling Fairy Rosebud, who is fighting Demon Alcohol, into Clown and Harlequin, Pantaloon and Columbine. This is achieved in what she calls, Gilbertianly, 'the revolving realms of radiant rehabilitations'. The text is compact of such speeches as: 'Now, Lady Angela, that we are alone, let me express the modest hope that the perfunctory embraces which the peculiar circumstances of the case have compelled me to bestow on you, have been conceived and executed with as much delicacy and personal repression as the unfortunate exigencies of the situation must justify.' No entertainment, you gather, for the 'new' drama: it was staged in the same month as the Court's first Vedrenne-Barker matinee of *Candida*, also a play in a vicarage but at St Dominic's, Victoria Park, E. Shaw, who disliked the 'glittering, noisy void' of pantomime, might not have been an enthusiastic visitor to the Garrick.

VI

In the First Folio of Shakespeare, the play of *Troilus and Cressida*, its pages unnumbered, is wedged between histories and   59 tragedies as if Heminges and Condell did not know where to put it. In Sheridan's *The Duenna*, Donna Louisa likens her converted Jewish lover to the blank page between Old and New Testaments. Similarly, we are doubtful where to place James Matthew Barrie (1860–1937) in the house of the Edwardian theatre. Uneasy in the drawing-room, hardly for the study, not entirely for the playroom, he refuses to be categorised. Aged forty when the century opened, with a background of a Scottish weaving family at Kirriemuir (his 'Thrums'), Edinburgh University, and English provincial journalism, he had been for a dozen years or so a figure in literary London: resolutely ambitious, for all the shy Scottish charm of which he was aware; ready, it seemed, for unending variation in the curlicues of a gently wreathing humour; capable, too, of dangerous sentimentality, and behind all a sudden chill, a momentary knowledge that he was playing games with life.

Theatrically, his work during the 1890s had been unimportant. But what are we to think later of a playwright, a stage illusionist, who began in 1900 with a shaky 'problem' drama, *The Wedding Guest*, and went on to the Regency-period romance of *Quality Street* (1902), the social fantasy of *The Admirable Crichton* (also 1902), the caprice of *Little Mary* (1903), the children's adventure of *Peter Pan* (1904), the mildly satirical *Alice Sit-by-the-Fire* (1905), the mature comedy of *What Every Woman Knows* (1908), and a number of one-act plays, sentimental or astringent, upon the edge? Sometimes, especially in the web of the self-indulgent directions with which his dialogue is muffled—never was such a man for italics—we can find him as difficult to read, in his fashion, as the dramatists of a later day who annotate chaos in their demotic gasps. But these are reading texts. Nearly always, in performance, we are conscious of the expert technician. When the fit is on him, he can charm any audience. On other occasions we can feel about his work as Polly, in *Caste*, did about red-currant jam: 'At the first taste, sweet; and, afterwards, shuddery.'[59] Or else we are walking in a garden of foaming honeysuckle beset by hidden and needled thorn.

The Wedding Guest remains an uncomplicated failure. Here a woman with a past, Kate Ommanney, seeking to enter the company of the Tanquerays and Danes, turns up at her former lover's wedding: the baby she leaves at her lodgings. (The lover is, equally, a man with a past, but, according to convention, it is the woman who pays.) The play is thoroughly naïve from the moment Mrs Ommanney enters[60] ('My father, who was a Cornish fisherman, educated me beyond my station, with the result that I needs must fly to London'), to the ultimate exchange between bride and bridegroom:[61] 'Paul!'— 'Margaret, what can I do to atone?'—'Help unhappy women.' A minor argument between a pair of elderly friends and competitors does prepare the way for a scene in *Mary Rose* twenty years on; otherwise *The Wedding Guest* might be by almost any other dramatist.

Quality Street (1902) returns us to Barrie: a blue-and-white Regency sampler, fairly well preserved; though a few threads in its affectionate cross-stitching have worked loose, it continues to be an amiably romantic recollection. The scarlet of the military beside the maidenly muslin may remind us of the Budmouth of Hardy's Hussars whose spurs 'clink! clink! up the Esplanade and down',[62] but everything else in the place where 'Phoebe of the ringlets' waits ten years for her Valentine ('Dear Phoebe Throssel, will you be Phoebe Brown?')[63] is, in one of his moods, routine Barrie, stage directions and all: 'By merely peeping, everyone in Quality Street can know at once who has been buying a Whimsy Cake, and usually why.'[64] There are far fewer whimsy cakes in *The Admirable Crichton* (1902) where Barrie in the theatre suddenly grows up. Here, during two years on a desert island in the Pacific, the social positions in a shipwrecked aristocratic household are reversed. The butler, who holds the views of Ulysses on degree, turns dictator; Lady Mary is prevented from becoming his consort only by the arrival at the wrong moment of a rescue ship. Crichton goes back to his butler's pantry and his Tweeny, and everyone else to the drawing-room of Loam House, Mayfair, as in the first act. A fantasy continually surprising, with a hard centre of ironical truth beneath the chocolate, it excited the Duke of York's audience when H. B. Irving's Crichton wooed Irene Vanbrugh's Lady Mary in the lines of Henley: 'Or ever the knightly years were gone / With the old world to the grave, / I was a *king* in   61

Babylon, / And you were a Christian slave.' The play bites deeper than it appears, but few questions were asked. After all, it was pure fantasy: servants did not behave like this. Some people were scandalised. 'It deals,' said Sir Squire Bancroft,[65] 'with the juxtaposition of the drawing-room and the Servants' Hall—always to me a very painful subject.' Or, as Max Beerbohm would exclaim in *Savonarola*:[66] 'O the disgrace of it!—the sandal, the incredible come-down!'

Good words when we consider that the next play is *Little Mary* (1903): Barrie's quality at this time fluctuated like a fever-chart. No one now revives a comedy that is, roughly, about the perils of over-eating—a vegetarian pamphlet, said Shaw—and is uncommonly trying to read. It did provide a useful catchword. That autumn, at the Gaiety, Gertie Millar was singing in *The Orchid*:[67]

> I've a jolly sort of uncle who is rather old and stout . . .
> And the only girl he takes with him whenever he goes out
> Is Little Mary, is Little Mary . . .

The play ends with an acutely embarrassing scene for a middle-aged peer and the eighteen-year-old girl who tells him:[68] 'I have so longed to mother you, lord, ever since I saw you in the shop. I can't do without mothering you.' That was Barrie's trouble. The idea of mothering (Moira Loney, Wendy Moira Angela Darling, Maggie Wylie) turned to an obsession. Certainly it dominated *Peter Pan; or, The Boy Who Would Not Grow Up*, a problem-child of the theatre since its première in 1904.

Though parents, generation by generation, have taken their children to *Peter Pan* as they were taken themselves, it has also engendered a near-hatred. Either you will hear nothing against the play or you boil over. True, up to Christmas 1971, it had suffered from a line of often slovenly annual revivals. Christmas inspires a conspiracy of friendliness; still, many of the performances in the marmoreal Scala, 'most beautiful of new theatres', now destroyed, could be simply glum. It is facile to blame the text. A reviser, trying to cut, must acknowledge that Barrie in the situation knew what he was doing. The best is irresistible. 'The cleverness of me!' Peter cries in an early strain of strutting chanticleer; and when the last line was written Barrie might have uttered an equally triumphant crow. The children's play which has now odder psychological implications than its dramatist could have considered, moves with an ordered irresponsibility. In the course of it nothing from the nursery shelf is lost: braves and buccaneers and adventuring children, a crocodile with a clock inside it, noonday comedy, midnight moonshine, a dash of sentiment and a heroic sweep, and over all, Peter Pan himself, boy eternal. One or two passages have a teeth-gritting mawkishness; but nothing could be better than Hook, terror of the Never Land (it is thus in the text), oily-curled scoundrel, heart of darkness, black sheep of Balliol, one of the last enchantments of the Restoration, as he reflects upon the possibility of a rich, damp cake or raps out: 'Split my infinitives!' (At least the modern theatre has rarely lacked good Hooks: Donald Sinden, Robert Eddison, Alastair Sim.) The Lagoon scene, with its famous 'To die will be an awfully big adventure,' was added for the first revival. Such a critic as Frank Swinnerton, who finds the line distressing, has said:[69] 'There is in *Peter Pan* something approaching an exploitation of the child mind.' It might serve as an examination-piece for psychiatrists, but we have no time to worry about that. In the text it is Barrie's most accomplished mingling of dialogue and pictorial stage direction:[70] 'What you see is the Never Land. You have often half-seen it before, or even three-quarters, after the nightlights were lit, and you might then have beached your coracle on it if you had not always at the great moment fallen asleep.' In the theatre it is a permanent prize, a permanent acquired taste, or neither ('Oh, for an hour of Herod!' said 'Anthony Hope').[71] *Peter Pan* is the Edwardian enigma.

Alice Sit-by-the-Fire (1905), no enigma, is as forgotten as *Little Mary*; it has its gentle satire in the opening talk between two young girls who go to the theatre to know what Life is. Little else: here, as frequently, Barrie (who could have explained something about life) appears to be spinning bedtime stories for his own rapt attention. One major comedy, *What Every Woman Knows* (1908), has not lost its audiences through nearly seven decades. It is a tale for feminists; a fable of conquest; a triumph for the managing and mothering Maggie Wylie (Hilda Trevelyan created her) who carried her sternly concentrated 63

Scots husband to the political heights. It flowers from a lovingly prepared first act into Barrie's most human play, his own quietly mischievous interpretation of the 'odd, odd triangle', and it is starred by such lines as 'There are few more impressive sights in the world than a Scotsman on the make'[72] and '[Charm] is a sort of bloom on a woman, If you have it, you don't need to have anything else; and if you don't have it, it doesn't very much matter what you have.'[73] Change the sex, and that can be said of Barrie himself. Briefly, he is proving in this play—he does not say it until nearly the last curtain—that every man in high places loves to think he has done it all himself; and his wife smiles and lets it go at that.

We do not hear in these days of *The Adored One; A Legend of the Old Bailey*. It attempted to treat a Criminal Court murder trial as whimsically amusing, an idea even Barrie (recently created a baronet) could not save. A revision of the first act, as a short play, *Seven Women*, is all that remains: one of the least of a group of brief pieces that vary between the average, the masterly, and the baffling. It is impossible to do much with *Old Friends* (1910) about a potential girl-dipsomaniac. *Rosalind* (1912; bravura part for a comedienne) is another red-currant-jam play; but *The Will* (1913), a study—in three rapid period flashes—of greed and degeneration, is sharply economical, and *The Twelve-Pound Look* (1910) even more so in its portrait of pomposity deflated. The new knight's first wife, who has gained her independence as a typist (the machine cost twelve pounds) begins the process. The spiritless second wife completes it:[74]

SIR HARRY: I'm busy, Emmy. (*He sits at his writing-desk*).
LADY SIMS (*dutifully*): I'm sorry; I'll go, Harry. (*Inconsequentially*) Are they very expensive?
SIR HARRY: What?
LADY SIMS: Those machines?
    (*When she has gone, the possible meaning of her question strikes him. The curtain hides him from us. . . .*)

There Barrie must be hidden from us. At the end of our period he had yet to go on to his other major works for the theatre—among them the haunted fantasies of *Dear Brutus* and

Mary Rose—which were away from the Edwardian world and owed nothing to any period.

The parlourmaid crackles back to lead us to the study: round its table, Mr Bernard Shaw, Mr Granville Barker, Mr John Galsworthy, and friends.

Notes

1. W. J. Macqueen Pope (1888–1960).
2. Preface to *Plays Pleasant* (1898). Bodley Head Bernard Shaw, Vol. 1 (1970), p. 376.
3. 'One Day: A Fragment' by Arthur W. Pinero. *The Theatre*, 1 January 1884.
4. *Real Conversations*: Recorded by William Archer (1904), pp. 21–2.
5. Alfred Brandon; Plymouth Repertory Theatre. Called wrongly Henty Beecham in *Shaw and Molly Tompkins*, ed. by Peter Tompkins (1961), p. 65.
6. *Real Conversations*, pp. 23–6.
7. W. Somerset Maugham: Andalusia; *Sketches and Impressions* (1905).
8. Sean O'Casey's *Rose and Crown* (1952), pp. 21–3.
9. *Trelawny of the 'Wells'* (1898), Act I.
10. *The Saturday Review*, 24 October 1903. Reprinted in *Around Theatres* (1953 edition), p. 289.
11. *His House in Order* (1906), Act 1.
12. Essay in *Theatre Programme* (1954), p. 228.
13. Preface to *The Times* (1891).
14. John Drinkwater: *Poems 1908–1914* (1917), p. 45: 'Lines for the Opening of the Birmingham Repertory Theatre'.
15. Irene Vanbrugh: *To Tell My Story* (1948), p. 70. Pinero objected to criticisms of his diction. 'Do all men talk nothing but the simplest colloquialisms, even in these days. The men of my acquaintance—certain of them—do not, at any rate.' (Letter, 13.10.1903, to William Archer (*The Collected Letters of Sir Arthur Pinero*, ed. J. P. Wearing; University of Minnesota Press, 1974, p. 192).) In the same letter Pinero says that he has attempted throughout *Letty* (and in other plays) 'to make the difference between the spontaneous utterance and the utterance which is the outcome of deliberate thought'. Thus, 'When Letty says "To my imperfect intelligence, etc." she is simply repeating what she has said to herself, if not to others, a hundred times.'
16. Sir George Arthur: *From Phelps to Gielgud* (1936), p. 141.
17. Irving Wardle on *Other People*.
18. *A Wife Without a Smile: A Comedy in Disguise* (1905), Act 3, p. 216.
19. A. E. W. Mason: *Sir George Alexander and the St James's Theatre* (1935), p. 138.
20. *To Tell My Story*, p. 74.
21. Max Beerbohm: *Letters to Reggie Turner*, ed. Rupert Hart-Davis (1964), p. 165.

22. *Sir George Alexander and the St James's Theatre*, p. 179.
23. *The Saturday Review*, 16 May 1908. *Last Theatres, 1904–1910* (1970), p. 369.
24. *Mid-Channel* (1910), p. 7.
25. *Ibid.*, p. 249.
26. *Sir George Alexander and the St James's Theatre*, p. 195.
27. *Mid-Channel*, p. 39.
28. *Ibid.*, p. 55.
29. *Ibid.*, p. 97.
30. James Agate: *At Half-Past Eight: Essays of the Theatre, 1921–1922* (1923), p. 124.
31. Fred Kerr: *Recollections of a Defective Memory* (1930), p. 152.
32. *Playgoers* (1913).
33. Bodley Head Bernard Shaw, Vol. IV (1970), p. 170.
34. Wilfred Denver in *The Silver King* (1882), Act II.
35. Lady Blanche in *Princess Ida* (1884), Act II.
36. *The Life and Letters of Henry Arthur Jones*, ed. Doris Arthur Jones (1930), p. 208.
37. George Rowell: *The Victorian Theatre* (1956), p. 109.
38. Reply to a questionnaire on dramatic technique from Professor Archibald Henderson of the University of North Carolina. Quoted in *The Life and Letters of Henry Arthur Jones*, pp. 434–5.
39. *The Life and Letters of Henry Arthur Jones*, p. 207.
40. *The Saturday Review*, 23 January 1904. In *Last Theatres, 1904–1910*, p. 177.
41. C. E. Montague: *Dramatic Values* (1911), p. 32.
42. William Archer: *The Old Drama and the New: An Essay in Re-Valuation* (1923), p. 298.
43. *The Divine Gift* (1913), Act III, p. 133.
44. *Ibid.*, p. 154.
45. *The Divine Gift*. Dedication, p. 29.
46. *Ibid.*, p. 38.
47. *The Collected Plays of W. Somerset Maugham*, Vol. 1 (1931), *Lady Frederick*, Act III, p. 67.
48. Rider Haggard: *She*, Chapter XXVII.
49. *Troilus and Cressida*, Act I, Scene III, lines 101 ff.
50. *The Collected Plays of W. Somerset Maugham*, Vol. 1 (1931), *Mrs Dot*, Act II, p. 133.
51. *Ibid.*, Preface, p. x.
52. *Ibid.*, *The Land of Promise*, Act III, p. 286.
53. A. V. Cookman in *The Year's Work in the Theatre, 1948–1949*, ed. J. C. Trewin (1949), p. 27.
54. *Shaw and Molly Tompkins*, ed. Peter Tompkins (1961), p. 62.
55. *The Plays of Hubert Henry Davies*, Vol. 1 (1921), *Mrs Gorringe's Necklace*, Act IV, p. 74.
56. *The Walls of Jericho* (1904), Act II.
57. Max Beerbohm: *Around Theatres* (1953 edition), p. 319; review of *The Rich Mrs Repton*.
58. *A Writer's Notebook* (1949), p. 186.

59. T. W. Robertson: *Caste*, Act I.
60. *The Plays of J. M. Barrie* (1928 edition). *The Wedding Guest*, Act I, p. 224.
61. *Ibid.*, Act IV, p. 271.
62. Thomas Hardy: 'Budmouth Dears', *The Dynasts* (1923 edition), Part III, Act II, Sc. 1, p. 367.
63. *The Plays of J. M. Barrie. Quality Street*, Act IV, p. 339.
64. *Ibid.*, Act I, p. 275.
65. *Sir George Alexander and the St James's Theatre*, p. 136.
66. Max Beerbohm: *Savonarola Brown* in *Seven Men*, collected edition, Vol. VII (1922); and in *Max in Verse* (Stephen Greene Press, Brattleboro, Vermont, 1963), p. 95.
67. *The Orchid* (1903). Musical play by J. T. Tanner, music by Ivan Caryll and Lionel Monckton.
68. *The Plays of J. M. Barrie. Little Mary*, Act III, p. 486.
69. Frank Swinnerton: *The Georgian Literary Scene* (1935); Everyman edition (1938), p. 88.
70. *The Plays of J. M. Barrie, Peter Pan*, Act II, p. 523.
71. Denis Mackail: *The Story of J. M. B.* (1941), p. 368.
72. *The Plays of J. M. Barrie. What Every Woman Knows*. Act II, p. 693.
73. *Ibid.*, *What Every Woman Knows*, Act I, p. 674.
74. *Ibid.*, *The Twelve-Pound Look*, p. 780.

67

CHAPTER THREE

The Study

I

Space given to dramatists of the period in the *Oxford Book of Quotations* can speak for itself. Pinero has only a single entry, and that from the 1890s; not, as one might have expected, Paula Tanqueray's line about past and future but her early 'What beautiful fruit! I love fruit when it's expensive.' (It might be the voice of a London playgoer.) Stephen Phillips who, according to turn-of-the-century critics, was on every lip, has merely the unremarkable 'A man not old, but mellow like good wine', from the third act of *Ulysses*; Charles Haddon Chambers gets his 'long arm of coincidence', one of those random phrases that endure; John Masefield is represented by a Centurion's 'Death opens unknown doors; it is most good to die', from *The Tragedy of Pompey the Great*; there is nothing at all from Henry Arthur Jones, nothing from the plays of Galsworthy or Granville Barker. But J. M. Barrie has fifteen entries from plays of our period, and Shaw has forty-six.

Bernard Shaw (1856–1950) was immensely quotable. He made it his business to say the unexpected. Even if, with him, the unexpected became the inevitable, it remained a good phrase.

He understood very soon that one way of being recognised was to be contrary. When he was seventy-four I heard him in a West country town where he had been invited to speak in favour of university education. He demolished university education in a thirty-minute exercise that delighted everyone and helped the cause; he was being Shavian. Shavianism could be perilous, but Shaw regarded humour as an essential solvent. The more people laughed, the more they would think of what he said; and no one in his era had more to say. During the late 1940s, when literary editor of a London Sunday newspaper, I would ask him sometimes for a book review. Though he began by writing briskly from Ayot St Lawrence, 'Strike me off your list of casuals; I am an extra-special', he did respond; and two reviews, each of nearly a full page, by a man on the edge of ninety, or over, proved a point he had never needed to prove. He was always an extra-special, and he stays so in the history of the theatre.

Dublin-born of an ineffectual father and an independent, romantic, musical mother, and formally educated only until he was fifteen, he was forty-four in 1900, a year younger than Arthur Pinero. Tall, lean, red-bearded, he was a cascade-talker. He had been an unpublished novelist (naturally everything was published later); he rose into a practised Fabian orator; and he reviewed books, music (with Wagner to Valhalla), and art with the same positive decision. Championing Ibsen, he wrote a study, not one of his best, of the man's 'quintessence', to him a playgoer's honey-dew or milk of paradise. He was a prose-writer with an exact ear; a creative revolutionary; presently an attacker of the commercial and romantic theatre of the Nineties. Having criticised most other things, it was clear that he would become a drama critic; during three years on the *Saturday Review,* 1895–8, he continued to write his own plays. Few managements responded; it was not then regarded as reasonable to incinerate one's audiences. The chronology is complicated and unimportant. The main fact is that Shaw marched suddenly to stage centre (and remained there) during the Vedrenne-Barker season of 1904–7 at the Royal Court Theatre in Sloane Square, off the West End beat.

When he was a drama critic his opponents thought of him as one of the poet Southey's 'March-of-Intellect boys'. In print no 69 man annoyed them more, and the knowledge that Shaw, keeping his temper serenely, could always argue them out of the field, fuelled their wrath. He derided the stage's fictitious morals, fictitious good conduct. He regarded sentimental drawing-room drama, society comedies, Ruritanian melodrama, as so much litter on the floor; and he conceived it his duty, in the words of the song, to clear up the straw in the passage so that life might begin again. It was largely owing to his generalship, and to Harley Granville Barker's—two dissimilar men making common cause—that the Theatre of Ideas did not fall apart in an Edwardian atmosphere apparently so inimical to it. Shaw would not obey the rules. Wrecking any drawing-room, he juggled with argument and social problem as the late-Elizabethans had done with image and metaphor; and he found that many playgoers enjoyed the change; 'a line of his own'. He obliged them to think of the false romance of war, marriage, medicine. He inverted traditional beliefs. He slammed away at politics and education. He went as far as possible from the mere

> simulation of the painted scene;
> Boards, actors, prompters, gaslight, and costume.[1]

He knew about the old methods and he would use any effect that helped him. But his was primarily a theatre of polemics, of apparently laughing debate. Having taken care to find the right thing to say, he said it (being in complete earnest) under a mask of levity. He did not regard drama as the setting-up of the camera to nature; it was the presentation in parable of 'the conflict between Man's will and his environment; in a word, of problem'.[2] Ivor Brown, in 1964, defined the vogue-word 'committed' as 'a word recently introduced to describe writers who, like Shaw, have strong opinions about social matters and are thus committed to one side in a conflict of opinion. . . . Nobody with a mind can be completely uncommitted. It is a matter of degree.'[3] Shaw added style to substance. In the preface to *Man and Superman* he declared himself: 'Effectiveness of assertion is the Alpha and Omega of style. He who has nothing to assert has no style and can have none; he who has something to assert will go as far in power of style as its momentousness and his conviction will carry him. Disprove his assertion after it is made, yet its style remains.'[4] In one sense, he has long reminded me of a preacher in my Cornish village (not far from Cadgwith where Shaw himself would stay), who cried: 'Friends, let the Word thump 'ee with great thumps!' Shaw's 'thumping' was done with an exact art. They have always cared for words in Dublin; Shaw more than most. With the ear of a musician he orchestrated his prose dialogue: none complained about him as about Pinero. But he could not pack into his plays everything that he wished, so his readers often fared better than his audiences. To most of his plays he appended a preface—a tract, an essay, a harangue, a fanfare, an encyclical—and this now and then could be more rewarding than the play itself which could seem ventriloquial and bloodless. At his most overflowingly copious, he would let his characters run on unwisely, and their longer overtly didactic passages are still apt to worry listeners. He realised this: when he saw that a debate was static he would try to help with some knockabout joke or by enlivening the stage pictorially—hence the cluster of uniforms in *Getting Married*. He loved ridiculous names (Ftatateeta). He knew, as Shakespeare did, that a good-humoured gibe against the English would certainly be applauded (Broadbent; Britannus).

Curiously, though he is revived more than any other dramatist, not all of his plays from the Edwardian world are actor-proof. Their narrative power is secondary. Shaw, thinly spoken, can often fail to hold the mind; there is a limit to a listener's concentration. Dangerous scenes are the last act of *Major Barbara*, a good deal of *Getting Married*, several passages in *Misalliance*, and surprisingly, I have come to believe now, *Man and Superman*. As we get it in performance, nearly always without the magnificent *Don Juan in Hell* interlude, it can seem like a cheerfully frivolous comedy of repartee, little else. *Don Juan*, on the other hand, is ninety minutes at action stations in the theatre of the mind. We ought not to be hyperbolical about everything that Shaw wrote. He was a lesser, a more self-indulgent man of the theatre than Ibsen. Repetition has dulled some of his work and familiarity has robbed some of his ideas of their first exhilaration. But, at his richest, he was an extra-special of the English stage. He led the Theatre of Ideas to a recognition that, a decade before, would have been unthinkable. We can speak of 71 him now in the words John Masefield, the Poet Laureate, wrote in 1946 for the ninetieth birthday:[5]

> After these ninety years we can survey
> Changes enough, so many due to him:
> Old wax-work melted down, old tinsel dim,
> Old sentimental clockwork put away.

It was an epitaph—he read it in his lifetime—that he must have valued.

II

Shaw's meeting with Harley Granville Barker (1877–1946) was vitally important to each of them. Charles Charrington recommended the young actor (an idea Henry Arthur Jones had already had)[6] for Marchbanks in the Stage Society's production of *Candida* (July 1900). Thereafter Barker was much in Shaw's mind as an actor and as a man—ardent if with relatively little sense of humour—who could be counted upon for a new independent theatre. Handsome, vital, Italianate, and, said Shaw,[7] 'always useful when a touch of poetry and refinement is needed', he had got about in the provinces, on the London fringe, and in the West End. He was a friend of William Archer and Gilbert Murray; he had written a play called *The Weatherhen* (1899) which St John Hankin, in *The Academy*, found 'wonderfully stimulating'. After meeting Shaw he appeared in some other special Shavian productions: the American Captain Kearney in *Captain Brassbound's Conversion* (1900)—hardly obvious casting—Napoleon in *The Man of Destiny* (1901), and Frank in *Mrs Warren's Profession*. Moreover, he had staged another play of his own, a late eighteenth-century comedy, *The Marrying of Ann Leete*, which then remained in obscurity until the Royal Shakespeare Company's unexpected revival in the autumn of 1975. When the piece, written in 1899, had a brief trial in 1902, various people vaguely admired it, not too explicitly. Shaw was explicit: 'By far the finest bit of literature since Stevenson's *Prince Otto*, and of a much more original quality of excellence.'[8] After seventy-three years *Ann Leete*

72

proved to be more durable than the text suggested. Writing at the end of one century about the close of another, the young Barker was trying to suggest something of the period's deep class distinctions, its political jobbery and expediency, and the dangerous stirrings of social rebellion: after all, the French Revolution had been going on over the water. Ann, who proposes suddenly to the gardener, is an early New Woman not easy to clarify; but in the RSC revival Barker's terse, charged, elliptical dialogue could sometimes rise sharply from the page. The play could have as epigraph a few words from the nearly inevitable source: 'How could communities . . . But by degree stand in authentic place?'

Barker's principal passion, like that of many young men with less staying-power, was for the uncommercial theatre, the National Theatre of the future, and as early as 1903 he had made tentative suggestions for a venture at the Court—at once conveniently outside the West End and conveniently near it. Nothing happened; but in the following spring his chance did arrive sooner than he had hoped. J. H. Leigh, a wealthy business man, who was an amateur actor and married to an actress, Thyrza Norman, who had been his ward, was putting on some 'Shakespeare Representations' at the Court, a pious exercise getting nowhere in particular. William Archer, most ubiquitous of theatre-men, proposed to him that he should ask young Granville Barker to act and produce. Barker came, but on his own delighted terms. He agreed with John Eugene Vedrenne, Leigh's manager, that he would stage *The Two Gentlemen of Verona*, of all comedies, and appear as Speed, of all parts ('Twenty to one then, he is shipp'd already, / And I have played the sheep in losing him!'), on condition that he could also do half-a-dozen matinees of Shaw's *Candida*. These were duly given in April and May 1904, Barker repeating his approved Stage Society performance of the sub-Shelleyan poet, Marchbanks, with Kate Rorke now as Candida, at the centre of what Shaw called 'an extraordinary ordinary play',[9] and Norman McKinnel as her husband, the parson Morell. From this beginning came the plan for a sustained matinee season 'under the management of Mr J. E. Vedrenne; the plays produced by Mr Granville Barker,' and the programme arranged so as to   73 avoid regular matinee days in the West End. Vedrenne, whose name would endure in a section of stage history that might have astonished him, was then aged thirty-seven, an excellent business man, precise and obsessively punctual.

Opening in October 1904 with six performances of the *Hippolytus* of Euripides in the rendering by Professor Gilbert Murray, the Vedrenne-Barker season was the nearest English parallel to the Théâtre Libre which a gasworks clerk, André Antoine, had started in Paris during 1887 in the Passage de l'Elysée des Beaux Arts. Both ventures encouraged a new school of dramatists, opposed the merely well-made play, and stood for naturalism in acting. The Court enterprise—before long it was capturing the evening bill as well—lasted for nearly three years, to the end of June 1907. It involved thirty-two plays by seventeen authors, and Bernard Shaw, as one would have expected, dominated the stage. He was forty-eight when Barker began to beat the drum for him. In one sense, he had long been his own drummer: his plays had been widely read, but it needed a run of performances to accustom the public to their sound. At the Court he became immediately the new Old Master of the theatre. Such works as *Candida*, *You Never Can Tell*, *Captain Brassbound's Conversion*, and *The Philanderer*, which had had various special, or technically private, performances elsewhere, were brought within the Vedrenne-Barker scheme. One that had to remain outside it was *Mrs Warren's Profession*, written in 1893, and, apart from a Stage Society production in 1902, unseen in London until 1925 after the lifting of the Censor's ban. Indicting the social conditions that fostered prostitution, the scandal of underpaid virtue and overpaid vice, Shaw created a prosperous brothel-keeper who had had what O'Casey, in another context, calls 'a sin-slushed career', and her daughter, an uncompromising New Woman of the time, who rejects tainted money to settle coldly in a Chancery Lane solicitor's office. It offers its Mrs Warren—in a first draft Mrs Jarman, one of the earlier names of Paula Tanqueray—ample opportunities for tirades and apologetics, but it has dwindled by now into a remote exercise. Shaw did not trouble the Court with a rather different piece; instead, it was acted at a Theatrical Garden Party. This (1905) was *Passion, Poison, and Petrifaction*, 'a brief

74

tragedy for barns and booths'. Brief enough—and what more tragic than the fate of the poisoned lover. He stiffens into a statue after tossing off, as antidote, a strong solution of plaster, once the bust of Lady Magnesia FitzTollemache. No one is likely to construct a thesis on the least-considered Shavian trifle.

Here is the full Court Theatre record, an important Edwardian document (it does not include the trial matinees of *Candida*.) Between 18 October 1904 and 29 June 1907 there were 946 performances of 32 plays by 17 authors. Because one triple bill and four double bills were included, the total number of performances of separate plays amounted to 988. Thus:[10]

PLAY	AUTHOR	Performances	
Man and Superman	Bernard Shaw	176	
You Never Can Tell	Bernard Shaw	149	
John Bull's Other Island	Bernard Shaw	121	
Captain Brassbound's Conversion	Bernard Shaw	89	
Major Barbara	Bernard Shaw	52	
The Doctor's Dilemma	Bernard Shaw	50	
Prunella	Laurence Housman & Granville Barker	48	
The Voysey Inheritance	Granville Barker	34	
Candida	Bernard Shaw	31	
The Silver Box	John Galsworthy	29	
Votes for Women!	Elizabeth Robins	23	
The Electra	Euripides	20	
The Hippolytus	Euripides	20	
The Return of the Prodigal	St John Hankin	19	
The Thieves' Comedy	Gerhart Hauptmann	9	
The Pot of Broth	W. B. Yeats	9	*triple bill*
In The Hospital	Arthur Schnitzler	9	
How He Lied to Her Husband	Bernard Shaw	9	
The Trojan Women	Euripides	8	
The Charity That Began at Home	St John Hankin	8	
The Reformer	Cyril Harcourt	8	*double bill*
The Campden Wonder	John Masefield	8	
The Philanderer	Bernard Shaw	8	
Don Juan in Hell	Bernard Shaw	8	*double bill*
The Man of Destiny	Bernard Shaw	8	

75

PLAY	AUTHOR	Performances
Hedda Gabler	Henrik Ibsen	7
Aglavaine and Selysette	Maurice Maeterlinck	6
The Wild Duck	Henrik Ibsen	6
Pan and the Young Shepherd	Maurice Hewlett	6 ⎫ *double bill*
The Youngest of the Angels	Maurice Hewlett	6 ⎭
A Question of Age	Robert Vernon Harcourt	2 ⎫ *double bill*
The Convict on the Hearth	Frederick Fenn	2 ⎭
		988

A few of these have vanished into the mists. *Votes for Women!*
which its author, the actress, styled 'a dramatic tract', was
applauded largely for a second-act suffragist meeting in
Trafalgar Square, with the handling of an overflowing stage
crowd, a technical problem Barker could approach masterfully,
though his planning sometimes became too mathematically
elaborate. Robert Vernon Harcourt, according to Desmond
MacCarthy,[11] wrote able society dialogue and had a sense of
situation without any notable skill in stage craft. But *A Question of
Age* was thin and had to be taken off after two performances; it
suffered at the first because the actress Fanny Brough left out a
passage that contained most of the plot. Cyril Harcourt's *The
Reformer*, like the other Harcourt's play, was also society comedy
that might have been a sop to the West End public. It always
startles me to find this dramatist in the Court list because for me
his name means simply another and even more trivial comedy,
from some years ahead (1914), entitled *A Pair of Silk Stockings*. It
used, though no one ever knew why, to be the mascot of my local
repertory theatre: whenever losses mounted, this arch chirrup
would restore the revenue. There was never a work, or for that
matter a dramatist, less suited to the Theatre of Ideas. Of others
on the list, Maurice Hewlett's two romantic plays by a novelist
without special feeling for the stage, formed a double bill that at
one point reduced the matinee receipts to £13.

III

But the main theme of the Vedrenne-Barker season, the Edwardian theatre in mid-channel, had to be Shaw. (It will be reasonable here to carry his work beyond the closing of the Court to the end of the period we call Edwardian.) He was obviously the Court's Life Force, 'erasing Shaw who made the folly die',[12] and who could wheedle with the sword-point. No one has compressed his achievement more succinctly than Ashley Dukes: 'He . . . stripped militarism of its glamour, history of its pomp, sex of its romance, science of its magic, and religion of its sorcery. Yet he [sought] to create as well as to destroy.'[13]

Candida: A Mystery, written in 1894 and published (as one of the *Plays Pleasant*) in 1898, is the most compact piece in the canon, a Shavian *Doll's House* with the husband as the doll. Shaw moves it along rapidly; its people never talk lengths of preface. The scene in which the mothering Candida's parson-husband, 'great baby' of a self-deceiving Christian Socialist (who does not realise that he is weaker than his wife), and her eighteen-year-old adorer, the poet Eugene Marchbanks, make their so-called 'bids' for her, has stayed both true and acutely theatrical. Eugene must have been a poor poet: Shaw does not help with his purple-winged archangels, tiny shallops, marble floors washed by the rain and dried by the sun, and so on. Not that it need disturb us; it is enough if the actor suggests a poet; Marchbanks, given his quality of fire and air, ceases to bring the Sixth Form to St Dominic's Parsonage and he has never been played better than by Granville Barker; next, perhaps, was Stephen Haggard in 1937. Desmond MacCarthy, searchingly evocative about plays, much less so as a rule about acting, has a fine passage on Barker:[14]

His voice possesses a curious individual quality which, while it limits the range of his impersonations, gives particular intensity to some. When he repeats her name, 'Candida, Candida, Candida,' there is not a touch of self-consciousness in the musical reiteration: he does not appear to be following the sound of his own voice like most actors at such times, but to be listening, detached, to his longing made audible. 77

It is an endearing play, not a customary epithet for Shaw. Our
only problem is how in the world Candida can be the daughter
of the egregious Burgess, a corkscrewing contractor, who talks
in the dramatist's most distressing phonetic Cockney, the sort of
jargon—on the page at least—repeated later in the Felix
Drinkwater of *Captain Brassbound's Conversion* and in *Pygmalion*.
Writers who have speculated on Lear's wife and Lady Macbeth's
youth should try to shape a play on the early years of Candida,
paragon of the parsonage; her mother must have been a
remarkable woman.

John Bull's Other Island (1904)—I take the major plays as they
came on at the Court—was an allegory of relations between
England and Ireland, as removed from *Candida* as anything
could be. Shaw had written it, at the request of W. B. Yeats, as a
patriotic contribution to the repertory of the Irish Literary
Theatre which would never have been its home. A man who
asked for this style of piece from Shaw was as daring as a high-
wire artist and less confident; *John Bull* in Yeats's theatre would
have been another Irish problem. Observe Larry Doyle's 'If you
want to interest [an Irishman] in Ireland, you've got to call the
unfortunate island Kathleen ni Hoolihan and pretend she's a
little old woman. It saves thinking. . . .'[15] Shaw put it modestly
when he described *John Bull* as 'uncongenial to the whole spirit
of the neo-Gaelic movement'.[16] Broadbent, Englishman among
the soft moist airs and the aborigines ('After all, whatever you
say, they like an Englishman')[17] is a large, bland ass, a
sentimental rhetorician, a buoyant balloon, who survives every
crack with a shillelagh. He is Shaw's revenge on those
traditionalists for whom the Other Island had remained a wet
western quagmire filled with jigging comic peasants, greasepaint Irishmen with the generic name of Pathrick O'Lunacy; in
John Bull the Saxon stranger is determined to sail down the
Blarney River. A visionary priest, Peter Keegan, who dreams of
heaven as 'a godhead in which all life is human and all humanity
divine: three in one and one in three', can be a sharp test for an
actor. Granville Barker created Keegan; but the part belongs in
memory to his successor, William Poel, best known as a
Shakespearian innovator; here he was suddenly inspired. *John
Bull* is among the least rubbed of the plays and, unhappily, one

of the least revived, even though at a Command Performance in
1906 King Edward VII laughed so much that he broke his chair.
When it is done with spirit, as at the Mermaid, London, in 1971,
it must be a Shavian triumph.

You Never Can Tell (1896) has always been ripe for revival.
Shaw wrote nothing kinder than this piece, steeped and
dulcified in good humour in spite of the dental surgery in its first
act (the time, anyway, is a 'fine August morning'). Explorers,
looking in cautiously at the Court to see what was happening in
the temple, could enjoy it without self-consciousness. It is
neither a sermon nor a demolition exercise; it is just what Shaw
said it was, a fashionable comedy for the theatre of its day, but
one with a mind behind the fashion. If ever a dramatist was
possessed by a secondary character, Shaw was by William the
Waiter, embodiment of sweet reason and the well-ordered life,
with a voice like the cooing of doves in immemorial elms. The
play is a point of rest; Shaw was in love while he was writing it,
and maybe that is why it reflects his benign view of the world
(even the tyrannical father softens), his amusement at the
philandering Valentine, five-shilling dentist, duellist of sex, and
his pleasure in the double turn for the twins. Yet, when Cyril
Maude chose it for the Haymarket, no one seemed to know what
the simple enough piece meant; it was abandoned after a
fortnight's abjectly floundering rehearsal by a sullen cast. Shaw
afterwards wrote a chapter for Cyril Maude's *The Haymarket
Theatre* (1903), briskly lampooning himself: 'In any other walk
of life than that of a dramatic author, I should expect him to
achieve a high measure of success.' In 1966 *You Never Can Tell*
was re-established at the Haymarket when Sir Ralph
Richardson's William found himself, on an August day in the
Nineties, guarding the family from Madeira that rediscovered
husband and father after eighteen years. Reviews were so
benevolent that the dramatist's own hand might have guided the
pens.

Strangely, one of the most regarded of all the plays, and the
most popular at the Court, *Man and Superman* (published, 1903;
Court, 1905, without the third act) is now inclined to limp in any
merely average performance. Arthur Bingham Walkley, of *The
Times*, never a persuaded Shavian, challenged Shaw to write a   79

Don Juan play, and the result was sub-titled—warningly—'a comedy and a philosophy': in the text it is encased between a vast preface and the self-indulgent essays and aphorisms of *The Revolutionist's Handbook and Pocket Companion*, which sounds like a concise crib to Shaw. In the text Ann Whitefield's pursuit of John Tanner can be wittily glinting (though the love chase by a woman worried Edwardians); today in the theatre each part needs exceptional virtuosity if the piece is not to lag. Shaw was more interested in his philosophy, the theme of creative evolution or the Life Force, self-knowledge through selective breeding of the Superman, than he was in Ann and Tanner who are merely instruments. Hard pounding for an Edwardian audience; yet the play—with Barker made up like the author—proved to be the core of the entire season. Its substance, however, is in the detachable third act, Tanner's dream (as Don Juan Tenorio) while he is held by some exceedingly Shavian brigands in the Sierra Nevada. The 'Shavio-Socratic dialogue' for the principals, who are now their Mozartian ancestors from *Don Giovanni*, is a fire of words that sparks and roars magnificiently in the Void near Hell. It gives to Juan such a speech as this:[18]

. . . There is the work of helping Life in its struggle upward. Think of how it wastes and scatters itself, how it raises up obstacles to itself and destroys itself in its ignorance and blindness. It needs a brain, this irresistible force, lest in its ignorance it should resist itself. What a piece of work is man! says the poet. Yes; but what a blunderer! Here is the highest miracle of organisation yet attained by Life, the most intensely alive thing that exists, the most conscious of all the organisms; and yet, how wretched are his brains! Stupidity made sordid and cruel by the realities learnt from toil and poverty: Imagination resolved to starve sooner than face these realities, piling up illusions to hide them, and calling itself cleverness, genius! And each accusing the other of its own defect: Stupidity accusing Imagination of folly, and Imagination accusing Stupidity of ignorance; whereas, alas! Stupidity has all the knowledge, and Imagination all the intelligence.

And presently:[19]

You forget that brainless magnificence of body has been tried. Things immeasurably greater than man in every respect but brain have existed and perished. The megatherium, the icthyosaurus have paced the earth with seven-league steps and hidden the day with cloud-vast wings. Where are they now? Fossils in museums, and so few and imperfect at that, that a knuckle bone or a tooth of one of them is prized beyond the lives of a thousand soldiers. These things lived and wanted to live; but for lack of brains they did not know how to carry out their purpose, and so destroyed themselves.

The extraordinary debate (in our time the best Juan was Esme Percy) was acted first at the Court for eight matinees in the summer of 1907; indeed it was the grand climax to the three years, though it seemed a waste to pair it with such a trifle as *The Man of Destiny*—'trifle' is the official description—early Shaw (1895) on the young Napoleon. Robert Loraine played Juan; Lillah McCarthy, the original Ann, Doña Ana; Michael Sherbrooke, the Statue; and Norman McKinnel, the Devil. No admirers of this scene—and it has been heard much less than it should have been down the years—can ever be fully at peace with the three-act compression that rockets from Surrey to Granada. Loraine in 1907 brought eloquence to eloquence. Shaw helpfully annotated the text for him like a symphony: 'The margin in the book twinkled with crotchets, crescendoes, and minims; with G clefs, F clefs, and pianissimos.'[20] Barker had always told his companies that the Shavian manner was that of Italian opera; and it is particularly so in the Edwardian plays. Shaw himself was the most potent of producers: as exacting as Pinero, a name not to be dwelt upon in Sloane Square, he could 'work' the plays in performance as they have rarely been managed since.

Major Barbara (1905) is, candidly, a 'discussion' which to Shaw meant something more dramatic than any Druriodrama or scandal in society. But it does need a superlative company as much as *Man and Superman* does. Max Beerbohm, who renounced his original belief that the plays were better on the page than the stage, never saw a variety of minor productions. *Barbara*, which might be called *Arms and the Woman*, can dip badly if such a cast as that of the Royal Shakespeare (1970) is not there to fortify us during the last act. Scored for cannon, tambourine, and drum, the play is, among other things, Shaw's denunciation of the crime of poverty, the worst of crimes beside which the others are virtues. Here are the explosives 81 manufacturer, Undershaft, who holds that man's first duty is not to be poor, and his daughter, the Salvation Army officer, who represents private charity, Undershaft is a millionaire, and that (work and money) is his religion, set against Barbara's of God and salvation. The strongest scene is in the Salvation Army shelter at West Ham in the second act; the most teasing is the prolix last act and Undershaft's victory; and the least expected character is a Professor of Greek, Adolphus Cusins, or 'Euripides'—acted first by Granville Barker and later by Lewis Casson—who becomes a Salvation Army drummer. He can hardly fail to beguile because Shaw founded him (not the drumming) upon Professor Gilbert Murrary.

Next, *Captain Brassbound's Conversion* (1899): it was originally *The Witch of Atlas*, a better title, for everything depends on Lady Cicely Waynflete's way of treating a perilous North African adventure. She is the sister-in-law of a judge apparently in mortal danger from the revengeful Brassbound but actually quite safe while Lady Cicely is there to treat men as children to be humoured. She is, as George Rowell has said, Candida-with-a-title in the middle of Morocco; and she does not invariably come off in performance. Ellen Terry's legendary charm was fitful at the Court, where Shaw had persuaded her to appear; and Ingrid Bergman in the most recent London revival (1972) was miscast as so English a figure.

Conversely, *The Doctor's Dilemma* (1906) seems to survive any production. There have been more profitable revivals of this than of either *Man and Superman* or *Major Barbara*, where the prefaces transcend the plays. But *The Doctor's Dilemma*, its title borrowed from a story by Hesba Stretton, is scarcely ever astray in the theatre. Easier than its companions, it is also, the redundant epilogue aside, better made: the Theatre of Ideas is more powerful when it agrees to an armistice with the Theatre Theatrical. It was a habit among Edwardian critics to set Shaw going, and he was replying here to William Archer's demand for a tragedy with a full-dress death scene. Hence what he declared to be the tragedy of the artist Dubedat, and his claim that, to people who could understand, the theme of a man of genius who was not also a man of honour must be the most tragic imaginable. The death scene, which duly arrives in the fourth act, is scorchingly difficult for an actor, written as it is in a tragi-comic mood and happening in the presence of Shaw's satirised doctors and the most inept idea of a journalist that even the Edwardian theatre was likely to have. We are not over-disturbed by the dilemma posed in the plot. One life can be saved: shall it be the amoral artist or the mediocre doctor? Shaw may have spread himself on the Dubedats, husband and wife, but posterity will probably remember the joke against the medical profession, Shaw waving to Molière. The humour is extravagant and stinging, and all the doctors are amply playable: the veteran who believes there is nothing new; the pathetic and humble-proud general practitioner, one of the horns of the dilemma; the Jewish doctor who found a promise of 'cures guaranteed' enough to win him a practice; a newly-knighted man of fifty who has never shaken off his youth; a surgeon whose advice to everyone is to have the nuciform sac removed; and Sir Ralph Bloomfield Bonington, 'B.B.', complacent ass with 'a head like a tall and slender egg' (1906, remember). 'B.B.' talks in the voice of Ralph Hodgson's tempter, 'Soft as a bubble sung / Out of a linnet's lung'; he is designed for trills and roulades, vocal capering, a sublime content. What more need man do than stimulate the phagocytes and talk at the same time in bland exclamation marks? Shaw wrote most of the piece in South Cornwall (the Lizard peninsula was then little known): after swimming at Cadgwith and staying at Ruan Minor there was every reason to make Dubedat's wife a Cornishwoman, Jennifer: 'It's only what you would call Guinevere'.[21] (Agreed, the woman would never have spoken of 'you east country people': Shaw's ear momentarily failed him.) In the theatre, as in the text, the play is compelling and various. Read it side by side with *His House In Order*, done at the St James's in the same year, and you have two faces, two techniques, of the Edwardian stage.

The Doctor's Dilemma was the last new major Shaw at the Court, *Don Juan in Hell* aside; but he did insist, regrettably, on a production of *The Philanderer* (1893), his tediously loquacious joke on the Ibsen vogue and the 'New Woman'. When the Thousand Performances ended in June 1907 a small financial balance remained. Though the enterprise had been precarious, 83 its prestige was so great that important actors would often play for a guinea a matinee.[22] The total cost of each set of six matinees was about £200: figures that today seem preposterous. Invariably playing and presentation were designed not to get in the way of the piece: the Court, first of all, was the dramatist's theatre, with producer and company pledged to interpret the author's text and not to regard it as material for firework-theatrics. There was fine acting in Sloane Square, Barker's own, that of Lillah McCarthy, Norman McKinnel, Dennis Eadie, Robert Loraine, Mrs Patrick Campbell (as Hedda Gabler), Lewis Casson, Ben Webster, Louis Calvert, Edmund Gwenn, Ellen O'Malley, Dorothy Minto, Laurence Irving, a score of others. Six weeks was the longest single run. 'The first thing we did,' Barker said, 'was to struggle against the long-run system, partly because we wanted to produce a lot of plays, and partly because we disagreed with it. It is bad for plays and bad for acting.' He and Vedrenne decided to go on to the Savoy Theatre for a season of some months which had no success whatever, failed to reproduce the Court spirit, and left the management penniless.

During this period Forbes-Robertson brought in for five weeks *Caesar and Cleopatra* which Shaw had written for him in 1898 and which he had staged in New York in 1906. Behind the chronicle was Shaw's pronouncement that the theatre wanted heroes in whom we could recognise our own humanity; men who reached the summit only at rare intervals, but who found the proper level on all occasions. He saw such a man as this in Caesar and knew that he had the right classic actor. At once complicated and loosely contrived, the piece has never done everything expected of it; certainly Shaw did not visualise the action with his usual clarity. There are three main parts: Caesar, who, Maurice Colbourne said[23] should be called Shavius Caesar—in performance he is a dignified, philosophic, gently humorous, and bloodless sage—a kitten-Cleopatra who, unless coaxed along tactfully, can be trying, and probably Britannus, Shaw's favourite jest, epitome of all the jokes made about the English: we feel that he foreshadows Mr Pooter of Holloway. There have been several hopeful revivals. Forbes-Robertson, who had all the calm nobility required, included Caesar in his farewell programme at Drury Lane in 1913, and such actors as Cedric Hardwicke, Malcolm Keen, and Laurence Olivier have interpreted the part. Even so, probably the most telling production was one at Birmingham Repertory in 1956 (Geoffrey Bayldon, Caesar; Doreen Aris, Cleopatra) which went to Paris and had later a brief showing at the Old Vic.

Getting Married, labelled 'a disquisitory play', was the last Shavian work by the Vedrenne-Barker management: it was done during a short and unsuccessful Haymarket season—largely planned by Shaw while Barker was absent —during the early-summer heat of 1908. The play is remorselessly debating Shaw, sustained by a group of people that, as soon as the night has begun, we must take for better, for worse, for richer, for poorer. He decided here to examine marriage from every aspect, religious or secular. As a concession to playgoers who wanted an occasional relief from the pressure of ideas, he provided a frail trellis of plot about a rebellious couple on their wedding morning. Having been reading subversive literature, they are inclined to drop the project, and their attitude, with much else, is discussed in (for its pictorial sake), the 'Norman kitchen' of the bride's father, the Bishop of Chelsea. Several 'public uniforms' enliven the static scene. Thus we have the Bishop in his apron, an Alderman in his robes, a liveried beadle, a chaplain in cassock and biretta, a scarlet General, a Mayoress in chain of office. That is merely for the surface. Having announced the subject for debate, Shaw sticks to it, quarrying steadily; the rest depends on the stamina of the individual playgoer. Not many discussions are invigorated by an unlikely Mayoress, described in a long, detailed stage direction containing the phrase, 'In a historical museum she would explain Edward IV's taste for shopkeeper's wives.'[24] The woman goes into a trance and into a speech that has daunted most actresses, though Googie Withers did control it in a 1967 London revival. Shaw has laid out his arguments almost like an ambitious landscape gardener laying out a park with its features and vistas and sudden surprises. One good character is the celibate chaplain, Soames, a former solicitor who combines fanaticism with legal formality, and who has the last exchange with the Mayoress. 'The thing one wants most,' she says, 'has 85 nothing to do with marriage at all.' 'Christian fellowship?' Soames suggests. 'You call it that, do you?' says the Mayoress; and he replies, 'What do *you* call it?'[25]

There was a good deal of fuss in 1909 about 'a sermon in crude melodrama', *The Shewing-Up of Blanco Posnet*, a single and unexciting act set in the wilder West in pioneer days. Shaw wrote it for Tree, but the Lord Chamberlain would not license it because some of the religious sentiments in a horse-thief's discovery of God struck him, inexplicably, as blasphemous. The Abbey Theatre company then did the little piece in Dublin and brought it to London for a special Stage Society performance. It was not licensed for another seven years. The much fuller *Misalliance* (1910) belonged to Charles Frohman's courageous repertory scheme (we shall return to this) at the Duke of York's, months recalled now for Galsworthy's *Justice*. *Misalliance* was less valuable. Its scene is a house at Hindhead, a locality well known to Shaw; its event 'a debate in one sitting' (during which the curtain is lowered—once now; it used to be twice—for the audience's sake). Principal debaters are a manufacturer and his children—Johnny Tarleton we have met—a former proconsul and his son, two visitors from a falling aeroplane, and another from a portable Turkish bath. The aviatrix is Lina Szczepanowska ('not an English name, is it?' asks her host),[26] and, for reasons of such plot as there is, the truculent rabbit from the Turkish bath proclaims himself as 'the son of Lucinda Titmus' (Shaw's names again). He also observes: 'Rome fell. Babylon fell. Hindhead's turn will come.'[27] Where *Getting Married* is, not surprisingly, about marriage, *Misalliance* is roughly about the relations between parents and children: the main misalliance is that between youth and age. For all its apparently flexible design, the construction is close, but here Shaw's hammer-hammer can become fatiguing. (For the benefit of people who insist that 'Who's for tennis?' was a catchword of the 1920s, I direct attention to Johnny Tarleton early in this play: 'Anybody on for a game of tennis?')[28]

Before the end of the period Shaw wrote three other plays at full-length besides some minor pieces of which *The Dark Lady of the Sonnets* (1910), special pleading for a National Theatre, has Shakespeare, a prowling word-fancier, in talk with Elizabeth of

England outside her palace at Whitehall. *Fanny's First Play* (1911) he would not acknowledge for three years, a mild joke he enjoyed, though everyone knew the identity of 'Xxxxxxx Xxxx' who had written 'an easy play for a little theatre'. Meanwhile it had as many as 622 performances at the Little and Kingsway under Lillah McCarthy's management (she had been married to Granville Barker since the middle of the Court season). Fanny attacks 'mere morality, or the substitution of custom for conscience'. The young, Shaw says, had better have their souls awakened by disgrace; youthful rebellion aerates a comedy (scene, Denmark Hill) that is still wise and appealing and helped by such a Shavian personage as a Duke's brother who is a footman. In prologue and epilogue we have the romantic Count from Venice, remotely elegant, living in spirit in the eighteenth century. His daughter (Fanny) has written a play that she wants acted as a birthday present, with real critics to discuss it; predictably, it shocks him. Though it may mean little now that Trotter is Walkley, Vaughan and Gunn are E. A. Baughan and Gilbert Cannan, and Flawner Bannal is any 'yellow-press journalist', the discussion is still speakable and valid. It has been much less performed than the fairly short but elaborately manœuvred *Androcles and the Lion* (1913), put on by Lillah McCarthy and Granville Barker at the St James's and decorated by Albert Rothenstein (Rutherston). Its study in religious experience probably angered veteran admirers of *The Sign of the Cross* and cognate Christian-martyr melodramas from another world. Shaw, with a serious purpose, keeps laughing; and that in the Wilson Barrett theatre would have been blasphemous. Certainly no matter for children whom Shaw was convinced would like his fantasy—as indeed they have done since, though whether they often ask why martyrs embrace martyrdom is arguable. Their parents have long argued over an incandescent and provocative preface—on the prospects of Christianity— that is more important than the play it introduces.

For every person who knows *Androcles*, a thousand must know *Pygmalion* (1913; London, 1914), especially since its re-incarnation as a musical play called *My Fair Lady*; alertly done, though the American librettists botched Shaw's most theatrical scene. In *His House In Order*, eight years before, Pinero's Nina   87

Jesson had left the stage with the furious 'I go to no park tomorrow; as God hears me, I do not.' In Shaw's comedy, his heroine, the Galatea whom her Pygmalion-Professor is teaching to speak like a Duchess, leaves the Chelsea tea-party after Freddy has asked 'Are you walking across the Park, Miss Doolittle?', with the shattering reply 'in perfectly elegant diction', 'Walk! Not bloodly likely!'[29] Even today, when anything can be said in the theatre, and is all the time, Eliza's single epithet from 1914 continues—if no longer shocking—to be as dramatically explosive as it was sixty years ago. All depends on the context.

Long before, in a *Man and Superman* direction, Shaw had described Ann Whitefield:[30] 'Turn up her nose, give a cast to her eye, replace her black and violet confection by the apron and feathers of a flower girl, strike all the aitches out of her speech, and Ann would still make one dream.' In *Pygmalion*, Eliza, dropping her apron and feathers, goes the other way and shows that a flower-girl can behave like a Duchess when she is treated as one. Her evolution is relishingly theatrical. Patterns of speech were an obsession with Shaw and he indulged himself by turning Eliza, in effect, to a Cinderella rescued by the Spirit of Phonetics. Higgins, the rescuer for experiment's sake, is a boor, but the comedy does not falter until the fourth and fifth acts when the transformation is complete and the newly-made Galatea rebels against Pygmalion. That is reasonable, but Shaw could have cut here: I have never really minded what happened to Eliza; whether she stayed with Higgins or, as we are told in a postscript to the published play, married the rather feeble Freddy and kept a flower shop in the arcade of a railway station not very far from the Victoria and Albert Museum.[31]

Scarcely first-rate Shaw, *Pygmalion* does have a splendid sequence of comedy scenes and the figure of Eliza's father, Alfred Doolittle, the golden dustman: one of the undeserving poor who runs up against middle-class morality, he ends as a middle-man himself. Still, in evoking *Pygmalion*, most of us revert to its third-act tea-party, that scene before Eliza's exit, bloody but unbowed. On an official test in a world bristling with aspirates, she makes a stately progress down a Long Walk of polite chit-chat, passing from the weather to the medicinal properties of gin. The Eliza of the last acts, in easy command of her vowels, can never be so endearing as Miss Doolittle in travail with the new small-talk and fluting gravely: 'My aunt died of influenza, so they said. But it's my belief they done the old woman in.'[32] Diana Rigg, in London (1974), showed that the part had lost nothing since Mrs Patrick Campbell and those tumultuous nights, with Sir Herbert Beerbohm Tree as Higgins, at His Majesty's Theatre before the outbreak of the first world war. We have heard too much of the offstage and rehearsal fights between Tree and Mrs Campbell with whom Shaw was infatuated as he had been with various other women, Ellen Terry for one. Mrs Campbell, though clearly an artist when she felt like it, became one of those dreary creatures, a conscious 'character'. St John Ervine wrote tersely: '[She] preferred temperament to talent, and threw away a career as a great actress so that she might provide slight people with topics of conversation because of her whims and whamsies.'[33]

IV

Eliza had come to stay. Shaw, when our period ends, had still a long journey: to *Heartbreak House*; *Saint Joan*; indeed to the end (AD 31920) of the pentateuch of *Back to Methuselah*; Lilith coming from the dark, looking to a day when Man's will has conquered, when the last stream between flesh and the spirit has been forded, and life (world without end) is a glory of pure intellect: 'the vortex freed from matter'.[34]

When the chasm opened in August 1914 Shaw was only fifty-eight, the world before him. He was, in his own person, a factory of thought, prompter of conscience, elucidator of social conduct—which was hardly what Pinero and Jones would have meant—and, in one of his *Methuselah* phrases, 'a whirlpool in pure intelligence'. At his crest (*Don Juan in Hell*) his debating manner was unmatched; at his most capricious (parts of *Getting Married*) he could write lengths of what Mr Polly called Eloquent Rhapsodooce. Nevertheless, from our distance, he stands like a pillar above the rest of the Edwardian stage. This said, we cannot forget that while Shaw was heading his forces at the Court and   89 elsewhere, the influence of the Edwardian Theatre Theatrical had not waned; a fight was on, but the stage was not controlled from the study. For the general playgoer, and in spite of some critical wishful thinking, it was the theatre of the great actor-managers, their government unaffected. Some critics were not quite certain what a Theatre of Ideas implied. Thus H. M. Walbrook with a resolutely mixed bag:[35]

The Theatre of Ideas has knocked at the door, and has been admitted. The victory of Mr Bernard Shaw and Mr John Galsworthy, and the success of such plays by other writers as *The Thunderbolt, An Englishman's Home, Nan, Diana of Dobson's, Hannele, The Blue Bird,* and *The Passing of the Third-Floor Back,* have meant a stirring of the waters. . . .

Actually, the drawing-rooms behind the gilt frames were as crowded as ever; romantics were unabashed; there was any amount of forthright speaking, and one found the usual men in possession. A distinguished theatre-man[36] has allowed me to quote from a letter he wrote some years ago:

My playgoing career, as an independent adventurer, started about 1905. I went to the theatre a dozen to fifteen times a year. For me it meant, first of all, Tree whose productions were a great and glowing excitement; I might be more critical of them today, but the impression they made on me in my boyhood convinces me of their intrinsic worth. Besides Tree, of course, there were Alexander, Bourchier, Cyril Maude, Oscar Asche, Lewis Waller. Alexander I saw several times, above all in *His House In Order.* For the Drury Lane melodramas one gladly queued six hours—no stools in those days. Though I was a devotee of the theatre, and I hope a fairly intelligent young man, I had not discovered the Theatre of Ideas and cannot remember that I ever knew about the existence of the Court Theatre season. About 1911 I saw *The Witch* in which Lillah McCarthy's performance has always remained with me as one of the greatest acting experiences in my life. From that moment the Theatre of Ideas held me, but in memory it does not lessen my estimate of the value and importance of the Edwardian Theatre Theatrical.

Of dramatists round the study table, Granville Barker was the most puzzling. Only thirty-seven when our period ends, he was then approaching the second marriage (to a rich American woman: he was divorced from Lillah McCarthy in 1917) that would remove him from the active stage, a few translations apart. The second marriage may not be the answer to a curious problem—why did Barker renounce his career? In any event, he preferred to gain new honour as a scholar and Shakespearian and to become an elder statesman in the shadows. His last part he acted in 1911. After 1914 he had only two single-handed productions in London. Yet as a producer he could be a near-genius, and as an actor (his Marchbanks 'moved with the slightly dangerous grace of a very high-bred wild animal') he had often an unforgettable presence. Naturally a theatre-man of his powers had to be a dramatist. His plays are now spoken about more than read or acted, though *The Voysey Inheritance*, from the Court (1905), has continued to hold the theatre. St John Ervine said of Barker that his 'besetting sin was his love of the rich and easy life'.[37] W. Bridges-Adams, who knew him well, said: 'Barker always loved the theatre. But in my belief—and I knew him for many years—he became what he had always intended to become':[38] that is, theorist, translator, Shakespearian, rather than practical man of the stage involved with it day by day.

In his role of one of the two chieftains of the Edwardian renaissance, we think of him first as a producer (director now): 'his powers of suggestion were enough to fill a rehearsal room with magic on the greyest morning.' As a dramatist, apart from the fantasy of *Prunella* which he wrote with Laurence Housman, a whimsical-sentimental piece taking the heart in one scene, the last, in its drenched melancholy of autumn. Barker's achieve-ment rests on three plays. In *The Voysey Inheritance* John Tanner's representative showed that he could talk for himself as well as being a handsome mouthpiece, though he never had Shaw's confident drive. The play is on the theme of absolute honesty. The Voysey law firm is built on the feats of a manipulative artist in embezzlement. What is the grandson, latest inheritor, to do? Having got to a strong theatrical position, Barker pauses and does not resolve it (to the Theatre Theatrical the ultimate crime): he is concerned less with dramatic thrust than with the numerous characters of the Voysey family, intricately idiosyncratic, who will probably be a collective preservative. Walkley, one feels, was right when he asserted, in effect, that the best things have nothing to do with matters of conscience, Shaw, or Nietzsche, but with the humours, feuds, and daily life of a prosperous suburban group.

Waste, Barker's domestic tragedy about a disastrous crossing of private life and political career, was banned (one of the causes of the later Censorship inquiry, 1909) because there was talk of an abortion: the Examiner of Plays said also that Barker 'must be prepared to moderate and modify the extremely outspoken reference to the sexual relations'[39] between Trebell, the hero, and a married woman. Today the ban seems nonsensical (there were probably complex political reasons as well). In November 1907 the Stage Society acted the play privately at the Imperial Theatre in Westminster where the Central Hall is now, Barker himself, on the night before his thirtieth birthday, appearing as the radical lawyer-politician whose career must be a sacrifice to the conventions. Aimée de Burgh was the mercilessly-pinned 'charming woman if, by charming, you understand a woman who converts every quality she possesses into a means of attraction, and has no use for any other'. A gloomy play's special merit is the shape of its dialogue, dignified but supple. Here, too, Barker (as he omitted to do in *The Voysey Inheritance*) has coupled an Edwardian care for design with his unusual regard for substance. 'I'm angry,' says one of the characters, 'just angry at the waste of a good man . . . oh! the waste.' The play's title became pointed; but the ban remained until the freer air of 1920 and it was another sixteen years before Barker's revised version had a public performance in London. The way in which he was regarded when *Waste* was new can be seen from the cast that gave (in January 1908) the then formal morning walk-through for copyright purposes:

Lady Davenport, Mrs W. P. Reeves; Walter Kent, Mr Gilbert Cannan; Miss Farrant, Miss Magdalen Ponsonby; Miss Trebell, Miss Clemence Housman; Mrs O'Connell, Mrs Bernard Shaw; Lucy Davenport, Mrs H. G. Wells; George Farrant, Mr St John Hankin; Russell Blackborough, Mr John Galsworthy; A Footman, Mr Allan Wade; Henry Trebell, Mr Laurence Housman; Simon, Mrs Granville Barker; Gilbert Wedgecroft, Mr H. G. Wells; Lord Charles Cantelupe, Professor Gilbert Murray, LL.D.; the Earl of Horsham, Mr Bernard Shaw; Edmunds, Mr Arthur Bowyer; Justin O'Connell, Mr William Archer.

Shaw was described as 'late of the Theatre Royal, Dublin' and Archer had a note 'his Last Appearance on any Stage'. Finally: 'Neither the Costumes nor the Scenery have been designed by Mr Charles Ricketts.'[40]

Barker's last major play, put on during the Charles Frohman repertory season at the Duke of York's in 1910, was *The Madras House* (seventeen women in a cast of twenty-five). It examines feminine repression, and in the third act, set in the 'rotunda' of the Bond Street dress-shop after which the play is named, considers from most angles the status of women and their future. It is civilised argument of a kind expected in the theatre of the new naturalism; a play fitted to a progressively rebellious period. Elsewhere there are tingling moments though the play is often detached and coldly ventriloquial; Barker stands away from his characters. Still, one does remember the emotionally frustrated Huxtable sisters in the house at Denmark Hill (a favourite suburb for the Theatre of Ideas):[41]

EMMA: ... It isn't exactly that one wants to get married. I daresay mother is right about that.
PHILIP: About what?
EMMA: Well, some time ago a gentleman proposed to Jane. And mother said it would have been more honourable if he had spoken to father first, and that Jane was the youngest and too young anyhow to know her own mind. Well, you know she's twenty-six. And they heard of something he'd once done and it was put a stop to. And Jane was very rebellious and mother cried. . . .

Where Barker, moving in Shaw's world, could be too eagerly voluble, John Galsworthy wrote more laconically. This dramatist (1867–1933), who had one piece in the Court repertory, *The Silver Box* (1906), finished in under two months, was basically a novelist with the solid family background of his own Forsytes and a fighting, reforming instinct. He was the most high-minded and sympathetic of men. James Agate's summary has truth in its exaggeration: 'The writer is in himself an entire Humane Society. He sides with the fox against the man in pink, the hen-coop against the marauding fox, the chickweed against the chicken, and whatever it is the chickweed preys on against that ferocious plant.'[42] When urgently moved he could move an audience. But he could not sustain the note all the time and his 93 lesser plays had to be diagrams for a company to fill out. Depressingly, he lacked any real sense of humour and much of his early work is now grey upon the page. From our period *The Silver Box*—his only Court piece—*Strife* (1909), and *Justice* (1910) do powerfully endure. In *The Silver Box*, immediately prosperous in the repertory of the new drama, he drove at social injustice ('One law for the rich . . .'). Briefly, a workman gets a month's hard labour when a rich young wastrel, whose offence has been much the same, is discharged. Coolly argued, the play had a barrister's reasoning and a dramatist's method. Writing about a Court revival, a reviewer in *The Academy* took his chance to stab at the commercial theatre of 1906:[43]

Mr Galsworthy . . . tackled the problem of putting his characters on to the stage simply and straightforwardly, without preoccupation. He did not think it necessary to have three doors and a french window to every scene, one of them (in the third act) leading to a bedroom, on the ground that stage rooms were like that. Nor did he think it necessary in the third act to work up to the venerable situation in which the wife visits the other man's rooms at twelve o'clock at night and is discovered (or not, as the case may be) by the husband.

Galsworthy's second play, *Joy*, which Barker also tried hopefully (but this was at the Savoy in 1907) proved to be the flimsiest butter-muslin. His two startling successes had yet to come. One, *Strife*, was a dramatic treatise on strikes which Barker (yet again) produced on behalf of the American impresario, Charles Frohman; done first at matinees, according to familiar habit, it soon went into a regular evening bill. The scene is a tin-plate works on the borders of England and Wales; the conflict is between Capital and Labour; and the main figures are the chairman of the works and the spokesman of the men, equally sincere, equally wrong-headed. The humanitarian Galsworthy, scrupulously balanced, guides us all over the battle-ground, to a directors' meeting, to the Labour leader's cottage, and to a fiery mass meeting outside the works. At the close, when neither side has won and there has been acute personal disaster, we are left to ponder on the futility of the whole wretched business:[44]

TENCH [the secretary]: D'you know, sir—these terms, they're the *very same* we drew out together, you and I, and put to both sides before the fight began? All this—all this—and—and—for what?
HARNESS [from the Union], *in a slow grim voice*: That's where the fun comes in!

Strife, in its way, bridged the years between Vedrenne-Barker and London's second repertory venture, Charles Frohman's at the Duke of York's in 1910. Where the Court had its near-thousand performances, Frohman, in a much larger and a central theatre, had only 128 of ten plays spread over seventeen weeks:

PLAY	AUTHOR	Performances
Justice	John Galsworthy	26
Misalliance	Bernard Shaw	11
Old Friends	J. M. Barrie	
The Sentimentalists	George Meredith	6
The Twelve-Pound Look	J. M. Barrie	
The Madras House	Granville Barker	10
Trelawny of the 'Wells'	A. W. Pinero	42
Prunella	Barker and Laurence Housman	17
Helena's Path	Anthony Hope and Cosmo Gordon-Lennox	2
Chains	Elizabeth Baker	14

Ironically, the Theatre Theatrical carried the season with a fluent revival of *Trelawny*. Several of the other plays we have met already. Of the others, the very slight *Helena's Path* (with country cricket-match) stood in the same relation to its neighbours as the Harcourt comedies did to the Court repertory. *The Sentimentalists* mildly rediscovered a porcelain-mannered, static, and unfinished pastoral, or early Victorian garden-play, by George Meredith, of all writers. And *Chains*, by a woman dramatist, was a wire-and-sandpaper study of a suburban clerk whose plan to escape to Australia is frustrated when he hears that his wife will have a child. He stays, chained, in the 'old grey solitary nothingness' at 55 Acacia Avenue, Hammersmith 95

('Acacia' appears, for some reason, to symbolise extreme dullness).

Today the aspiring programme, financially a failure, is remembered because of *Justice*, magnificently produced by Barker, with which the season began and in which Galsworthy was directly a propagandist. He would say later, in the preface to the Manaton edition of his plays, that he was not conscious of any desire to secure direct reform. 'His only ambition in drama . . . is to present truth as he sees it, and, gripping with it his readers or his audiences, to produce in them a sort of mental and moral ferment whereby vision may be enlarged, imagination livened, and understanding promoted.' In *Justice*, a tragedy fiercely realistic, solitary confinement is attacked in a scene whose fame is out of proportion to its brevity. A young clerk, momentarily tempted, has committed forgery. He goes to penal servitude (the blindness of justice again). In a short wordless scene we watch him beating furiously on the door of his tiny cell. Not a word is spoken; the impact startles. After curtain-fall at the première, the gallery audience and some of those in other parts of the house stayed in the darkened theatre until half-an-hour before midnight, shouting 'We want Galsworthy!'[45] Barker had at length to assure them that the dramatist had gone. Winston Churchill, then Home Secretary, saw and admired *Justice* and, because of it, the penalty of solitary confinement was reconsidered. St John Ervine, writing after forty-five years, remembered the occasion for Barker's mastery as a producer: 'In the court scene, during Falder's trial, immense effect was obtained by the lighting of lamps in the court as the evening closed on the final episodes. . . . The lights, one after the other at intervals, were turned on; and the accumulated result of the illumination was strong enough to be vividly remembered by one enthralled spectator.'[46] The modern theatre has overlooked the play. A London revival in 1968, expertly cast, did not run, though (possibly because) its revelation of what Galsworthy called 'nothing if not a picture of blind justice'[47] was as agonising as it used to be.

Little else before the war was anywhere near Galsworthy's best work. His compassion continued to be evident in such average and now rarely-dusted plays as *The Eldest Son* (1912), *The*

Pigeon from the same year, *The Fugitive* (1913), and *The Mob* (1914), the last an assault on jingoism that failed because the man on whom much depended came out in the theatre as a tedious egotist. Otherwise, we might say of these pieces—in words from a source[48] that might have baffled Galsworthy—that they were all 'well-seasoned, straight-grained, and free from large or defective knots, or worm-holes'. *The Eldest Son*, fashioned as competently as any of them, uses the old story of the son of the house and a servant, here the baronet's heir and a lady's maid. Again and again—however painful Sir Squire Bancroft found it—Edwardians reverted to class distinction; it was a subject anyone as sensitive as Galsworthy had to discuss. 'Unless we're true to our caste,' barks Sir William, 'and prepared to work for it, the landed classes are going to go under to this infernal democratic spirit in the air.'[49] But all will be well at the house in the Shires. Freda refuses Bill three minutes before the night ends.

An apparent intruder in the study is St John Hankin (1869–1909), whose name figures in the copyright performance of *Waste*. It has ceased now to appear as a matter of right in surveys of the stage, yet his manner is more accomplished and pungent than that of the early Somerset Maugham. He straddles between the theatres of entertainment and ideas. In life he could be restless and demanding, and his plays keep a quinine-tang, though there is nothing of it in the bland set of *Dramatic Sequels* he wrote for *Punch* in the ebbing century: additional acts to such plays as *Hamlet*, *The School for Scandal*, and *The Second Mrs Tanqueray*. (A third and redoubtable Mrs Tanqueray whom we do not meet is now the mistress of Highercoombe: 'Your weddings are always so furtive', says Cayley Drummle to Aubrey.)

Hankin's principal plays may live, though it was his habit to demolish, not to build. He wrote for the Court where Barker did both *The Return of the Prodigal* (1905) and *The Charity That Began at Home* (1906). Barry Jackson, founder of the Birmingham Repertory, had a confirmed belief in *The Cassilis Engagement* (1907), a comedy effectively ruthless. The chatelaine of Deynham Abbey manages to break her son's engagement to a bookmaker's daughter, Ethel Borridge (the classes again), 97 simply by inviting the unlucky girl and her appalling mother to stay, and boring them to death by calculated sweetness and the routine of a country house. Uncompromising as it can be, it will carry an audience if Mrs Borridge is kept within reasonable bounds. Personally, I prefer *The Return of the Prodigal* in spite of Shaw's dislike—he was angry with Barker for doing it—and the faint response to a glittering cast, led by John Gielgud, in the 1948 revival. Mockingly, Hankin presents a prodigal son who is not ashamed of himself. He can remind one of Kipling's[50]

> The fatted calf is dressed for me,
> But the husks have greater zest for me,
> I think my pigs will be best for me,
> So I'm off to the Yards afresh.

This Eustace returns for a few days to the bosom, more or less, of his wealthy cloth-manufacturing people in Gloucestershire, only (after suitable financial arrangements) to strike off again, as insolently charming and unredeemed as when he arrived. He is a prodigal who neatly inverts the old conventions, such as 'People in the Colonies always do write for money'. Eustace prefers to seek the fatted calf in person. After deflating both his pompous father and brother, he slips off again into the unknown—to London at least—with hush money of £250 a year, to be paid quarterly. 'Make it three hundred, Father,' he suggests without luck, 'and I won't write!' (In the 1948 revival he took £650 a year and said, 'Make it a thousand'.) We hear much of Hankin's cynicism. Undeniably he looked at society with bitter amusement, but sometimes he can reach the heart. Here are a few speeches from a fourth-act scene for the prodigal and his unmarried sister who might have an affinity with the Huxtable sisters of Barker's Denmark Hill:[51]

VIOLET (*quietly*): You think my life happier than yours, then?
EUSTACE: Isn't it?
VIOLET: No. *Your* life is your own. You can do as you please with it, use it or waste it as you think best. You are free. I am not. You think, because I stay quietly at home, doing the duty that lies nearest me and not crying out against Fate, therefore I've nothing more to wish for! Would *you* be happy, do you suppose, if you were in my case? I live here down in Chedleigh from year's end to year's end. Mother

1. *Herbert Beerbohm Tree as Shylock in* The Merchant of Venice, *His Majesty's Theatre,* 1908

2. *Dennis Neilson-Terry (Oberon) above Titania (Christine Silver)
and Nigel Playfair (Bottom) in Granville Barker's production of*
A Midsummer Night's Dream, *Savoy Theatre*, 1914.
Donald Calthrop (Puck) is on the right

3. *A scene from Cecil Raleigh and Henry Hamilton's Drury Lane melodrama, The Sins of Society, 1907. The pawnbroker (Oscar Adye), who has placed a diamond tiara in a cardboard box, is looking for sealing-wax. While his back is turned Lady Marion Beaumont (Constance Collier) changes the box with the tiara for a duplicate which she has filled with coal.*

4. *H.B. Irving as Dr Jekyll in* Dr Jekyll and Mr Hyde, *founded by J. Comyns Carr on the story by Robert Louis Stevenson, Queen's Theatre, January* 1910

5. *H.B. Irving as Mr Hyde in the Comyns Carr
version of Stevenson's* Dr Jekyll and Mr Hyde,
Queen's Theatre, January 1910

6. *Gerald du Maurier as the Duc de Charmerace in* Arsène
Lupin, *by François de Croisset and Maurice Leblanc, at
the Duke of York's Theatre,* 1909

7. *Annie Russell as Barbara Undershaft and Oswald Yorke as Bill Walker in Act Two of Bernard Shaw's* Major Barbara *at the Royal Court Theatre, November* 1905

8. When, at the invitation of the Prime Minister (H.H. Asquith), the third act of Shaw's John Bull's Other Island was played at 10 Downing Street on 30 June 1911, before King George V and Queen Mary, Granville Barker (the original Keegan) appeared as Larry Doyle. He is standing (second from L.) in a scene from the performance. Among the others are Louis Calvert (far L.) as Broadbent, and J.D. Beveridge and Wilfred Shine (respectively third and second from R.) as Father Dempsey and Barney Doran

9. *Smith, the parlourmaid (Marie Löhr), pours the wine for Thomas Freeman (Robert Loraine) in the second act of Somerset Maugham's* Smith, Comedy Theatre, 1909

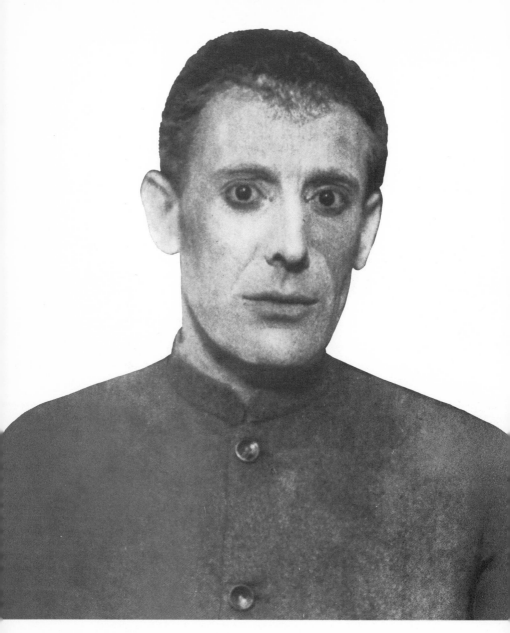

10. *Dennis Eadie as Falder in John Galsworthy's*
Justice, *Duke of York's Theatre*, 1910

11. *Henry Ainley and Evelyn Millard in Stephen Phillips's*
Paolo and Francesca, *St James's, 1902. The garden
scene at the end of Act Three. Francesca: 'Here is the
place where I had ceased to read'*

12. Hilary Jesson: 'Let Nina, if she will, add her tribute to Filmer's.' A scene from the second act (in the drawing-room at Overbury Towers) of Pinero's His House In Order, St James's, 1906. In the foreground, L. to R.: (on sofa) Bella Pateman (Lady Ridgeley) and E. Lyall Swete (Sir Daniel Ridgeley); George Alexander (Hilary Jesson) and Irene Vanbrugh (Nina Jesson), standing centre; and, seated on right, Nigel Playfair (Dr Dilnott) and Dawson Milward

13. THEIR LOVE AFFAIR, an operetta in tableaux by J. Comyns Carr. St James's Theatre, 1908. (1) Louis Calvert as James Mortimore; (2) Mabel Hackney (Mrs Laurence Irving), L., as a needy music-teacher's wife, Phyllis, who has destroyed the will that leaves a large estate to Helen Thornhill (Mrs Patrick Campbell's daughter, Stella Campbell, R.)

Dover Street Studios

14. *A scene from* The Blue Bird, *Maurice Maeterlinck's fairy play, translated by Alexander Teixeira de Mattos, Haymarket Theatre, 1909. Tyltyl sees that all things have souls*

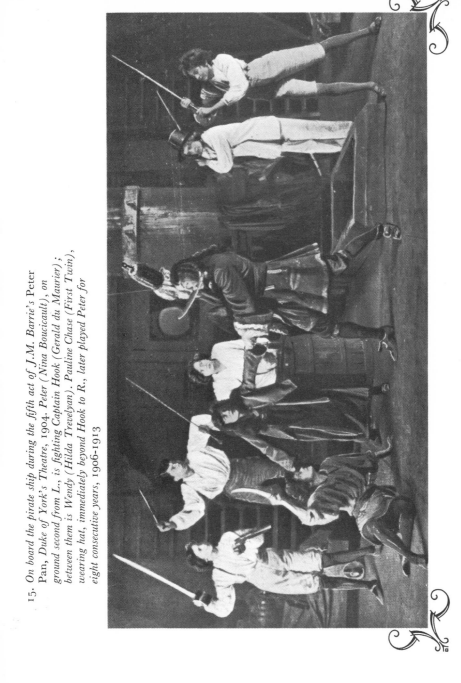

15. On board the pirate ship during the fifth act of J.M. Barrie's Peter Pan, Duke of York's Theatre, 1904. Peter (Nina Boucicault), on ground second from L., is fighting Captain Hook (Gerald du Maurier); between them is Wendy (Hilda Trevelyan). Pauline Chase (First Twin), wearing hat, immediately beyond Hook to R., later played Peter for eight consecutive years, 1906-1913

16. Marie Lloyd
(Matilda Wood)

17. George Robey
(George Edward Wade)

18. Vesta Tilley
(later Lady de Frece)

never leaves home. She doesn't care to pay visits. So I cannot either. I may sometimes get away for a few days, a week, perhaps, but very seldom. And as Mother grows older I shall go less. Soon people will give up asking me when they find I always refuse. And so I shall be left here alone with no friends, no real companionship, merely one of the family, obliged to know the people they know, visit the people they visit, not a grown woman with interests of her own and a life to order as she pleases.

EUSTACE: But you'll marry—

VIOLET: Marry! What chance have I of marrying now? When we hadn't so much money, and Henry and Father weren't so set in taking a position in the County, there was some chance for me. Now there is none. . . . It's all very well for Henry. He is a partner in the firm. He will be a very rich man. He can marry Stella Faringford. Oh, we are to be great people! But you don't find Sir John Faringford's son proposing to *me*! No! He wants a girl of his own class or else an heiress, not a manufacturer's daughter with a few thousand pounds. So the great people won't marry me and I mustn't marry the little people. Father wouldn't like it. He hardly lets Mother ask them to the house nowadays. And so the years go by and my youth with them, and I know it will be like this always, always.

EUSTACE: Poor old Vi! And I thought you were quite contented with your bazaars and your old women. Why don't you speak to the Mater?

VIOLET: What's the use? Mother wouldn't understand. She married when she was twenty-one. She doesn't know what it is for a girl to go on living at home long after she's grown up and ought to have a house of her own. So I stay on here knitting socks for old Allen and working *your* handkerchiefs, and here I shall stay till Mother and Father are both dead. . . . And then it will be too late.

Believing that he might be suffering from a fatal disease, Hankin committed suicide, by drowning, in the summer of 1909. Shaw described him then as 'a most gifted writer of high comedy of the kind that is a stirring and important criticism of life', and dedicated a volume of plays to 'the memory of my fellow worker'.

V

The Return of the Prodigal was in the programmes of the Gaiety, Manchester, the first English provincial Repertory. Between 1907 and 1913 four major Repertory Theatres were opened, but the movement had a flinty path ahead; the Theatre of Ideas could not yet be cocksure. In the year 1908, with the Court glowing in the minds of its former 'congregation', and vigorous provincial risings either achieved or imminent, these were some of the productions in London and outside it:

London: *My Mimosa Maid*, 'Riviera musical incident,' Prince of Wales's; *Pete*, by Hall Caine and Louis N. Parker, Lyceum; *Fanny and the Servant Problem*, by Jerome K. Jerome, Aldwych; *Susannah—and Some Others*, by Madame Albanesi, Royalty.

Outer London: *Love's Golden Dream*, by Frances Delaval, Royal, Stratford (characters included Harold Tre-Wynne, Vashti de Marconi, P. C. Penryn, and Tommy Tittlemouse); *Beau Brocade (the Highwayman)*, by Baroness Orczy and Montague Barstow, Coronet; *He's a Jolly Good Fellow*, by Arthur Shirley and E. Vivian Edmonds, Dalston (Lord Vernon, Bertie Splashington, Julie Flonflon, Little Harold).

Provinces: *The Goddess of Destruction*, romantic military drama by Terence Nerrey, Queen's, Liverpool (Lord Lionel Welford, Mrs Teresa Towzer, Count Boris Torvineff, and Ischar Viborsky); *The Woman from Russia*, 'domestic play of passion, virtue, and honour,' by Fred G. Ingleby, Alexandra, Sheffield; *The Empty Cradle*, domestic drama, author unnamed, Royal, Bilston (Carnaby Bloodworth, Hon. St Clair Selby, Misery, Sarah Puddicombe).

Not to speak of *The Power of Lies*, *For Love of a Women*, *The Outcast of the Family*, *A Desperate Marriage*, *Married to the Wrong Man*, *How Women Ruin Men*, *Grit*, *Foiled*, and *A Repentant Sinner*, at various places and on various stages. There were also electric theatres that specialised in 'the rock-steady representations of the present-day advance in animated photography'.

Meanwhile, Miss A. E. F. (Annie Elizabeth Fredericka) Horniman, oblivious of all these matters, declared open the provincial repertory movement in what one of her first actors called 'a city of thrusting prosperity,' Manchester. Herself a Londoner, then in her late forties, her moderate fortune (which rumour made far larger than it was) derived from the family tea business. From youth she had an instinctive feeling for the theatre, not an art her relatives admired. Self-effacingly, when she had the chance and the means, she became a pioneer of the Theatre of Ideas, financing in 1894 the London production, a 'fruitful failure', of Shaw's *Arms and the Man* (it was not in her Manchester list). Miss Horniman was a friend and helper of W. B. Yeats; and during the spring of 1904, in Dublin, she bought and subsidised for the Irish National Theatre Society the building, once a mechanics' institute, that became the Abbey and opened its doors at Christmas that year. (More of this later.) When she parted company with the Irish Players after 'acting for years as fairy godmother to a singularly ungrateful theatrical Cinderella', she settled during 1907 in Manchester; a woman of much presence, candour, and generosity, who found the northern city, with its care for the arts, thoroughly congenial to her. She wanted her repertory theatre—even if she disapproved of the word, it established itself in spite of her—to have a regular change of programme, to be catholic in choice, and (though here there had to be marriage of convenience) not to be governed by one school of dramatists. Miss Horniman and her director, B. Iden Payne, promised

an especially widely open door to present-day British writers, who will not now need to sigh for a hearing, provided only that they have something to say worth listening to, and say it in an interesting and original manner.[52]

The enterprise began in the oblong ballroom that was known as the Midland Hotel Theatre and then established itself in 1908 at the transformed Gaiety, a name that must have brought a chuckle from George Edwardes in London. Miss Horniman's theatre, the first in Britain with every seat numbered and reserved, was decorated simply in white and red; no gilt, no flock wallpapers. The stage was framed by mottled marble. The orchestra had neither brass nor drums. You would not find an advertisement curtain at the Gaiety, and the theatre's own announcements in local newspapers were as direct as possible, 101 without hyperbole. (Miss Horniman's grandfather was a Quaker: the spirit endured.) At once the Gaiety set out to educate Manchester in the new drama, represented by a fresh and thriving regional school—a Pennine chain of such authors, through the years, as Harold Brighouse, Allan Monkhouse, Stanley Houghton—and a solid fortification of approved plays from London's theatre of doctrine. Naturally, the Gaiety welcomed the new realism. Though it ranged far, it also experimented relishingly with kitchen-dresser drama, rebellion in small sitting-rooms, domestic volcanoes erupting in middle-class streets. Plenty of other things, romantic, even frivolous; but the Manchester School was a no-nonsense academy that showed the very age and body of the time its form and pressure. (Some titles, such as *The Amateur Socialist, Unemployed*, and *The Subjection of Kezia*, did sound as if the dramatists were walking up a cinder-path in the rain.) The company, at various times, fostered players who would honour the London stage: Sybil Thorndike, Lewis Casson (who followed Payne as director), Edyth Goodall, Esme Percy, Herbert Lomas, Milton Rosmer, Ada King. The Gaiety's fame outran Manchester; five or six times there were London seasons (two visits to North America as well). Its most publicised piece was *Hindle Wakes*, produced in 1912 eighteen months before the author, Stanley Houghton, died. By chance it opened in London where the Gaiety players, under Lewis Casson, did it for the Stage Society; thereafter it had a couple of performances in the company's season at the Coronet in Notting Hill Gate; and it went on to the West End to run steadily at the Playhouse through a burning summer.

Houghton had already written in 1910 a carefully-poised play of rebellion against paternal authority, *The Younger Generation*. *Hindle Wakes*, with parents and children in conflict, was at heart a Lancashire feminist variant on the inevitable Edwardian theme, marriage between the classes. 'Should Fanny marry Alan?' was the famous poster of 1912 and Houghton's plot was debated fiercely wherever playgoers met. It is, briefly, a tale of two weaving families in the Lancashire town of Hindle. Nat Jeffcote and Chris Hawthorn had been fellow-weavers as young men. But Nat prospered and bought the mill; Chris remained in his employ. Now, when Fanny Hawthorn has spent a stolen week-end at Llandudno with Alan Jeffcote, it is clear, according to the rules—also an inevitable Edwardian phrase—that there can be only one sequel. Fanny and Alan must marry immediately; he must make an honest woman of her. So the parents think; so Alan's betrothed, Beatrice, thinks; so at last does Alan himself. Fanny does not agree. Proudly, she asserts her independence; she will have no man she cannot respect. Her defiance still rings:[53]

ALAN: But you didn't ever really love me?
FANNY: Love you? Good heavens, of course not! Why on earth should I love you? You were just someone to have a bit of fun with. You were an amusement—a lark.
ALAN (*shocked*): Fanny! Is that all you cared for me?
FANNY: How much more did you care for me?
ALAN: But it's not the same. I'm a man.
FANNY: You're a man, and I was your little fancy. Well, I'm a woman, and *you* were *my* little fancy. You wouldn't prevent a woman enjoying herself as well as a man, if she takes it into her head?
ALAN: It sounds so jolly immoral. I never thought of a girl looking on a chap just like that! I made sure you wanted to marry me if you got the chance.
FANNY: No fear! You're not good enough for me. The chap Fanny Hawthorn weds has got to be made of different stuff from you, my lad. My husband, if ever I have one, will be a man, not a fellow who'll throw over his girl at his father's bidding. You're not man enough for me. You're a nice lad, and I'm fond of you. But I wouldn't ever marry you.

Again:

I'm a Lancashire lass, and so long as there's weaving sheds in Lancashire, I shall earn enough brass to keep me going. I wouldn't live again at home after this, not anyhow! I'm going to be on my own in future.

So many girls were going to be on their own. But Houghton's Fanny astonished the average Edwardian for whom the Lancashire mill-girl was another accepted stereotype, as in the song from the musical comedy of *The Orchid* (1903):[54]

Liza Ann is a neat young lass,
And she's working up at Briggs's mill,—

103

Ev'ry morning at six o'clock
You can see her walking up the hill.

'A neat young lass', but not Fanny Hawthorn. The play lived. In London, at a 1949 revival, playgoers were still asking whether Fanny should marry Alan; it was, in effect, another triumphant première for Houghton (who died young in 1913). The Nat Jeffcote that night was Herbert Lomas, who had created the part in 1912, and whose powerful voice had always had in it the wind of the Pennines and the clacking of looms.

St John Ervine's *Jane Clegg* (1913) was also a Gaiety find. The young Ulsterman, who at one point managed the Abbey, Dublin (to which he was not inordinately addicted) became a both kindly and contentious London drama critic. In later years he wrote a trinity of stage best-sellers, but his reputation in the theatre moves with *Jane Clegg* and—out of our period—the later *John Ferguson*. Jane Clegg is a woman who has finished with forgiveness. Her husband is a commercial traveller, a flashy, furtive, slinking little man. When he deceives her yet again, she dismisses him; by chance she has the means to do so, and, unlike some wives condemned for life to the same worthless man, she takes her chance. Ervine was speaking from life, of life: a joyless play, unassailably theatrical. Sybil Thorndike was the first Jane: her husband, Henry, was Bernard Copping, a precise and endeared artist in English repertory.[55] The Gaiety also staged *Mary Broome* (1911) by Allan Monkhouse, of the *Manchester Guardian*, C. E. Montague's lieutenant in a group of probing, literate Manchester drama critics that also included the not so grave James Agate. *Mary Broome* was interesting because Monkhouse had turned to a period obsession. Maidservants were heavily on the mind of an Edwardian dramatist. They were either segregated behind the green baize door and brought out as needed to dress the stage; they were unrestrainedly comic; or they caused alarm by marrying, or refusing to marry, into the family. Down the century there had been examples, Israel Zangwill's *Merely Mary Ann* (1904), a snobbish exhibit; Maugham's *Smith* (1909), Galsworthy's *The Eldest Son*. Now Monkhouse, gentle, compassionate man, wrote *Mary Broome*, set at first in 'the drawing room of a biggish suburban villa'. Mary appears almost at once, 'a comely young woman in the housemaid's usual afternoon dress and with the housemaid's usual self-possession'.[56] A girl of dignity and sense, she is married presently to the son of the house, a vain and feeble 'literary man'; we are glad when, after her child's death, she goes off to Canada with a faithful admirer. It is warmly-felt play, still of value as another glance at the wakening Edwardian conscience.

A rising further in the North was the Scottish Repertory Theatre in Glasgow. It opened in April 1909, under Alfred Wareing, as 'Scotland's own theatre, financed by Scottish money, managed by Scotsmen, established to make Scotland independent of London for its dramatic supplies'. On the whole, an unambiguous statement. With much else, it offered sixteen new plays in its first four seasons. Few were written in permanent ink, and I doubt whether Scots still tingle with pleasure when they realise that Glasgow, with a piece called *Barbara Grows Up*, 'turned its attention to the creation of a national drama'. But Wareing, in his Citizens' Theatre, was a concentrated zealot; if he did nothing else—and he did—he would be thanked for presenting Chekhov's *The Seagull* for the first time in Britain (1909): the George Calderon translation, Mary Jerrold as Arkadina. It was too early yet for Chekhov; audiences could not yet understand these plays that hold autumn in their eyes, these people with their ecstasies and rash-embraced despairs. Wareing was bold, and he trusted his own boldness—practically two years before the disastrous Stage Society production of *The Cherry Orchard* in London. This so exasperated its Sunday-night house that at the last curtain the theatre was nearly half empty. As late as 1925, we can remember, Henry Arthur Jones said after the Fagan revival that the play 'gave him the impression of someone who had visited a lunatic asylum and taken down everything the inmates said'.[59]

The Scottish Repertory had to close at the outbreak of the war; and within three years Miss Horniman yielded unwillingly in Manchester. By the early 1920s the Gaiety, from the blossoming spring of the Theatre of Ideas, had dwindled to a cinema. Still, two other theatres, each born during our period, survived to lead English repertory through the decades (there are many challengers now). The older was the Liverpool

Playhouse, opened in 1911 with *The Admirable Crichton* after a preliminary season elsewhere that began with *Strife*, also produced by Basil Dean. It was Liverpool's own venture, belonging to 1,300 shareholders; after some preliminary pitch-and-toss, intensified by the war, it settled into a theatre of steady distinction that, like the Gaiety, would send to London many famous names (Ronald Squire, Cecil Parker, Diana Wynyard, Michael Redgrave).

The other major Repertory was in Birmingham. It was this that would most excite historians between the wars, and all because of one man's bounty. His native city never fully understood or appreciated Barry Vincent Jackson, though his theatre in Station Street, with the narrow, sharply raked auditorium, would be internationally praised. I have written the story in detail. Let me say now that Jackson, with his constant alacrity of spirit, founded the Repertory 'to serve an art instead of making that art serve a commercial purpose': a theatre that the poet John Drinkwater, Jackson's close friend, called 'the captive image of a dream'.[58] Where Miss Horniman's fortune was from tea, Jackson's came from the firm of provision merchants (the Maypole Dairies) that his father had founded. George Jackson allowed Barry—named after the actor Barry Sullivan—to indulge his feeling for the arts. It was an hour when ice-floes were cracking; in various parts of the land, groups in love with the stage but dissatisfied with what they saw, popular London plays reproduced as by a copying-press, had begun to think and plan creatively. In Birmingham Jackson formed a celebrated amateur company, the Pilgrim Players. He was resolved to have a professional theatre; in October 1912 he saw work beginning on a restricted patch of land behind New Street Station; and remarkably, in the following February, the Birmingham Repertory opened its doors with *Twelfth Night*. That evening Barry Jackson, six feet tall, urbanely commanding (but now a little shy), came out before the curtain to read the rhymed iambics of Drinkwater's ode. This ended with the words,

> We have the challenge of the mighty line—
> God grant us grace to give the countersign[59]

and from that moment the Birmingham Repertory Theatre moved forward into history 'to kindle and to bless'.[60] Half-a-dozen of its early choices were poets' plays. It is time to close the study door and move further back through the spaces of the Edwardian house to the music-room where the poets congregate.

Notes

1. Elizabeth Barrett Browning: *Aurora Leigh* (1856).
2. Preface to *Mrs Warren's Profession:* The Bodley Head Bernard Shaw, Vol. 1 (1970), p. 250.
3. Ivor Brown: *What is a Play?* (1964), p. 14.
4. *Man and Superman*: Epistle Dedicatory to Arthur Bingham Walkley: Bodley Head Bernard Shaw, Vol. 2 (1971), p. 527.
5. John Masefield: 'On the Ninetieth Birthday of Bernard Shaw' in *GBS 90: Aspects of Bernard Shaw's Life and Work*. Edited by S. Winsten (1946), p. 17.
6. Doris Arthur Jones: *The Life and Letters of Henry Arthur Jones* (1930), p. 205.
7. *Ibid.*, p. 211.
8. Letter to William Archer (27.8.1903) in *Bernard Shaw: Collected Letters 1898–1910*, ed. by Dan H. Laurence (1972), p. 359.
9. Interview drafted by Shaw: Bodley Head Bernard Shaw, Vol. 1 (1970), p. 595.
10. Desmond MacCarthy: *The Court Theatre, 1904–1907: A Commentary and a Criticism* (1907), p. 124.
11. *Ibid.*, p. 26.
12. John Masefield in *GBS 90*, p. 17.
13. Ashley Dukes: *Drama* (1926), p. 97.
14. MacCarthy: *The Court Theatre*, p. 72.
15. *John Bull's Other Island*: Bodley Head Bernard Shaw (1971), p. 910.
16. *Ibid.*, Preface for Politicians, p. 808.
17. *John Bull's Other Island*, Act III, p. 971.
18. *Man and Superman:* Bodley Head Bernard Shaw, Vol. 2 (1971), p. 652.
19. *Ibid.*, p. 653.
20. Winifred Loraine: *Robert Loraine* (1938), p. 90.
21. *The Doctor's Dilemma:* Bodley Head Bernard Shaw, Vol. III (1971), p. 357.
22. Sir Lewis Casson in BBC talk, July 1951.
23. Maurice Colbourne in *The Real Bernard Shaw* (1949), p. 134.
24. *Getting Married:* Bodley Head Bernard Shaw, Vol. III (1971), p. 622.
25. *Ibid.*, p. 661.
26. *Misalliance:* Bodley Head Bernard Shaw, Vol. IV (1972), p. 193.
27. *Ibid.*, p. 219.
28. *Ibid.*, p. 169.

29. *Pygmalion:* Bodley Head Bernard Shaw, Vol. IV (1972), p. 730.
30. *Man and Superman:* Bodley Head Bernard Shaw, Vol. II (1971), p. 549.
31. *Pygmalion:* Bodley Head Bernard Shaw, Vol. IV (1972), p. 794.
32. *Ibid.*, p. 728.
33. St John Ervine: *Bernard Shaw: His Life, Work, and Friends* (1956), p. 443.
34. *Back to Methuselah:* Bodley Head Bernard Shaw, Vol. V (1972), p. 630.
35. H. M. Walbrook: *Nights at the Play* (1911). Preface, pp. ix–x.
36. Charles Landstone, former Deputy Drama Director, Arts Council of Great Britain.
37. Ervine, p. 344.
38. From broadcast talk on 'The Lost Leader', included in *A Bridges-Adams Letter Book*, ed. by Robert Speaight (1971), p. 87.
39. C. B. Purdom: *Harley Granville Barker* (1955), p. 73.
40. *Ibid.*, p. 76.
41. Granville Barker: *The Madras House* (1910), Act I.
42. James Agate: *A Short View of the English Stage* (1926), pp. 79–80.
43. Quoted by H. V. Marrot in *The Life and Letters of John Galsworthy* (1935), p. 201.
44. *The Plays of John Galsworthy* (1929): *Strife*, Act III, p. 156.
45. Marrot, p. 255.
46. Ervine, pp. 343–4.
47. Marrot, p. 261.
48. Stationery Office report on Squeegee Heads (1935).
49. *The Plays of John Galsworthy; The Eldest Son*, Act 1, p. 171.
50. Rudyard Kipling: 'The Prodigal Son (Western Version)': Inclusive Edition of the Verse (1928 edition), p. 562.
51. *The Return of the Prodigal* (1905), Act IV.
52. Rex Pogson: *Miss Horniman and the Gaiety Theatre, Manchester* (1952), p. 26.
53. *Hindle Wakes* (1912), Act III.
54. *The Orchid:* musical play by J. T. Tanner; music by Ivan Caryll and Lionel Monckton, Gaiety (1903).
55. Bernard Copping (d. 1939): leading man at the Plymouth Repertory for many years, and Director, 1929–33.
56. *Mary Broome* (1911), Act I.
57. Doris Arthur Jones: *Life and Letters of Henry Arthur Jones* (1930), p. 350.
58. John Drinkwater: *Poems 1908–1914* (1917): 'The Building,' p. 23.
59. *Ibid.*, 'Lines for the Opening of the Birmingham Repertory Theatre', p. 26.
60. 'Barry Jackson' (J.C.T.), *The Sketch*, 25.2.1953.

CHAPTER FOUR

The Music-Room

I

Henry Arthur Jones, in his Preface to *The Divine Gift*, wrote acidly of playgoers' 'sheep-like impulse to do what and go where the other sheep are doing and going. When I was a boy tending my father's sheep, as I drove them along, some old bell-wether would take it into his head suddenly to jump five feet high and six feet wide over a three-inch trickling ditch. Every sheep, as it came up, would jump exactly the same height and distance. How often do we see the public jumping for months together five feet high over a three-inch puddle!'[1]

Ungrateful words, coming as they did from a dramatist who needed his public. Yet they were true enough; and often, as we have known in any decade, drama critics have been caught doing the same thing over the latest modish obstacle. Certainly, though we must be fair to the 'puddle', which here was a fair-sized stream, the critics—both literary and dramatic—were jumping high when Stephen Phillips was the theatre's pride in the daybreak of the century and after. He was the dramatist of the dreaming keels of Greece, the golden shuttle and the violet wool, the 'smell of cedar sawn and sandalwood',[2] the twitter of the brown bird in the leaves, a singing of dead poets from their graves, the black pine and the bending wheat, the souls that flashed together in one flame, the 'huge and random elemental blow'.[3]

Born in 1866, third cousin of the Shakespearian actor-manager Frank Benson, and a cousin of the poet Laurence Binyon, he was a Peterborough Canon's eldest son in a family of thirteen, nine sons and four daughters, and his early education was at Stratford-upon-Avon Grammar School (there had been a good precedent). Six feet four inches in height and looking like a Roman gladiator, he had auburn hair, enormous intent eyes, and a set of the mouth that could be oddly bitter. As a young actor (and inveterate practical joker) with Benson, he had misused—by listening to himself—a baritone that was potentially fine. Later, as a transiently famous dramatist, he may not have listened to himself enough. Always the sound of the words meant more to him than their precise meaning. With Benson he was applauded both as the Ghost in *Hamlet*—a part he would play later with Martin Harvey—and as Prospero, though he soon grew tired of repetition: as Prospero a time came when he would suspend his staff above the orchestra as a fishing-rod and describe under his breath to Miranda the fish he had caught from various instruments. When he left the Benson company and, for a while, the stage, he taught history at an Army crammer's, work that would be a hyphen between his careers as actor and dramatist. Already he was considering a play, though he had not planned as yet 'the deliberate rebellion against the Elizabethan theatre' that he would try to express in work instantly labelled neo-Elizabethan. Before this he published a number of poems—*Marpessa* was the richest—that Ivor Brown hit off nearly forty years later: 'If a youth of any verbal profusion and talent for pastiche had soaked himself in Tennyson, dined in Soho with a bottle of the more vehement Chianti, and let drive, he could hardly help hitting the target.' Hence Brown's parody:[4]

Air such as fans Olympus, murmurous air
Cool as a maiden's fingers on the brow
Of purple-dark Parnassus when the grape
Is passionate for plucking, air that thrills
To play on Tempe's rivulets and pass

Cascading into coronals of foam.
Such air am I. . . .

Phillips, at length and inevitably, turned to the verse drama which for two centuries had had an uncommonly bad time. There had been the midnight magnificence of Shelley's *The Cenci*, banned from public performance; a few plays by Byron, the closet-work of Beddoes, not much else. The spirit of the nineteenth century is in a phrase from George Darley's *Ethelstan; or, The Battle of Brunanburgh* (1841). Froda and Gorm, pirates, meet on Another Part of the Field, and Gorm speaks: 'Well happ'd on, brother-ranger of the brine!' Through the period tushery ruled. Blank verse was made for the chlamys, the toga, plate-armour; it was all revival, no begetting; blank verse in the letter only, the lingo without the inner fire. Tennyson, a major poet, knew nothing at all of dramatic construction and owed what success he had on the stage to Irving's manipulation of *Becket*. During the early 1890s Henry Arthur Jones wrote a fourteenth century narrative, *The Tempter*, which Tree put on at the Haymarket (1893). It was desperate stuff mostly in the idiom of those brother-rangers of the brine. 'My dear young friend,' said the Devil, 'you're in a plaguey mess,'[5] and he could have been judging the verse.

A few years later Phillips arrived, to be covered at once by a creaming surge of hyperbole. Drama and literary critics had had a corporate vision on the road to Damascus. The early poems were compared with Sophocles, Landor, Swinburne, and Tennyson. Tree staged *Herod* (1900) and Phillips was ranked with Marlowe, Webster, Chapman, and (so William Archer murmured) 'the elder Dumas speaking with the voice of Milton'. Alexander did *Paolo and Francesca*, previously published, at the St James's in 1902, and Dante rose beside it. So, frenziedly, forward, until—as one would have expected, though this may be hindsight—Phillips, who in private had rashly dissipated his powers, passed from the life of the stage. That would still be some time ahead; at first there were intimations of immortality.

Herbert Beerbohm Tree, in 1900, had called *Herod* 'a grand play to go bankrupt on'. He was a manager to suit Phillips, a fantast of the theatre, eccentric in the grand manner, able to transform mediocre parts by a chameleon-skill in character-playing. In production he usually thought too precisely on the event and took realism to its limit. 'Civil as an orange', says Beatrice of Claudio in *Much Ado About Nothing*, and there at His Majesty's, stage centre, was an orange-tree, to ensure that no one lost the point. Nothing if not theatrical, he responded to the staginess in Phillips; and *Herod* (in the text an errata slip says, sadly, 'For "Aha!" read "Ah!"'') was certainly stagey:

> But O, the raining of the blooms;
> The cymbals and the roarings and the roses!
> I seemed to drink bright wine and run on flowers . . .[6]

and

> HEROD: Why am I bowed thus—I that am Herod? Come,
> I'll take you in my arms. I'll have your lips
> By force, and chain your body up to me;
> I am denied your soul, but I will slake
> The thirst of the flesh, and drink your beauty deep.
> MARIAMNE (*repulsing him*): I'll not endure your touch! Your hands
> are curved
> From that fell throttle . . .[7]

(Normally, these things did not happen in an Edwardian drawing-room.) Phillips said that when he read the third act of *Herod* to Tree, the manager 'at the outset was bored, sceptical, and wanted nothing so much as to get through with it. Gradually he grew more and more interested and excited, until I came to the passage where trumpets are heard in the distance. "Ha!" he said to his secretary, "you see the reason of that?" Then he turned to me and said: "Have you ever been on the stage?" He didn't know that I began life as an actor, but he divined it in that one touch!'[8] In the same interview with Archer he said that he sought for unity of effect where the Elizabethans sought for multiplicity. Strangely, Phillips believed that he was getting away from the Elizabethans when all the time he echoed 'the singing of dead poets from their graves'.

For a while the trumpets were very close. *Paolo and Francesca*, though confined like *Herod* to a restricted group of colours and metaphors, was on the whole a better play; and Phillips was seldom at a loss for the sounding line. I have always wondered whether 'The strucken casement of chop-fallen age', which you will find nowhere in Shakespeare—Frank Benson used to spatchcock it into a speech on one of his hazier nights—might not have derived from these florid adventures. It has the air. For the sake of *Paolo* ('The very palace rocks, / Remembering at midnight),[9] rather than of *Herod* and the flamboyant *Ulysses* (1902), with little of the surge and thunder of the Odyssey, we ought not utterly to discard Phillips. There could be a certain zest in his tours of Herod's palace, of Renaissance Italy, or of Hades and Ithaca ('As sharks to him that drowns, / They make towards me, sidelong swimming shapes').[10] His was a minor talent, a sidelong, swimming shape, but he did try. A few lines from the beginning of *Paolo* can speak now for the kind of straightforward stage effect that he provided and the Edwardians loved. On the night of 6 March 1902, not long after the St James's curtain had risen upon the crowded, shadowy hall of the Malatesta castle at Rimini, 'hung with weapons, banners, and instruments of the Chase', a whisper of 'Lord Malatesta' ran among the Guests, Citizens, Soldiers, and Retainers, and George Alexander, as Giovanni Malatesta, Tyrant of Rimini, came swiftly along an upper gallery and down the steps.[11] He paused. 'Peace!' he cried:

> Peace to this house of Rimini henceforth!
> Kinsmen, although the Ghibelline is fallen,
> And lies out on the plains of Trentola,
> Still have we foes untrampled, wavering friends,
> Therefore on victory to set a seal,
> Today I take to wife Ravenna's child,
> Daughter of great Polenta, our ally;
> Between us an indissoluble bond.
> Deep in affairs my brother I despatched,
> My Paolo—who is indeed myself—
> For scarcely have we breathed a separate thought—
> To bring her on the road to Rimini.

Doors at the far end of the gallery swung apart in a flash of sunlight, and leading by the hand Francesca (Evelyn Millard), 'all dewy from her convent fetched', there entered in gold armour a youth from the brush of Giorgione. Flowers were cast over them. Francesca knelt to Giovanni who kissed her on the

113

forehead. Presently the crowds dispersed. Giovanni—using an excuse that might have occurred to Aubrey Tanqueray in Rimini—observed:

> Three delegates from Pesaro, Francesca,
> Expect my swift decision on the tax . . .

and, for a moment, his brother and Francesca were left alone. She spoke, and Henry Ainley answered her in a voice that itself shone like the noonday:

FRANCESCA: O, Paolo,
  Who were they that have lived within these walls?
PAOLO: Why do you ask?
FRANCESCA: It is not sign nor sound;
  Only it seemeth difficult to breathe;
  It is as though I battled with this air.
PAOLO: You are not sad?
FRANCESCA: What is it to be sad?
  Nothing hath grieved me yet but ancient woes,
  Sea-perils, or some long-ago farewell,
  Or the last sunset cry of wounded kings.
  I have wept but on the pages of a book,
  And I have longed for sorrow of my own.

Thence to the later scenes; to the play's most compelling speech by the childless Lucrezia ('I, with so much to give, perish of thrift! / Omitted by His casual dew');[12] to Paolo's cry as he looked back on the sunset-towers of Rimini; the garden scene ('So still it is that we might almost hear / The sigh of all the sleepers in the world');[13] and the final passion and ecstasy, with the last Websterian echo, 'Hide them. They look like children fast asleep.'

Through the years *Paolo and Francesca* has obstinately recurred. But little else. *The Sin of David*, written in 1904 and not seen until H. B. Irving, Sir Henry's son, staged it ten years later, put the sombre tale of David, Bathsheba, and Uriah the Hittite into a Cromwellian setting in the Fenland, and broke into such typical Phillippics (the wife speaks) as this:[14]

> How e'en the Fenland hath grown fairyland
> And all these levels gleam as passionate
> As the high gardens of Assyrian Kings

or this (the lover in another echo-chamber scene):[15]

> Apart we two did wander inland; now
> Listen, the ocean of infinity!
> Life hath no more in it.

Indeed, not much. Phillips did rally for a moment when he wrote *Nero* (1906). We may remember it now for lines spoken with relish by Tree as the Emperor:[16]

> Rome hath no critics! I would write a play
> Lived there a single critic fit to judge it.
> Whether a dancing-girl kicks high enough—
> On this they can pronounce: this is their trade.
> With verse upon the stage they cannot cope.
> Too well they dine, too heavily, and bear
> The undigested peacock to the stalls.

It was luckless for Phillips's future that so much of his verse would blend and blur in the mind. Thus any playgoer who knew the dramatist for *Paolo and Francesca*, *Herod*, *Ulysses*, and *Nero*, might have found lingering in memory something like this mosaic (no two lines are found consecutively in any play):

> *An amphitheatre of marble hills in a glimmering light of dawn.*
> HE: O liquid language of Eternity!
> The delicate air and flowery sigh of you:
> About thee is the sound of rushing wings
> As now at last, sleepless and without rest,
> Towards thee I move: now am I free and gay.
> O breathing of balsam and of citron groves,
> Aloe and cinnamon and cassia balm!
> In this cool air and fragrance ere the dawn,
> And poplars shivering in a silvery dream,
> I am an-hungered for that human breast:
> You only in this universe I want.
> SHE: I am deaf with praises, and all dazed with flowers.
> *She touches abstractedly the strings of a mandolin.*
> HE: Day in a breathless passion kisses night.
> SHE: The peril hath a glitter for thy sake.
> HE: All hangs upon the fervour of farewell:
> Under some potion gently will I die.

SHE: But me this fraught expectancy allures:
Look up! and with a smile I'll bind you fast.
Enter from one side Kinsmen and Retainers. Exit Marriage procession of Kinsmen, etc.

Still, in general, Phillips had one virtue the long roll of sub-poetic dramatists had wanted. He kept a plot running and he wrote the kind of highly simplified Elizabethan rhetoric acceptable without strain. If not a master of narrative, he could at least link a sequence of melodramatic incidents. Away from his work, he was more tragic than his own inventions; he grew moody and farouche, living in obscure seaside lodgings or at Ashford in Middlesex, a resolute drinker unhappy at home for all his wife's devotion, a man against society. Hopefully, managers would still make a plan for him. Thus the generous Martin Harvey gave in 1909 a showing to a prose drama, *The Lost Heir*, a free version of Scott's *The Bride of Lammermoor*. (Long before, Herman Merivale had treated it for Irving in the blankest verse.) The new piece survived for only three weeks. Martin Harvey recalled that it was hard to pin down their dramatist. They wanted the part of Craigengelt, soldier of fortune, to be enlarged; but though 'enthusiasm for the task blazed in his eyes',[17] no one could get Phillips to begin it. The only method was the oldest: to trap him in the greenroom and to keep him there, fortified, until the work—apparently excellent but never used—was finished. In the following year he wrote *Pietro of Siena*, a brief medieval drama about a conqueror in love with his enemy's sister and talking of 'a voice that stole on us / Like strings from planets dreaming in faint skies'.[18] The actual dilemma is a cheap variant of *Measure for Measure* ('He is not such a coward / That he would put his life into the scales / Against his sister's shame');[19] the play never very flexible, stiffens into a waxwork anecdote.

By then Phillips, a man with 'a pallid sturdiness . . . like a bewildered edition of Napoleon Bonaparte',[20] had become a tarnished name; he had squandered himself and he was on the rim of penury. When he died in December 1915 in his fiftieth year, one of the castaways of literature, he left an estate of five pounds. He should have left, too, a mark upon the conscience of some of his critics who had merely toyed with him, overpraising his casual dew, then letting him pass into near-oblivion. It is curious now to read his declaration to William Archer in 1901:[21]

My whole case, as against the Elizabethan drama, is that I claim to be judged rather by the cumulative effect of a whole work than by isolated and even irrelevant patches of splendour. In regard to painting, for instance, one does not say, 'This is a great picture in right of that one beautiful head, though all the rest is crude and out of drawing.' The whole effect is the only true effect. But the English nation is suspicious of anything in which the effect is not rendered obvious by partial failure—as, in a circus, they will give the loudest applause to the man who has once or twice failed to go through his hoop, if only he ultimately succeeds. That a play, then, should be smooth, limpid, and concentrated, arouses in them a certain instinct of resentment. So, at least, it sometimes seems to me.

'Smooth, limpid, and concentrated.' Something, maybe, in that.

II

Though Phillips had few rivals on the commercial stage, there were aspirants enough. Success breeds imitation; and managements found themselves with a variety of manuscripts thought by their authors to be smooth, limpid, and concentrated, and a great many other things. Mostly they were formal Elizabethan-Jacobean pastiche. No facile dramatist could resist the blank-verse drug. It did not bother them—if, in fact, they ever realised it—that in the cheerful nonsense of *The Admirable Bashville; or, Constancy Unrewarded* (1901; first professionally acted, 1903) Shaw had put all the tricks into impeccable iambics ('My cousin ails, Bashville; procure some wet';[22] 'A lovely woman, with distracted cries. . . . Approaches like a wounded antelope'; 'And bid the driver hie to Downing Street').

Oscar Asche took no notice. The thunderous Old Bensonian put on a group of poets' plays during his three years at the Adelphi, aided by a largely Bensonian cast trained in verse-speaking and with Otho Stuart as his partner. Among these productions were an actor James Bernard Fagan's *The Prayer of* 117 *the Sword* (1904), Comyns Carr's *Tristram and Iseult* and Rudolf Besier's *The Virgin Goddess* (both in 1906). The first of these, about a young monk, medieval Italian, who breaks his vows to help a distressed lady, was conscientious sub-Phillips: 'Now do I know the mysteries of the stars / The message that the winds have told the trees', and so on. It contained a professional Fool who irritated Max Beerbohm with the kind of quip that Max himself later fixed wickedly in *Savonarola*: 'How many crows may nest in a grocer's jerkin?'—'A full dozen at cock-crow, or something less under the dog-star, by reason of the dew which lies heavy on men taken by the scurvy.'[23] Carr's efficient *Tristram* variation suggested that the romantic lovers' blank verse vocabulary was limited, though his play did have the right panoply of regal halls and Tristram's ship. Among the cast were Sir Dinas, Sir Sagramore, Sir Andrew, and Sir Morganore; and the dramatist had conscientiously considered the immensities without meeting any fresh thought on life and death and love. Rudolf Besier's *The Virgin Goddess*, more applauded than the others, was a new Greek tragedy, inspired no doubt by Gilbert Murray's classical versions at the Court. Preserving the unities, and staged against blue skies and sunlit marble, it had a fevered first-night reception and critical cheers next day. It ran to miserable business for five weeks. Besier, who never tried blank verse again, did not model his play strictly upon Greek drama: 'It was made for performance and on the modern stage, and should be judged as an acting play.'[24] We have had no chance to see it acted. In the text a few of its lyrical choruses have a ring; the narrative of a Queen's death as a sacrifice, slain by her lover, is told more urgently than memorably. There is too much in this vein:[25]

Alas!
Would I were stone, and not this flesh and blood
That burns and shudders in the cruel gin
Which those high powers whose sport is human pain
Cunningly baited for mine overthrow.

Later, at His Majesty's (1907), Asche and his wife, Lily Brayton, valiantly performed Laurence Binyon's austere tragedy of *Attila*; but this too had not much life in the theatre and little beyond its first run. Asche replaced it by *As You Like It* and a Forest of Arden with two thousand pots of fern—the characters walked through fern in places two feet high—large clumps of bamboo, and cartloads of autumn leaves and moss-grown logs.

Verse drama for the Edwardians had, in effect, to be a moss-grown log set as far off in time as possible. Nobody talked of Westland Marston's *The Patrician's Daughter* from 1842, a tragedy of the spiritual conflicts of modern life in which an Earl's daughter and her lover, a young Radical statesman, addressed each other in measured decasyllabics. ('Blank verse and parasols!' said the actress, Mrs Warner; 'Is that not quite a new combination?')[26] Dickens, of all people, rushed into a verse prologue: 'Awake the Present! Shall no scene display / The tragic passion of the passing day?'[27] In theory, the Edwardians, like the early Victorians, enjoyed a night of resonant platitudes. In practice, having temporarily accepted Phillips, they felt that duty had been done. The swashing costume play went better, as Fred Terry and Julia Neilson knew, in language that passed for prose ('I bade my gossip come hot-foot i' the morn': *Dorothy o' the Hall*). If relatively few verse dramas reached the public stage—even then, more than in previous decades—closet-dramatists were printing every word. Allardyce Nicoll has quoted selectively.[28] Thus, the beginning of W. G. Hole's *Queen Elizabeth* (1904):

> See, here we stand, six proper men and bold,
> A-tremble lest her Grace's farthingale
> Should rustle in the passage ere arrives
> Our spokesman, Burleigh.

John Masefield once established the dimmer poetic drama in a single line from a play he said a friend of his had sent him: *Curtain rises and discovers housemaid scrubbing the floor.* She speaks: 'O heaven, the misery of a double life!'[29]

III

Masefield himself (1878–1967), who later would be Poet Laureate for over thirty years, was a man of unfaltering charity 119 and compassion, with a voice like a salt-water ballad—he had been a merchant sailor in his youth—and clear, long-sighted blue eyes. He wrote of a story-teller's power: 'Of the books which delight, and persuade by delight to the use of books, my own favourites are stories . . . I prefer them to be touched with beauty and strangeness.' He said, too, that he liked tributaries to come in upon the main stream, and 'exquisite bays and backwaters to open out, into all of which the mind can go exploring.'[30] There is not much room in the theatre for the bay and backwater; but we continue to explore Masefield's plays in memory. He never employed a set of faded images to start the stock response. L. A. G. Strong said of him during his life, and with reason: 'He has not written meanly, coldly, or carelessly.' As a dramatist who knew instinctively the power of what he called on a famous occasion 'the acted passion beautiful and swift',[31] Masefield wrote nearly twenty plays. Only two at full-length are within our period (I omit *The Witch*, his treatment of the Norwegian *Anna Pedersdotter*), but these are two that should endure—*The Tragedy of Nan* and *The Tragedy of Pompey the Great*. Prose plays, they live in the poets' drama.

Granville Barker, Masefield's secure friend, put on at the Court his earliest short piece, and one of the most disturbing, *The Campden Wonder*, done oddly after Cyril Harcourt's trifle, *The Reformer* (1907). It disturbs us to read because Masefield did not try to soften his narrative: period 1660, based on Cotswold history. It is the tale of a drunken, envious, and perverted elder son who confesses falsely to a murder, implicating both his mother and his prosperous elder brother, so that all three are hanged. Whereupon the supposed victim appears. Minor though it is, and unacted now, it is rightly bound up in a volume with the equally uncompromising *Tragedy of Nan*. But *Nan*, in its union of realism and heightened speech, can be profoundly touching; Masefield's compassion shines through it as the lighthouse-ray of The Lizard used to shine through the windows of my native village on a stormy night. Dedicated to W. B. Yeats, staged by the Pioneers in May 1908, and afterwards acted for matinees at the Haymarket under Barker's direction—he was not at his easiest with the 'peasants'—*Nan* is set in Regency Gloucestershire on a remote farm at Broad Oak on Severn. Its heroine, living with an uncle and a relentless aunt, is an orphan whose father had been hanged for sheep-stealing. Her weathercock-lover is a deplorable weakling; at the last, driven to desperate means, she finds a tragic splendour. As Strong said, the play comes near to 'that impassioned fusion between sordid circumstances and mystical reality' at which all of Masefield's work was aimed. Nan's only stay is a crazed ancient, the Gaffer. His visionary ramblings, speech influenced by the prose of J. M. Synge, Masefield's friend, can be hazardous in the theatre; H. R. Hignett, Benson-trained, who created the part and who was acting it still in 1943, never let emotion waver. The old man shows to us the high tide of Severn[32] as it sweeps up under a harvest moon, covers mudbanks and sandbanks, comes with a flash 'like a swan a-gettin' up out of the pool', and swirls on, curling and toppling, with a bright crown upon it:

> The salmon-fishers'll lose their nets tonight. The tide 'll sweep them away. O, I've known it. It takes the nets up miles. Miles. They find 'em high up. Beyond Glorster. Beyond 'Artpury. Girt golden flag-flowers over 'em. And apple-trees a-growin' over 'em. Apples of red and apples of gold. They fall into the water. The water be still there, where the apples fall. The nets 'ave apples in them.
>
> NAN: And fish, Gaffer?
>
> GAFFER: Strange fish. Strange fish out of the sea.
>
> NAN: Yes. Strange fish indeed, Gaffer. A strange fish in the nets tomorrow. A dumb thing. Knocking agen the bridges. Something white. Something white in the water. They'd pull me out. Men would. They'd find my body. (*Shuddering*) I couldn't. I couldn't.

Ill-tempered things have been written about *Nan*. Certain passages never came right: the wicked aunt is too like a figure from Grimm. But what counts is the impact in the theatre as we share Masefield's anger at cruelties practised upon the helpless.

The Stage Society acted *The Tragedy of Pompey the Great* in 1910. Sombrely quiet, it has only its directness in common with *Nan* (Masefield had nothing foggy in his mind). This is classical, not domestic, tragedy. Pompey is a idealist with more of Masefield in him than the historic original, just as Shaw's Caesar is ineradicably Shavius. A chronicle without bombast, it describes Pompey's resolve to fight with Caesar, then marching upon Rome; the triumph of his leadership at Dyrrachium, his overthrow by the generals of his staff, defeat at Pharsalia, and his murder at Pelusium. Most of the action is, classically, offstage; *Pompey* is a play of the mind. Masefield, who as a narrator born always admired the convention, makes invigorating use of a Messenger's battle-speech. Elsewhere, language can be marmoreal; the marble does not always gleam. After a cold beginning, the play gathers nobility and we pause at Cato's: 'There are two Romes, Metellus. One built of brick by hodsmen. But the Rome I serve glimmers in the uplifted heart; it is a court for the calm gods, that Rome. Let me not shame that city. Advance the eagles.'[33] We have later the scene with the body of Valerius Flaccus which Pompey crowns with laurel and adorns with the purple; the elegiac lines of the Centurions; and the slave Philip's song, often anthologised, on the night before Pharsalia:[34]

> Though we are ringed with spears, though the last hope is gone,
> Romans stand firm, the Roman dead look on.
> Before our sparks of life blow back to him who gave,
> Burn clear, brave hearts, and light our pathway to the grave.

Masefield alone could have written the last act on board a merchant vessel at Pelusium. We are told what has passed, in the first line for a chantyman ('heard off, amid a click of pawls'), 'Old Pompey lost Pharsalia fight', to which, a few seconds later, the sailors, heaving at the forward capstan reply: 'And Caesar now is the world's delight. / And I'll go no more a-roving, / With Pompey the Great.'[35] Presently Pompey goes ashore and to his death, remembering the grey owls in his quiet childhood valley at Alba; and the tragedy closes on the seamen's chorus, sung like an ordinary halliard chanty, to the tune of 'Hanging Johnny':

THE CHANTY: For the gods employ strange means to bring their will to be.
CHORUS: Away, i-oh.
THE CHANTY: We are in the wise god's hands and more we cannot see.
CHORUS: So away, i-oh.
A VOICE: High enough.
THE MATE: Lie to. (*The Seamen lay to the fall.*) Make fast. Coil up.
A VOICE: All clear to seaward.
122   THE CAPTAIN: Pipe down. (*The Bosun pipes the belay.*)[36]

When had Roman tragedy ended like this? Certainly not in anything the Edwardians knew. *Nan* apart, Masefield had always to be an acquired taste in the theatre; his loyal followers had to search for special performances. Though technically it is just out of our period, I have to speak of *Philip the King* (staged in the autumn of 1914) in which news of the Armada reaches Spain: a brief play set in a small dark cell in the King's palace, and yet clenching within its half-hour the Armada's pride, endurance, and failure ('Our broken galleons house the gannet-birds');[37] the overwhelming of the entire chivalry of Spain. It contains one of Masefield's most driving poems, 'The wind and sea were fair', in which a Messenger—still that usage—in the rhythm of Drayton's ballad of Agincourt, tells how the fire-ships flamed through the Spanish fleet in Calais Roads. The tragedy burns like flame in frost; but today, as with practically all of Masefield's work for the theatre, *Nan* excepted, it is seldom given a hearing. The plays are read, not acted, though television once did justice to *Pompey*. Gravest of plays, it does have moments when, as a stage direction demands, we hear 'a shaking blast from a trumpet. . . . The air rings.'[38]

IV

While John Masefield was not a man for the decorated play, James Elroy Flecker (1884–1915) would not leave a line uncharged. He belongs to our period, even if his two plays—one to be famous, one pushed unfairly aside—were not acted until long after his death of consumption at a Davos sanatorium in the New Year of 1915. Three of his grandparents had a central European Jewish background. His father was the headmaster of an evangelical public school, Dean Close at Cheltenham; the family went there two years after the boy (originally christened Herman Elroy; he disliked his first name) was born at Lewisham on a day in 1884 as dark and foggy as Victorian London could show. It was a glum welcome for the man who, of all English writers of his day, would be the poet of the sun; of pictures printed as sharply as the noon shadow upon marble; of the swan-peaks over Syria, and Greece and its 'leafy 123 rood of song'. To the end he was inlaying, polishing, refining. His Oriental drama of *Hassan*, an Arabian Night of Haroun's Caliphate, more than once passed through the refining fire. He wrote to Edward Marsh in June 1913 from Leysin in Switzerland:[39]

I am going to cut the farce clean out—or modify it greatly, and be less heavy with the Oriental expressions. On the other hand, I shall not worry over much about the requisites of the Stage. A lot of rot is talked about literary plays not succeeding. It usually means that plays which are written in lifeless blank verse on Boadicea or Savonarola, and which are infinitely boring to read, are not good stage plays . . . I am only going to try and keep *Hassan* interesting; then if it's good enough the stage can adapt it or adapt itself to it. . . .

The basis of the play was an old Turkish farce which Flecker transformed to an exercise in the romantic-macabre overlaid by arabesques of Oriental imagery. It is a baffling piece, a basically cruel melodrama, that in the theatre has always promised more than it performs. There are passages of extreme beauty, the epilogue at the Gate of the Moon, Bagdad (the Golden Journey to Samarkand—'softly through the silence beat the bells')[40] written first as a detached poem; the ghazel to Yasmin ('How splendid in the morning glows the lily'); some of the speeches of the poet Ishak ('Thy dawn, O master of the world, thy dawn'), and the scene for the ghosts by the fountain, so difficult to stage. In the theatre *Hassan* seldom makes its sharp tragic effect: the blade is muffled where it should strike cleanly. Basil Dean, always loyal, finally directed it with great splendour at His Majesty's (the right theatre) nearly nine years after Flecker's death; but in spite of various attempts at revival, *Hassan* has not established itself firmly. Though it tempts us still, we cannot really think now, as J. C. Squire did, that it contains 'some of the loveliest and most terrible spectacles which an English poet has ever imagined for the stage'.[41]

I prefer the earlier and much less professional *Don Juan* (1910) which has had few performances: a wild piece, the familiar legend in a modern English frame, the Theatre of Ideas pressing upon the theatre of Stephen Phillips (but Flecker was a far better poet). *Don Juan* reaches the stage in glistening shreds. *Hassan*, more of a theatre play, lacks the same odd tremor of expectancy. In *Don Juan* we seem always to be on the edge of revelation, sun over the crest, sail above the horizon, a world behind the opening door: it is the hour (in a line from *Hassan*) when 'the lilies open on the lawn'. To catalogue the absurdities is easy enough—politics can be fatal to a poet—but one can admire the play not for its doctrine but the music there; not for its character-drawing which is thin, or for its construction which is hit-or-miss. Some of its shreds must continue to excite: Juan's declamation, 'I am Don Juan. curst from age to age / By priestly tract and sentimental stage'[42] (which we find, detached, in the Collected Poems); the epithalamium ('Smile then, children, hand in hand / Bright and white as the summer snow'),[43] something hard to fit persuasively into the structure; and the speech for the dying patriot ('Day breaks on England down the Kentish hills') that ends:[44]

> Though she send you as she sent you long ago,
> South to desert, east to ocean, west to snow,
> West of these, out to seas colder than the Hebrides, I must go
> Where the fleet of stars is anchored and the young Star-captains
> glow.

This, we find, has to be treated not as lyrical but as dramatic verse. The dying patriot is, surprisingly, a Conservative Prime Minister shot on the Thames Embankment. Explaining the poem to a friend who had read it out of context, Flecker wrote: 'The patriot has been shot; and as he dies, very mistily he thinks of England from East to West. . . . The blood is suggested by his own blood and is a piece of mental wandering, quite in keeping dramatically.'[45] Show-pieces apart—the fairy-tale, 'There lived a king I know not where',[46] is another, told to a little girl on the outskirts of Gloucester—*Don Juan* has a few shining pages of rhymed dialogue between the hero and the fisher-girl Tisbea. Here occurs the couplet: 'Kiss long and deep, while guardian overhead / The noiseless constellations turn and tread.'[47] Both Bernard Shaw ('It is too good to be shelved')[48] and the poet Herbert Trench, then at the Haymarket Theatre, recognised the merits of the play; but today it has to be a lonely curiosity, though I have seen it quite well done and, on television, 125 excellently. Flecker was poet first, dramatist second; unlike so many poets who have turned hopefully to the stage, he can get us to listen to the self-indulgence of his golden journeys.

V

That indefinable personage, the average Edwardian playgoer (*His House In Order, Man and Superman, Raffles, The Arcadians*), knew nothing of what was going on in the secluded gravity of Max Gate, near Dorchester. There Thomas Hardy, in his sixties, worked for years on the chronicle of *The Dynasts*, 'an epic-drama of the war with Napoleon, in three parts, nineteen acts, and one hundred and thirty scenes'. It was the ultimate closet-play: 'Enter the Ancient Spirit and Chorus of the Years, the Spirit and Chorus of the Pities, the Shade of the Earth, the Spirits Sinister and Ironic with their Choruses, Rumours, Spirit-Messengers, and Recording Angels.'[49] When it appeared in three parts, between 1903 and 1908, a storm of comment from the literary critics accompanied it like part of its entourage, or a derisive hooting from the pavement, but it was not considered seriously in terms of theatrical production though its form was dramatic. It took the advent of the European war for any director to work upon *The Dynasts*; inevitably, the name was Granville Barker; and he could offer only a selective impression. Hardy himself, in his determinedly untheatrical way, had suggested[50] that if it were ever staged, there might be 'a monotonic delivery of speeches, with dreamy conventional gestures, something in the manner traditionally maintained by the old Christmas mummers. . . . Gauze or screens to blur outlines might still further shut out the actual.' Sometimes a charmingly innocent genius, Hardy might have been describing the effect of routine Edwardian verse drama.

In part at least, *The Dynasts* should one day test the resources of the National Theatre. (Some years after Hardy's death it found on radio a fittting stage of the imagination.) It is an extraordinary assemblage of styles, in blank verse—often grimly blank as Hardy presses on with factual information—prose, 126 rhyme, and metrical patterns of many kinds. At the back of its

Napoleonic narrative is the complex philosophical framework of creation and fate, the Overworld with the controlling Immanent Will. Most readers, I think, remember this less than the marvellous sequence of aerial stage directions so interwoven with the text. One of the simplest: 'A view now nocturnal, now diurnal, from on high over the Straits of Dover, and stretching from city to city. By night Paris and London seem each as a little swarm of lights surrounded by a halo; by day as a confused glitter of white and grey. The Channel between them is a mirror reflecting the sky, brightly or faintly, as the hour may be.'[51] Hardy the poet is in full virtuosity, as in 'The Night of Trafalgar', the threnody of Albuera, the rondeau for the Chorus of Pities before Salamanca, 'My love's gone a-fighting' in the Casterbridge scene, and the startling Chorus of the Years before Waterloo:[52]

> Yea, the coneys are scared by the thud of hoofs,
> And their white scuts flash at their vanishing heels,
> And swallows abandon the hamlet-roofs.
>
> The mole's tunnelled chambers are crushed by wheels,
> The lark's eggs scattered, their owners fled;
> And the hedgehog's household the sapper unseals . . .
>
> Trodden and bruised to a miry tomb
> Are ears that have greened but will never be gold,
> And flowers in the bud that will never bloom.

To quote from so vast a work is only to flake a grain or two from a monolith. Inevitably the texture is uneven; but *The Dynasts*, in careful choice, ought not to defy a flexible modern treatment: the Duchess of Richmond's ball, for example, and that moment when the drums are heard: 'there echoes into the ballroom a long-drawn metallic purl of sound, making all the company start'. Hardy's work, belonging technically to the Edwardians, is timeless. It defies even one of Max Beerbohm's most celebrated and affectionate parodies, 'A Sequelula to *The Dynasts*' (1912): 'The spirit of Mr Hardy is visible as a grey transparency swiftly interpenetrating the brain of the Spirit of the Years and urging him in a particular direction, to a particular point.'[53]

VI

All this while much was happening across the Irish Sea. When Flecker was trying to re-model the National Anthem, he wrote, a little desperately: 'Erin's island lawn / Echoes the dulcet-drawn / Song with a cry of Dawn . . .'.[54] Not a good poem; Dublin would have read it ironically. Turning it to our own purpose, the 'cry of dawn' could have come from the Abbey; during nearly ten years before 1914 it had been acting as a national theatre, creating a legend for itself in what had been an inconspicuous mechanics' institute. It had grown from the Irish Literary Theatre and, later, the Irish National Theatre Society; opened just after Christmas 1904, thanks—as we have seen—to Miss Horniman, and bound up with the names of W. B. Yeats, Lady Gregory, and J. M. Synge, the Abbey was vaguely amateurish in direction, extensively publicised, and usually exciting. It housed a thriving company of native players able to speak, to listen, and, when they were listening, to stand still, as critics noticed on early and applauded visits to London. There were the brothers Fay, W. G. and Frank; a young comedian, Arthur Sinclair, connoisseur of the pause; Sara Allgood, majestically simple and moving (but in later life a terror to uncertain novices), and her sister Maire O'Neill: 'One all simplicity,' said Yeats, 'her mind shaped by folk song and folk story; the other sophisticated, lyrical, and subtle.'[55]

Yeats, as a dramatist, demanded a union of beauty and simplicity and would have nothing of conventional and stagey opulence; excesses that would have been impossible at the Abbey. His plots rose from Celtic legend, their action secondary to a continually varied music of speech. A master of the poetic-symbolic, one surrendered to him as to an incantation: no flamboyance, no theatrical tricks, only the vague, murmuring dark, the plumy sea, the wool-white foam, long-throated swans, Time's old lanthorn, the years like great black oxen (a later dramatist Sean O'Casey's favourite line), a speckled heathcock on a golden dish, the blossoming apple-stem, the mists of the ultimate west, and the Old Woman who was Ireland and who, as she walked down the path, became 'a young girl, and she had the walk of a queen'.[56] This was the poet's theatre of *Cathleen ni Houlihan, The Shadowy Waters, On Baile's Strand, Deirdre*, much else. Often we remember less what happens than what is said, as in Cuchulain's speech to Conchubar in *On Baile's Strand*:[57]

> You will stop with us,
> And we will hunt the deer and the wild bulls;
> And, when we have grown weary, light our fires
> Between the wood and water, or on some mountain
> Where the Shape-Changers of the morning come.
> The High King there would make a mock of me
> Because I did not take a wife among them.
> Why do you hang your head? It's a good life:
> The head grows prouder in the light of the dawn,
> And friendship thickens in the murmuring dark
> Where the spare hazels meet the wool-white foam.
> But I can see there's no more need for words
> And that you'll be my friend from this day out.

But John Millington Synge (1871–1909) was the greater dramatist of the Irish renaissance. Yeats, who asked for beautiful and appropriate language, did not realise that the truest fulfilment would be not the Celtic-myth verse plays but what was called popularly the Synge-song, the prose rhythms of the tragedy of *Riders to the Sea*, of which C. E. Montague wrote, '[It] takes you straight into black tragedy; you step through one door into darkness'; the peasant sketch, *The Shadow of the Glen*, which owed much to the maidservants of an old Wicklow house whose talk drifted up to the author through a chink in the kitchen ceiling; and the unexampled *Playboy of the Western World*. Synge, Wicklow-born, was twenty-eight when Yeats, meeting him in Paris, recognised his genius and urged him to return to Ireland to look and to listen. Synge went west, to the Aran Islands. At his death in Dublin twelve years later he left half a dozen plays; in the second, the brief *Riders to the Sea* (1904), he had reached his meridian in tragedy: the compressed result of his study of 'the eternal life of man spent under sun and in rain and in rude physical effort, never changed since the beginning'. Maurya, the old woman of the western island, who has only one   129 son left of all her family, knows that her Bartley, too, must inevitably perish. The sea takes him. Maurya says slowly: 'They've all gone now and there isn't anything more the sea can do to me.' The play moves to its end in a swell of emotion like an incoming wave:[58]

> Michael has a clean burial in the far north, by the grace of the Almighty God. Bartley will have a fine coffin out of the white boards, and a deep grave surely. What more can we want than that? No man at all can be living for ever, and we must be satisfied.

Irishmen complained neither about this play nor about the strong emotion of the posthumous and unrevised *Deirdre of the Sorrows*. But some of them could not endure *The Playboy of the Western World*. 'You've a fine bit of talk, stranger,' says Pegeen, 'and it's with yourself I would go.' Though listeners have gone with Christy Mahon down the years, in the birth-pangs of the *Playboy* its fine bit of talk infuriated myopic patriots. The Abbey first night (26 January 1907) brought hisses, the second an angry hullabaloo. The cast could not have been bettered: W. G. Fay as the playboy, Arthur Sinclair, Maire O'Neill as Pegeen, Sara Allgood. Then why the wrath? Some Dubliners held that Synge had defamed his country in his comic-ironic treatment of parricide, his uncompromising view of the peasant character, and—a more exact complaint—the use of the word 'shift' in the speech: 'It's Pegeen I'm seeking only, and what'd I care if you brought me a drift of chosen females, standing in their shifts itself, maybe, from this place to the eastern world?'[59] Irish-American spectators (as late as 1911–12) also rioted when the Abbey company toured with it. It was all very silly; the *Playboy*, it has been said wisely, is as much and little of an insult to Ireland as *Don Quixote* is to Spain.

Christy Mahon has come to the country shebeen near a village on a wild coast of Mayo, boasting that he has killed his father 'in a distant place . . . a windy corner of high, distant hills'. For a time the awed locals treat him as a hero ('making a mighty man of me this day by the power of a lie'). In the Irish theatre's most famous scene, he woos Pegeen Mike, the publican's daughter, in language that justifies Synge's claim in 1907: 'In a good play every speech should be as fully flavoured as a nut or an apple, and such speeches cannot be written by anyone who works among people who have shut their lips on poetry':

CHRISTY: . . . When the airs is warming, in four months or five, it's then yourself and me should be pacing Neifin in the dews of night, the times sweet smells do be rising, and you'd see a little, shiny new moon, maybe, sinking on the hills.

PEGEEN (*looking at him playfully*): And it's that kind of a poacher's love you'd make, Christy Mahon, on the sides of Neifin, when the night is down?

CHRISTY: It's little you'll think if my love's a poacher's or an earl's itself, when you'll feel my two hands stretched around you, and I squeezing kisses on your puckered lips, till I'd feel a kind of pity for the Lord God is all ages sitting lonesome in His golden chair.

PEGEEN: That'll be right fun, Christy Mahon, and any girl would walk her heart out before she'd meet a young man who was your like for eloquence, or talk at all.

CHRISTY (*encouraged*): Let you wait, to hear me talking, till we're astray in Erris, when Good Friday's by, drinking a sup from a well, and making mighty kisses with our wetted mouths, or gaming in a gap of sunshine, with yourself stretched back unto your necklace, in the flowers of the earth.

PEGEEN (*in a low voice, moved by his tone*): I'd be nice so, is it?

CHRISTY (*with rapture*): If the mitred bishops seen you that time, they'd be the like of the holy prophets, I'm thinking, do be straining the bars of paradise to lay eyes on the Lady Helen of Troy, and she abroad, pacing back and forward, with a nosegay in her golden shawl.

PEGEEN (*with real tenderness*): And what is it, I have, Christy Mahon, to make me fitting entertainment for the like of you, that has such poet's talking, and such bravery of heart?

CHRISTY (*in a low voice*): Isn't there the light of seven heavens in your heart alone, the way you'll be an angel's lamp to me from this out, and I abroad in the darkness, spearing salmons in the Owen or the Carrowmore?

PEGEEN: If I was your wife I'd be along with you those nights, Christy Mahon, the way you'd see I was a great hand at coaxing bailiffs, or coining funny nicknames for the stars of night.

CHRISTY: You, is it? Taking your death in the hailstones, or in the fogs of dawn.

PEGEEN: Yourself and me would shelter easy in a narrow bush (*with a*   131 *qualm of dread)*; but we're only talking, maybe; for this would be a poor thatched place to hold a fine lad is the like of you.

CHRISTY*(putting his arm round her)*: If I wasn't a good Christian, it's on my naked knees I'd be saying my prayers and paters to every jackstraw you have roofing your head, and every stony pebble is paving the laneway to your door.

PEGEEN*(radiantly)*: If that's the truth, I'll be burning candles from this out to the miracles of God that have brought you from the south today, and I with my gowns bought ready, the way that I can wed you, and not wait at all.[60]

This is their last talk together. Christy's bellicose father, by no means dead, arrives before the end of the play, and after various alarums he and his son go off together. Christy is a conqueror after all; ready to move 'romancing through a romping lifetime from this hour to the dawning of the judgment day'. Pegeen, left behind, can only say simply, 'Oh, my grief, I've lost him surely. I've lost the only Playboy of the Western World.' Into the piece Synge wove some of the phrases he had learned from herds and fishermen along the coast between Kerry and Mayo, or from beggar-women and ballad singers nearer to Dublin.[61] Yet he was not a mere dramatic reporter, employing the purple patch to mend the pale fabric of his speech. He was a dramatic artist of the most agile imagination who never shut his lips on poetry. This is writing that sounded, in the dimness of the verse drama, like an exaltation of larks. It was as freshening, in its far different manner, as Shaw's prose had been to the to-and-fro of the London stage. Dublin was lucky because it had Yeats also. Put *The Playboy* beside Phillips's *Nero* or Besier's *The Virgin Goddess*, and we know how London playgoers (not that many of them would have noticed it) were deprived. Synge, who was engaged to Molly Allgood (Maire O'Neill), died young, in 1909, and was buried in Dublin. The grave, dark-haired man, with the voice guttural and quick, the humorous mouth beneath its bushy moustache, and the 'eye at once smoky and kindling'[62] (John Masefield, his friend, speaks) left in his plays an enduring statement. He and Yeats were planetary; but several of the dramatists who wrote for the Abbey sparkled bravely in its firmament. To this day, when the theatre has the west in its eyes, we look for an exhilarating use of words, a skirmish of wit, or both. In her day, Augusta, Lady Gregory (1852–1932), who talked of the Irish people's 'incorrigible genius for myth-making', was most prolific of all in comic invention. In many of her published plays—*The Gaol Gate* for one; *Spreading the News*, *The Rising of the Moon*—the dialogue seems to lie as naturally on the page as buttercups powder a field. In performance, granted the right cast (for her work has never been entirely actor-proof), her 'Kiltartan' speech is irresistible in movement and idiom.

VII

In London the modern poets' drama did not progress once Stephen Phillips had spent himself. In effect, he described himself in a stage direction at the beginning of *Nero*: 'A meteor strikes across the sky.'[63] The provinces, their new Repertory Theatres aside, kept to an old routine. Classical drama was another matter. Outside London Shakespeare was usually on the move; and in the West End and round it, between the New Year of 1900 and the summer of 1914, there were some 150 Shakespeare revivals, passing from the morocco-bound, extra-illustrated editions of Tree to the frequently capricious austerity of William Poel.

It is the first business of a manager to fill his theatre. Certainly Herbert Beerbohm Tree filled the auditorium of His (Her) Majesty's as well as the stage, and though we may wonder now at his methods as an 'upholsterer' or 'poodle-trimmer'—the words once used for Charles Kean—we know also that they suited the time and the spectators. Spectators rather than listeners, though, wisely, Tree never under-cast his plays: he was not an actor-manager in the evil tradition, a carp environed by minnows. Still, for him Shakespeare had to be pictorial; in spite of occasional experiments, he was obstinate about this through life. He began the century as he meant to proceed, with *A Midsummer Night's Dream* (1900), densely arboreal, its woods well-rabbited, and the play fortified by 'every available atom of Mendelssohn's entrancing sounds'. His love for Shakespeare was genuine; for years he had annual festivals at His Majesty's. Even so, his work is recollected now for extraneous things, 133 mostly visual: for Olivia's *Twelfth Night* garden, grassy terraces, real fountains, box hedges, steps, statues, today a composition only for incredulous bewilderment; the deposed Richard II on a white horse, entering London behind Bolingbroke, a mob yelling, stones hurtling, the Duke of York's speech recreated; Benedick, up a tree, throwing down oranges at Leonato, Claudio, and Don Pedro while they discussed him; flying witches in *Macbeth* and a precipitous zigzag of stairs for the sleepwalking; and an ornate *Antony and Cleopatra* tableau of the Queen robed and crowned in silver as the goddess Isis, and carrying a golden sceptre and the symbol of the sacred golden calf, as she moved in procession through the streets of Alexandria. Tree wrote at the time of a *Henry VIII* (1910), quite as extravagant as anything that Charles Kean did: 'I claim that not the least important mission of the modern theatre is to give to the public representations of history which shall be at once an education and a delight. To do this the manager shall avail himself of the best archaeological and artistic help his generation can afford him, while endeavouring to preserve what he believes to be the spirit and intention of the author.'[64]

Whether he kept the spirit and intention must always be arguable. Thus his *Antony and Cleopatra* opened with the fourth scene of the first act, Caesar's house in Rome; moved to Alexandria, with the immediate entrance of the lovers ('If it be love indeed, tell me how much'), and then used Enobarbus to speak what should have been the play's first lines (for Philo), 'Nay, but this dotage of our general's o'erflows the measure.' So in other plays, *The Tempest* for one, where Tree's Caliban became the star and, at the end, crept from his cave 'in mute despair' after Prospero had spoken a cut version of 'Ye elves' and sailed away towards Italy. This was the end of the play at His Majesty's:[65]

PROSPERO:　　　　But this rough magic
　　I here abjure, I'll break my staff,
　　Bury it certain fathoms in the earth,
　　And deeper than did ever plummet sound
　　I'll drown my book.

FINAL TABLEAU
Prospero breaks his staff, at which there is lightning and thunder, followed by
darkness. Through the darkness we gradually see once more a picture of the
Yellow Sands enveloped in a purple haze. The Nymphs are again singing 'Come
unto these yellow sands.' But their music is broken by the homing-song of the
sailors, and we see the ship sailing away, carrying Prospero and the lovers, and
all their train. Caliban creeps from his cave, and watches the departing ship
bearing away the freight of humanity which for a brief spell has gladdened and
saddened his island home, and taught him to 'seek for grace'. For the last time
Ariel appears, singing the song of the bee. Taking flight at the words 'Merrily,
merrily shall I live now', the voice of the sprite rises higher and higher until it is
merged into the note of the lark—Ariel is now free as a bird. Caliban listens for
the last time to the sweet air, then turns sadly in the direction of the departing
ship. The play is ended. As the curtain rises again, the ship is seen on the horizon,
Caliban stretching out his arms towards it in mute despair. The night falls, and
Caliban is left on the lonely rock. He is a King once more.

As Robert Speaight has said: 'It had not occurred to Tree that
the one person whose back [Caliban] would have contemplated
with relief was Prospero.'[66] Both as manager and as actor—he
was better in weakness than in strength—he treated his plays in
the spirit of the Byronic couplet: 'I like your moral and
machinery; your plot, too, has much scope for scenery.'
Nothing could be done with him when he had made up his
mind. Bridges-Adams said of the more academic Edwardians:
'They preached austerity to Tree, and might as well have
preached to an orchid.'[67]

His way was the general Shakespearian method of his time,
though few had his resources. We have seen how Oscar Asche
dealt with Arden in *As You Like It*. This pleasantly childish giant
(remarkably, Angelo in *Measure for Measure* was one of his best
performances) did a variety of picture-book productions
including a *Merry Wives of Windsor* (1911) which he directed at
the Garrick as a snowy Christmas-card, the stage four inches
deep in salt, everyone in mufflers and gloves or mittens, and
wood fires crackling. He had ample reason for this because the
Merry Wives has many wintry hints ('a raw, rheumatic day';
'laugh this sport o'er by a country fire'; Herne the Hunter 'all
the winter time, at still midnight . . .' and so on). But innovation
in a play presumed to be familiar can be fatal; critics, holding 135

The Merry Wives to be a play of early summer, reacted angrily. Lewis Waller, as actor-manager, was less ornate than Tree or Asche (though the *Henry V* scene in Picardy, by the flooded Somme, lingered in many minds). He depended on his personality as the day's romantic blazon, with a voice that rang like bell-metal. As Henry he would invariably 'arrive upon the scene full tilt. . . . He would lean against the farthest wall, and just before his actual cue came, give himself a push with his hand and travel towards the door, archway, or whatever it was through which he must go. He never just stepped upon the stage.'[68] Waller was a capable, virile actor. H. B. Irving, with the hereditary imaginative glint, was a better one; it was unfair that he had to walk in the shadow and the memory of his father. His stage versions, notably his *Hamlet*, could be severely cut, but this was so with most of the London Shakespeare of the time. Like the mangled Myrmidons of Achilles, the texts could be 'noseless, handless, hack'd, and chipp'd'. In *Othello* (Lyric Theatre, 1902), Johnston Forbes-Robertson, a dignified, high-bred Moor, emasculated the piece in his resolve to omit 'passages and scenes . . . of a character which might prove distasteful to a modern audience'.[69] Single words, too. 'Whore' was unspeakable. When Desdemona asked: 'Am I that name, Iago?' Emilia said: 'He called her wanton.' The Hamlet of his age and never less than melodious, Forbes-Robertson had always a gravely moving, thoughtful reserve, whereas at that time another romantic, Martin Harvey, could work himself into a high fever. Harvey did begin to break with conventional staging; but, generally, we can summarise Edwardian revivals as Shakespeare of the picture-frame, with lopped texts, performances large, slow, and declamatory, and representational colour-plate sets filled (Desmond MacCarthy's phrase in another context) with 'the loosely agglutinated sticks and straws' of needless spectacle. Occasionally there were such scenic restraints as the superb Charles Ricketts settings, Stonehenge-manner, for *King Lear* (Haymarket, 1909; Norman McKinnel's mediocre Lear; a text that cut even 'poor naked wretches'); yet, as a rule, we do not summon immediately the names of the highly professional scenic artists who dressed the Edwardian stage. Ellen Terry's son, Gordon Craig, major influence on another generation, was not in tune with the Edwardians; from professional self-exile in years ahead he would inspire others to adapt for the theatre the great visions—his cry against naturalism—that he was seldom allowed to oversee himself. Early, in 1903, he had designed for his mother a *Much Ado About Nothing* at the Imperial in Westminster; the church scene, influenced by the paintings of Taddeo Gaddi, was suggested by a great altar crowded with enormous candlesticks, by a gigantic crucifix, its upper part lost in shadow, and by a pool of light cast upon the floor from an imaginary stained-glass window above the proscenium arch. Some years later, in 1908, Tree, transiently and fantastically, considered Craig as a designer for *Macbeth*. The tremendous simplicities that arrived were promptly scorned by the veteran scene-painter, Joseph Harker, wrathful at the ignoring of everyday theatre problems. When Tree did reach *Macbeth* in 1911 it was in his customary Romantic Decorated style.

Maybe unfairly, for the popular Shakespearians were at once the voices and the children of their time, the two men of the period most honoured now, for different reasons, were William Poel and the ubiquitous Harley Granville Barker. Poel, tall, thin, aquiline zealot with longish grey hair and a scholarly stoop, was a wayward, idiosyncratic figure in a world of materialism; a Shakespearian who hated the picture-frame, the green mould of otiose business, and a languidly funereal spacing of the verse. His Shakespeare, that of his Elizabethan Stage Society, was meant for a permanent, two-levelled architectural set, an inner stage behind a traverse curtain, a wide, projecting unlocalised platform stage, Elizabethan dress with a few period modifications, and highly-coloured, musically-inflected speech of great range and suppleness. He cast the plays orchestrally. His actors had to learn the score, to concentrate upon his close vocal analyses of every line, his 'tunes' and key-words. Granville Barker put it this way:

In the teeth of ridicule, he [Poel] insisted that for an actor to make himself like unto a human megaphone was to miss, for one thing, the whole merit of Elizabethan verse with its consonantal swiftness, its gradations sudden or slow, into vowelled liquidity, its comic rushes and stops, with, above all, the peculiar beauty of its rhymes.

Poel's actors, preoccupied with the verse, had as little time for anything else as he had for the run of theatrical tricks, salted stages, dissolving sphinxes, cascading streams, trampled ferns, and witches in flight. At his apogee his productions had a fine directness, impetus, and simplicity; at his worst they could be maddeningly capricious; for no conceivable reason he would cut and transpose ruthlessly. During our period he was happiest with a *Measure for Measure*, done (1908) at the Gaiety, Manchester, and at Stratford—something that profoundly impressed the young Barry Jackson—and with a famous *Troilus and Cressida*. In this, at the King's Hall, Covent Garden (December 1912) the Greeks were Elizabethan soldiers, the Trojans wore masque costumes of the period, and Thersites was played (by a woman) as the camp jester, dressed as a clown and speaking with a Scots accent. *Troilus*, though there had been an inconspicuous production at the Great Queen Street Theatre in 1907, was little known except to students. It has always seemed odd to me that when W. S. Gilbert wrote his last Savoy-opera libretto in 1895–6, *The Grand Duke; or, The Statutory Duel,* he chose *Troilus and Cressida*[70] as the coming production for the players in the Grand Duchy of Pfennig-Halbpfennig. Not, I imagine, that Poel had even heard of this. His *Troilus*, in retrospect, was important—among much else—because Edith Evans, a milliner then, an amateur from Streatham, played Cressida, calling up miraculously the wanton of the Greeks, the encounterer glib of tongue; suggesting beauty without being, in the conventional sense, beautiful; taking a scene and holding it with an intuitive, zestful truth.

Now, when *Troilus and Cressida* is regular in the repertory, we must wonder how playgoers felt that night when the contention over Argive Helen rose from the text, and with it the speeches of Ulysses shaped, in their cold wisdom, like frost-flowers on a January pane. Here there were disasters, for Poel, in his crankiest, least sensitive vein, absurdly dismembered such a speech as 'Time hath, my lord, a wallet at his back' (Ulysses to Achilles). Moreover, he cut from one of the key speeches of Cressida the lines beginning 'When water drops have worn the stones of Troy.' Certain of his vagaries could be incomprehensible: Archer once called him a 'non-scenic

Beerbohm Tree'. Still, wilful though he could be, Poel never relaxed his search for the 'tuned tongue', the plasticity of the Elizabethan stage: he worked for those who came after him. Bridges-Adams wrote of him, long after his death: 'He was the Father of the Puritan Revolution in the theatre—a Dionysian ascetic, secretly at odds with himself, I fancy, until the white fire of *Everyman* fused him into one. . . . As obstinate as a mule and as brave as a lion.'[71]

Tree, who could be agreeably unpredictable, invited Poel to stage *The Two Gentlemen of Verona* at His Majesty's during the Shakespeare festival of 1910: it was like asking a stern Quaker to the rites of an uninhibited pleasure-dome. Poel took it calmly; his production revived enchantingly the quiet, youthful piece so often mishandled. Yet the occasion had its oddities; and Bridges-Adams's description of his first meeting with Poel, as reported by Robert Speaight, says much.[72]

He [Bridges-Adams] found Poel wrapped in a grey muffler, nibbling at a biscuit and sipping a glass of milk. In front of him a lady, shimmering with sequins and no longer in her first youth, was in an attitude of visible distress. Poel's voice was raised in querulous criticism: 'I am disappointed,' he said, 'very disappointed indeed. Of all Shakespeare's heroes Valentine is one of the most romantic, one of the most virile. I have chosen you out of London for this part, but so far you have shown me no virility whatsoever.'

Not long before the *Troilus and Cressida*, Granville Barker, who had once played Richard II for Poel, had staged in September 1912 the first of three celebrated Shakespeare revivals, *The Winter's Tale* at the Savoy. Barker wanted, in effect, to find the right mean between Poel and Tree. He disliked cumbrous spectacle and traditional mechanics. He wished to prove how Elizabethan stagecraft and its virtues could be employed in a modern theatre and how, without injuring continuity, a play could be 'decorated'. No cuts: only six lines were taken from *The Winter's Tale*. The play had to live from the first, and its poetry, the heart of the drama, to be fully expressed. At the Savoy Granville Barker used three acting areas: a fairly small one at the back within a false proscenium that reduced the depth and width of the stage; a second one, four steps lower, that was 139 spanned by the proscenium arch and covered the front of the stage proper; and a third, slightly lower again, an apron twelve feet deep in the centre, eleven feet deep at the sides, that spread out over the orchestra pit. The area could be divided by curtains, as needed. Players would approach the middle stage and forestage through proscenium doors. From the forestage they could deliver set speeches naturally and swiftly to the audience. There were no footlights. Hard white lighting came from projectors principally in front of the dress circle. Norman Wilkinson's backgrounds were unrealistic; mainly draped curtains (in the palace of Leontes 'a simple harmony of white pilasters against dead-gold curtains'); for Bohemia, an alarmingly stark shepherd's cottage; costume designs by Albert Rothenstein (Rutherston) were Renaissance-classic and in strong tones of emerald, magenta, lemon, and scarlet. Speech for those days was extraordinarily swift; Leontes and Hermione, Henry Ainley and Lillah McCarthy, discovered every nuance in the verse with Barker's directing mind behind them insisting on thought governing speech, on variation of pace and colour and pitch. Many playgoers, who had not learned the Elizabethan art of listening, were dubious; it was true that in order to make his points, Barker had forced some of them in a production entirely foreign to the taste of the period. *Twelfth Night*, in Wilkinson's black-and-silver, and a formal garden (with Noah's Ark trees) for Olivia, was much better received—the play, anyway, is easier—and this time Barker, who found a compelling rhythm, heard less about speed. Stock business was sponged from the text; Toby and Andrew, often fooled to shreds, were recognisably gentlemen; and Ainley's Malvolio appeared as a priggish egotist, unsentimentalised.

So forward, after a year's lapse, to a *Midsummer Night's Dream* which again set Barker at the very pulse of argument. In the heart of the Wood near Athens was a rough green velvet mound, white-flowered; above it an immense terra-cotta wreath of flowers from which depended a light gauze canopy where fireflies and glow-worms flickered; behind, curtains lit in various changing tones of green, blue, violet, and purple, with a backcloth of green rising to a star-spangled purplish-blue. The idea was to keep the Immortals' midnight wood utterly apart from a more or less realistic and relatively severe palace scene. Barker used old English folk-tunes. Peter Quince's earnest players lost all their withered gags. But argument circled round the fairies. Barker wrote:[73]

The fairies cannot sound too beautiful. How should they look? One does one's best. . . . They must not be too startling. But one wishes people weren't so easily startled. They mustn't warp your imagination—stepping too boldly between Shakespeare's spirit and yours. It is a difficult problem; we (Norman Wilkinson and I—he to do and I carp) have done our best. One point is worth making. Oberon and Titania are romantic creations: sprung from Huon of Bordeaux, etc., say the commentators; come from the farthest steppe of India, says Shakespeare. But Puck is English folk-lore.

How was this resolved? Barker had the fairies' hands and faces gilded; they wore bronze tights, and they moved always like marionettes. Desmond MacCarthy[74] called them 'ormolu fairies, looking as though they had been detached from some fantastic, bristling old clock'. Debatable; but never less than creatures of another world. Puck (Donald Calthrop) wore scarlet and had red berries in his yellow hair.

These productions were the beginning of a gale that would swell inexorably until one day it whirled before it in irretrievable ruin the sagging canvas pavilions of spectacular Shakespeare, the marble canopies, and the paint-encrusted cloths. But in August 1914 the war set its period to Barker's experiment. Though, like Poel's, his work would be eternally influential, he would stay with Shakespeare in the study, never—if we except the Gielgud *Lear* of 1940—approaching him again officially in the theatre. He was the elder statesman in retirement, the leader who preferred to abdicate.

VIII

In his Preface to *A Midsummer Night's Dream*, for the Savoy, Barker spoke of 'a company inspired by such scholarly ideals as Benson could give'. Frank Benson, unselfconsciously, was a noble figure of the Edwardian stage—of the stage, indeed, in three reigns. For thirty-odd years, rarely broken, he conducted 141 the festivals at Stratford-upon-Avon, but his incessant touring established him: 'Poor players or begging friars, we go up and down the land that the people may never go without an opportunity of seeing Shakespeare played by a company dedicated to his service.' He did not lightly use such a word as 'dedicated'. Looking like the noblest Roman of them all, he could have been a Greek in Periclean Athens. As an actor-manager he led the most astonishing company of young players, able again and again to renew its strength, that the land had known. As a business man he was hopelessly unpractical. As an actor he could be magnificent on his night (Henry V; Macbeth; Richard II, haunted artist, lost, spoilt child, a performance that inspired a superb notice by C. E. Montague). But his power, with the aid of his wife, Constance, not herself a good actress, was in leading and invigorating his company. He had been actor and athlete at Oxford. He won the Three Miles against Cambridge; in Balliol Hall he played Clytemnestra in the Greek text of the *Agamemnon* of Aeschylus, a production he helped to plan. Irving gave him a few weeks as Paris in the Lyceum *Romeo and Juliet* (1882); he did some haphazard provincial touring; and suddenly he took over a company (Shakespeare, Old Comedy, melodrama) that its manager had abandoned at Cupar in Fifeshire. This was the origin of the Bensonian 'band of brothers'.

From 1886, with short gaps, Benson usually conducted those brief festivals in the modern-Gothic Memorial Theatre, an endeared 'striped sugar-stick' opened by the Avon at Stratford on the drenching night of Shakespeare's birthday, 1879. There, moving across the wide arch of the ranged empire, he would put on every play in the canon except *Pericles* (John Coleman did it after a fashion in 1900), *Troilus and Cressida* (which Poel brought for a matinee in 1913), and *Titus Andronicus*. There he led a changing group of players that would people the classical stages of the period: Ainley, Asche, Arthur Whitby, Matheson Lang, Randle Ayrton, Dorothy Green, dozens more. There the heads of the English theatre, Ellen Terry to Tree and Forbes-Robertson, came to act for special performances. None could refuse Benson; always he could coax 'great leviathans to dance on sands'. At the beginning of the century he had his London

Shakespeare seasons at the Lyceum and the Comedy, not very successful for he lacked the panoply of the metropolitan managers. Max Beerbohm, with a piece of mannered raillery, did great disservice to Benson by reviewing the company in terms of a cricket team. Benson believed in physical fitness, but the suggestion that he was entirely obsessed by sport is one of the legends that have grown into the English theatre. Tolerant though he was, Benson disliked it.

Actually, in continued touring—sometimes with two or three companies on the road—no one did more for Shakespeare: service recognised when he received the accolade in 1916 at the tercentenary matinee in Drury Lane. King George V knighted him (and not with a property sword, another myth) as, still in the bloodstained robes of the murdered Caesar, he knelt in the Royal Room behind the Royal Box. But when our period ends he was F. R. Benson, an actor whose theatrical life was a sierra. He would startle an audience—usually during some night of routine on a remote stage—and on the next night he could be out of key, fumbling, gravelled for a word. It was a pity that London and its critics seldom knew the true excitement: moments when, as if a torch had been thrust into resinous timber, news would run through the dressing-rooms and the company, regulations defied, would gather in the wings to listen to a leader it adored.

Benson, playing in London, was away from Stratford for the century's first festival, 1900; carelessly for him, he let a leathery old actor, John Coleman, stage the Levantine tour of *Pericles*. Coleman had made much of this into a melodrama of his own ('Thou art a stranger here' someone observes). He did not hesitate to 'expunge the first act, to eradicate the banality of the second, to omit the irrelevant Gower chorus, and altogether to eliminate the obscenity of the fourth act'. Himself—he was seventy-two—he played the handsome shipwrecked Prince in wrinkled pink fleshings with green wool gummed here and there to represent seaweed. Bensonians, sent down to compose the cast, watched and listened in incredulous rapture. It was the only unintentionally comic turn in a sequence of Stratford festivals that, until the first world war, offered little but splendour. The Coleman botch would have been more to the 143 taste of such a manageress as Mrs Millicent Bandmann-Palmer. She was a bold little autocrat who appeared as Hamlet in northern manufacturing towns; just as happy in *East Lynne* or *Jane Shore*, she treated her nightly speech of thanks as another star part. Osmond Tearle's solidly capable Shakespearian company was about at the very beginning of the century; but, next to Benson, Ben Greet was the classical manager the provinces knew best. A bulky, competent actor with a floss of white hair, he was absolutely untiring whether in Britain or in the United States (where the young Russell and Sybil Thorndike toured with him). Though, because of his absences abroad, he could not match Benson's consistency and developing tradition, Greet was an unexampled pastoralist: his company would play practically anywhere. Barry Jackson[75] wrote to me once of a Greet production he remembered from his youth: a *Midsummer Night's Dream* in rural Warwickshire, with Dorothea Baird and the brothers Quartermaine: 'A wet day, clearing at sundown with a slight mist and a full moon. Being young I had sported a new pair of chamois gloves, and, applauding spiritedly, vanished in a cloud of French chalk.' These were days when small-part actors, paid twenty-five shillings a week and equipped with the necessary 'Shakespearian shoes', tights, and a variety of wigs—provided, among much else, by themselves—would dutifully learn the cut texts and prepare for anything.

IX

In 1904, Benson, wistfully recalling his Oxford *Agamemnon* (in the Greek), took on tour the complete Oresteian Trilogy (in translation). It was an hour for Greek drama. Gilbert Murray—the original of Shaw's Cusins, 'Euripides', in *Major Barbara*—was beginning his sequence of translations. Barker staged two at the Court, the *Hippolytus*, done earlier elsewhere by another management, and the *Electra*. Murray did more than anyone to revive for a modern theatre these plays from what Ivor Brown called 'the primal, sudden, and superb thrust at civilisation which sprang from the waters of the Ionian Sea with the flash of a sword and the beauty of a flower'. Though one could only indicate Greek drama within the Edwardian confines, Murray's texts—in time neglected by the professional stage—kept a still unbroken power and music. One day the fluent, rhymed translations would be criticised as diffusely Swinburnian. But I call Ivor Brown again,[76] as expert witness: 'If Greek plays are acted now in English, the version chosen may be some bare-bones, prosaic stuff which convinces you that, whatever Greek tragedy may have been intellectually, it had no pulse of poetry, no leap of metre, no warmth of phrase. This is too absurd to last. In a few years Murray will be back in justified favour.' Martin Harvey used Murray's text of the *Oedipus* of Sophocles when in 1912 Max Reinhardt directed the play at the Opera House, Covent Garden, with the great crowd of 300 Thebans storming up through the auditorium in a black-and-white surge. 'Not an average West End occasion,' a critic said; and we can echo him as we move on finally to the cluttered play-room at the core of the Edwardian house.

Notes

1. Henry Arthur Jones: *The Divine Gift* (1913). Preface, p. 44.
2. *Ulysses* (1902), p. 44.
3. *Ulysses*, p. 14.
4. Quoted by James Agate in *Ego 2* (1936), pp. 294–5.
5. *The Tempter* (published 1898).
6. *Herod* (1901), p. 24.
7. *Ibid.*, pp. 68–9.
8. *Real Conversations* recorded by William Archer (1904), p. 81.
9. *Paolo and Francesca* (1902), p. 97.
10. *Ulysses*, p. 77.
11. *Paolo and Francesca*, pp. 11–18.
12. *Ibid.*, p. 25.
13. *Ibid.*, p. 85.
14. *The Sin of David* (1904), p. 41.
15. *Ibid.*, p. 36.
16. *Nero* (1906), p. 41.
17. *The Autobiography of Sir John Martin Harvey* (1933), p. 372.
18. *Pietro of Siena* (1910), p. 14.
19. *Ibid.*, p. 28.
20. Ben Travers: *Vale of Laughter* (1957), p. 57.
21. *Real Conversations*, p. 80.

22. *The Admirable Bashville* (1901): Bodley Head Bernard Shaw, Vol. 2 (1971), p. 447.
23. *Savonarola* (1917; *Seven Men*, 1919); or *Max in Verse* (Stephen Greene Press, Brattleboro, Vermont, 1963), p. 82.
24. Rudolf Besier: *The Virgin Goddess* (1906) in *Great Modern British Plays*, ed. J. W. Marriott (1929), p. 310.
25. *Ibid.*, p. 353.
26. *The Journal of William Charles Macready, 1832–1851*, ed. J. C. Trewin (1967), Introduction, p. xxi.
27. Macready's *Journal*, p. 190.
28. Allardyce Nicoll: *English Drama 1900–1930* (1973), p. 297.
29. John Masefield: *Recent Prose* (1932 edition), p. 136.
30. John Masefield: *I Want! I Want!* (1944), p. 13.
31. Masefield: Prologue for the Opening of the second Shakespeare Memorial Theatre at Stratford-upon-Avon: April 1932.
32. Masefield: *The Tragedy of Nan* (1909), pp. 51–2.
33. Masefield: *The Tragedy of Pompey the Great* (1910), 1922 edition, p. 33.
34. *Ibid.*, p. 63.
35. *Ibid.*, p. 65.
36. *Ibid.*, pp. 86–7.
37. John Masefield: *The Collected Poems* (1932 edition), p. 355.
38. *The Tragedy of Pompey the Great*, p. 52.
39. Letter quoted in *The Golden Journey: A Biography of James Elroy Flecker* by John Sherwood (1973), pp. 182–3.
40. Flecker: *Hassan* (1922; Penguin edition, 1948), p. 122.
41. J. C. (Sir John) Squire's Introduction to *Hassan*, 1922.
42. Flecker: *Don Juan* (1925), p. 110.
43. *Ibid.*, p. 142.
44. *Ibid.*, pp. 94–5.
45. Letter from Flecker to T. M. A. Cooper (23.11.11) in Geraldine Hodgson's *Life of James Elroy Flecker* (Blackwell, 1925), p. 167.
46. *Don Juan*, p. 27.
47. *Ibid.*, p. 16.
48. In Hellé Flecker's Preface to *Don Juan* (1925) letter written 6.3.1911.
49. Thomas Hardy: *The Dynasts*. (1923 edition), p. 1: Fore Scene.
50. *Ibid.*, Preface, p. xi.
51. *Ibid.*, Part II, Act I, Sc. ii, p. 149.
52. *Ibid.*, Part II, Act VI, Sc. viii, p. 483.
53. Max Beerbohm: *A Christmas Garland* (1912, Collected Edition, Vol. V, 1922), pp. 53–6.
54. *Collected Poems of James Elroy Flecker* (1935 edition), p. 235.
55. W. B. Yeats: *The Irish Dramatic Movement* in *Dramatic Personae* (1936), p. 182.
56. Yeats: *Cathleen Ni Houlihan* (1902) in *The Collected Plays* (1952 edition), p. 88.
57. Yeats: *Collected Plays: On Baile's Strand* (1904), p. 266.
58. J. M. Synge: *Riders to the Sea* (1905) in *Plays, Poems, and Prose* (Everyman edition, 1940), p. 30.
59. *The Playboy of the Western World*: Everyman edition, p. 163.

60. *Ibid.*, pp. 154–6.
61. Preface to *The Playboy*, p. 108.
62. John Masefield: *Recent Prose* (1932 edition):*John M. Synge*, pp. 181–2.
63. Stephen Phillips: *Nero* (1906), p. 3.
64. Sir Herbert Beerbohm Tree: *Henry VIII and His Court* (1911).
65. *The Tempest* arranged for the stage by Sir Herbert Beerbohm Tree (1904); 50th performance Souvenir).
66. Robert Speaight: *Shakespeare on the Stage* (1973), p. 126.
67. W. Bridges-Adams: *The Irresistible Theatre* (1957), p. 205.
68. W. Macqueen Pope: *Ghosts and Greasepaint* (1951), p. 102.
69. *Othello* edition (1902); quoted in *Shakespeare on the English Stage, 1900–1964* (Trewin, 1964), p. 22.
70. W. S. Gilbert: *The Savoy Operas* (1952 edition): *The Grand Duke*, p. 631 *passim*. The date of the performance is presumed to be 1750.
71. W. Bridges-Adams (31.1.1948) to Arthur Colby Sprague. Quoted in *A Bridges-Adams Letter Book* (1971), ed. with a memoir by Robert Speaight, p. 35.
72. Robert Speaight: *William Poel and the Elizabethan Revival* (1954), p. 121.
73. Granville Barker in preface (p. ix) to Savoy acting edition of *A Midsummer Night's Dream* (1914).
74. Desmond MacCarthy: Reprinted in *Theatre* (1954), p. 53.
75. Barry Jackson: letter to J. C. Trewin, 5.2.1959.
76. Ivor Brown: *The Way of My World* (1954), pp. 66–7.

CHAPTER FIVE

The Play-Room

I

When our period opened, Shaw was finding himself, or getting others to find him; he had no need to be told. Granville Barker, unhyphenated as he would be until 1918, was in the wings. Pinero and Jones adhered strictly to their own rules of battle. Stephen Phillips was Dante and Milton. Barrie was still unsure. Fourteen years on, though a programme-hoarder might discover the same names (he would be hard-pressed to get a Phillips), their relative positions would have changed. The Theatre of Ideas was no longer hole-and-corner. Repertory was not an esoteric word. The Theatre Theatrical was repeating its effects. Shakespeare was becoming more than an actor-manager's game. Certain things had remained more or less constant: musical comedy, melodrama, pantomime; the general to-and-fro of the Central London and provincial stage; the scurry of the play-room: all part of the Edwardian scheme.

Consider one (1902–3)[1] of several volumes of drama criticism by J. T. Grein, a gentle, ebullient London Dutchman who, though he fostered the experimental theatre of his day, was ready from his front-row stall to examine practically anything. Almost every play he notices in this book has long been lost: for example, *The Heart of Achilles*, Russian melodrama by the prolific Louis N. Parker, with Boyle Lawrence ('The authors invent a conspiracy to deliver India into Russian hands; they invent a fateful telegram abstracted by a young ne'er-do-well from a Russian statesman'); *Memory's Garden*, by Albert Chevalier and T. Gallon, 'acidulated sugar-water'; *All on Account of Eliza*, a 'rustic comedy' by Leo Dietrichstein, with real rain so slow in coming that a comedian whispered anxiously 'Turn it on! Turn it on!'; *The Little French Milliner*,[2] not surprisingly from the French; a comedy entitled *The End of a Story*,[3] its second act 'on the banks of the Avon, Stratford of the Bard; a villa, cosy with creepers, honeysuckle, a canary'; *The Lord of His House*, phlegmatic husband and impulsive wife, a former admirer's arrival, and the usual consequences; *The Hedonists*,[4] *Mrs Willoughby's Kiss*,[5] *Captain Kettle*,[6] *The President*,[7] *Eleanor* (by Mrs Humphry Ward; 'like a desiccated novel'), and so on. Infrequently, recognition gleams: *If I Were King* (Justin Huntly McCarthy), with George Alexander as Villon, a romantic indulgence that even then pined for the unwritten music of Sigmund Romberg; *The Princess's Nose*, simply because of Henry Arthur Jones's eccentric title; and *The Admirable Crichton*, which Grein, stuffily, did not like at all: 'Was it necessary to contrast a very lowly type of kitchenmaid with refined society?' Grein did not have a chance to see—and no one had—such a distillation of the period as an anonymous dramatist described in a letter to Cyril Maude, then in Haymarket management:[8]

Dear Sir.—I have written a play and for some weeks I was unable to decide whether to send it to you or to Mr Tree. Finally, however, as I hope you will be glad to hear, I decided on you.

It is a naval play, and I was well qualified to write it, having been a surgeon in the Navy, addicted to writing, a keen amateur actor, and a persistent playgoer.

The leading part (your part) is that of a naval officer, who is supposed to be the son of a bishop by a woman who had been in the ballet. But nothing is definitely known. Anyhow, your two characteristics are, a passion for practical joking, and fitful moments of religious devotion. In Act I, owing to one of your jokes, a midshipman is killed, which so works on you that you resign your commission and in an ecstasy of religious enthusiasm enter a monastery. Here all goes well for a time, but eventually your inbred love of practical joking reasserts itself, and in a sudden fit you play pranks in the monastery, and again accidentally kill a young monk. It now transpires that you are the son of the Father Superior, and you learn this in a highly dramatic scene. 'Who then,' you demand, 'is my mother?' Upon this the Mother Superior (hitherto of unsuspected virtue) comes forward and says 'I am' (*sensation*).

This, of course, alters things, and your child (you have a young illegitimate son) appears on the scene, and the action becomes both exciting and involved.

This is only a crude character sketch, but if you *feel* the idea, will you kindly suggest what fees I should receive? The writing is—if I may say so—of extraordinary brilliance, and in the words of the company manager, 'There's money in it.'—Yours faithfully . . .

Everywhere, away now from Grein and the son of the Mother Superior, and wandering down the bypaths, one is environed by names that mean less than they should: *The Mummy and the Humming Bird* (1901),[9] *The Altar of Friendship* (1903),[10] *The Lady of Rosedale* (1904), *The Indecision of Mr Kingsbury* (1905).[11] Such pieces as these dwell only in the files or in Professor Allardyce Nicoll's massive play-list.[12] *Billy's Little Love Affair* also. This (1903) was by H. V. Esmond, and the *Play Pictorial* printed 'some bright lines':

MRS GREAVES: Don't keep chipping in. I like being depressed—it's the only comfort I've got . . .

and

JACK: Other people are such brutes.
SIR HARRY: Eh?
JACK: Especially other women.
SIR HARRY: Let me recommend you to cling to the latter part of your statement all through your married life. It will protect your wife from chloral.

Other titles linger for other reasons. The Edwardians loved costume-plays: the stalls needed powder, and so they had, very simply, *When Knighthood Was In Flower*;[13] or, more strenuously, *The Scarlet Pimpernel*, elaborated by Fred Terry and Julia Neilson,[14] and *Monsieur Beaucaire*,[15] with Lewis Waller as Duke-into-barber, and the stain of blood that was like a red, red rose.

Patriotism was certainly in flower. In *An Englishman's Home* by Guy du Maurier, Gerald's brother (Wyndham's, 1909), the troops of Her Imperial Majesty the Empress of the North invaded England, and Myrtle Villa, Wickham, became a beleaguered castle. It was pleasant to hold the gorgeous East in fee, so Edward Knoblock fulfilled the need with the arabesques of *Kismet* (1911), and Harry M. Vernon and Harold Owen with a sinister Oriental melodrama, *Mr Wu*. Probably more than any of these, playgoers talked at one point about Jerome K. Jerome's *The Passing of the Third Floor Back* (1908), albatross or golden millstone round the neck of Johnston Forbes-Robertson. The Theatre of Ideas shivered: Max Beerbohm said that blasphemy paid;[16] but the piece went on and on: its scene a Bloomsbury boarding-house, its principal a new guest, a man of ineffable dignity and benevolence, formally frock-coated. He moves among a selection of disagreeable types (Bully, Hussy, Rogue, Shrew, Cad, and so forth), changes their hearts, and vanishes as quietly as he had come while the little maidservant, her arms outstretched, stands in the form of a cross. Forbes-Robertson found that he could not drop the play. In his memoirs he sought, courteously, to be grateful. He and his wife, Gertrude Elliott (who played Stasia, the 'slavey'), were 'gradually deeply impressed by the elevating nature of the theme'.[17]

II

None of these pieces would have raised the temperature of the Examiner of Plays. But through the period, and especially with the flourishing of the Theatre of Ideas, the Censor's unpopularity grew. Official objections to Granville Barker's *Waste*, Edward Garnett's *The Breaking Point* (about an unmarried girl's fear of pregnancy), and Shaw's *Blanco Posnet* were progressively exacerbating. Eventually in 1909 a Joint Select Committee of the Lords and Commons met to review the whole question; and there had never been so strong a cast of witnesses: Shaw, Barker, Galsworthy, Gilbert Murray, for writers who had belonged to the Court; Forbes-Robertson, Tree, Alexander, 151

Squire Bancroft, among the managers; Pinero and Gilbert for elder statesmen of authority; Archer and Walkley for the critics; several more besides. By no means everyone attacked the Censorship; the managers and many actors were for it. At this remove, only a single exchange sticks in the mind:

> *Bernard Shaw:* I contend that the more you improve it [the Censorship] the more disastrous it will be, because the more effectually will it stop the immoral play, which from my point of view is the only play that is worth writing.
> *Mr Hugh Law:* By 'immoral' all through, you mean non-customary.
> *Mr Shaw:* Yes, I mean non-customary.

Consider the resonances there. What was ultimately recommended does not matter now; Shaw said, with reason, that it illustrated the art of contriving methods of reform that left matters exactly as they were. The Lord Chamberlain's office continued to anger senior dramatists until the period ended in August 1914; then the long interregnum after which the day's theatre would shake itself and begin again. Between 1909 and 1914 the most publicised conflict was transient; strangely, it involved a quiet regional writer, Eden Phillpotts, primarily a novelist.

Granville Barker, in 1912, was going to produce Phillpotts's *The Secret Woman* at the Kingsway. This dramatist was not one of the Court party, though in the mid-1920s he would have a connection with the theatre when his Devon comedy, *The Farmer's Wife*, ran there for years. In those days he was content to stay in the pastures round Little Silver, to rule his own demi-paradise, and to employ the full speech of Devon, no rustic-type, stock-pot substitute. Unluckily, he wrote too much, confining himself to a parade of rural repartee, misogyny, feasting, idyllic sentiment, and ultimate matrimony. He did it with skill, and he has been under-valued. Before the war he was more redoubtable: the author of the Dartmoor novels, a cycle—twenty in all—that would continue until 1923. A few plays, too, though these, except one, were uncontentious. The exception was *The Secret Woman* when he was forty-nine. At Barker's suggestion he had adapted it from his novel. On the eve of production the Lord Chamberlain refused a licence,[18] demanding that two speeches should be cut, one of them by a husband to a wife: 'You won't understand. An angel from heaven wouldn't understand. It would take a devil from hell to do that—according to what you believe. The way of a man's body. . . . My flesh and blood's a bit too much for you and always was. And a bit too much for me sometimes.' Phillpotts, on principle, would not cut. Barker, Shaw, Murray, Masefield, Galsworthy, Henry James, George Moore, Quiller-Couch, Barrie, Pinero, most of the leading authors and dramatists, supported him in a united letter of protest in *The Times*. Special free performances had to be given to keep within the law. Inevitably, there was a rush for the novel which had been only moderately received. The play itself—with Janet Achurch miscast—was like a mediocre print of a fine portrait. Its one living passage was the beginning of the woman's revelation to her son in the second act:

Presently I stopped on the hill and listened to a night-jar churn out his queer talk. And then I saw Halstock lying dark over the river, and something made me slip down to the water and across the stepping-stones and climb up the Glen. Somehow I knew he was there; and I laughed to myself to think how I'd surprise Anthony if I chanced upon him. So I went behind a rowan and waited for moonrise. She came up behind the cleave all silver-bright, and the darkness was full of light and the silence was full of peace. My last peace in the world, Michael boy! But I thought 'twas good to be there. I said to myself, 'You'd be wiser, Ann Redvers, if you comed out like this of a night sometimes after the bustle of day, and let your soul take rest at the edge of the dark.'[19]

That, and Joshua Bloom's dictum, 'The grave be a very wonderful state in my judgment—but for the getting there,' are the real Phillpotts.

III

There were better things. Some today are simply titles: Mrs W. K. Clifford's *The Likeness of the Night* (1901), which Madge Kendal (off-stage one of the most imperious of English actresses) momentarily burnished as a loving wife who committed suicide   153 so that her wayward husband might be happy elsewhere; Cicely Hamilton's romantic *Diana of Dobson's* (1908), opening in the dormitory of living-in drapers' assistants who, like housemaids, were on the Edwardian conscience; Rudolf Besier's *Don* (1909), sympathetic tale of a quixotic idealist; and the same author's *Lady Patricia* (1911), with Mrs Patrick Campbell to burlesque both herself and the kind of woman she had so long impersonated. Here she was a mooning dryad who lived in a foam of rapture and guelder roses, spent most of her time in a summer-house half-way up an oak-tree, and drew a performance that, in the play's own idiom, could rightly be hailed as corking.

One or two other plays have been preserved on radio or television. Among them are two by Arnold Bennett. Determined to be the precise professional in anything he attempted, Bennett for years had been trying to write plays—some, unsuccessfully, were with Phillpotts—and before 1914 five of them competently arrived. The most durable would be a three-period family narrative, *Milestones* (1912; construction by Edward Knoblock, specialist in dramatic architecture) and *The Great Adventure* (1913), based on Bennett's novel, *Buried Alive*. There he did use engagingly his gift for the realistic-romantic: the central figure, a famous artist in search of peace, allowed his valet to be buried in Westminster Abbey with full state while he himself retired to Putney and the care of Janet Cannot. Bennett's other work could be structurally unsure. The people were there; the world they inhabited was often canvas and three-ply. When they left the stage they walked only into the wings—unexpectedly, remembering the variety and solid truth of the novels.

Magic (1913), which Shaw persuaded G. K. Chesterton to write, was amiable nonsense with a pearl of absent-minded Dukes: it reappears occasionally. But we do not hear now of *Typhoon* (also 1913), adapted freely from the Hungarian of Melchior Lengyel by Laurence Irving, second and fated of Sir Henry's remarkable sons. He also played, with a startling dignity and subtlety, Takeramo, the intellectual Japanese in Paris, who ceremoniously commits hara-kiri after a tragic emotional and racial entanglement. No English actor had Irving's understanding of the Oriental mind: it was a very long flight from *The Mikado*. A play at once theatrical and psychologically wise, *Typhoon* was not in the long-run list. Length of run has never been a safe index to quality; but here—to tell its own Edwardian stage story—is a summary of productions between 1900 and 1914 that lasted (an arbitrary figure) for 350 performances or more:

PLAY	THEATRE	DATE	PERFORM-ANCES	TYPE AND AUTHOR
The Arcadians	Shaftesbury	28.4.1909	809	Musical Comedy by Mark Ambient and A. M. Thompson; music by Lionel Monckton and Howard Talbot
The Bad Girl of the Family	Aldwych	27.12.1909	452	Melodrama by Frederick Melville
The Belle of Mayfair	Vaudeville	11.4.1906	416	Musical Comedy by C. H. Brookfield and Cosmo Hamilton; music by Leslie Stuart
Bunty Pulls the Strings	{ Playhouse { Haymarket	4.7.1911 18.7.1911	617	Scottish comedy by Graham Moffat
The Catch of the Season		9.9.1904	621	Musical play by Seymour Hicks and Cosmo Hamilton; music by H. E. Haines and Cosmo Baker
A Chinese Honeymoon	Strand	5.10.1901	1,075	Musical play by George Dance; music by Howard Talbot
The Chocolate Soldier	Lyric	10.9.1910	500	Comic opera by Stanislaus Stange; music by Oscar Straus

155

PLAY	THEATRE	DATE	PERFORM-ANCES	TYPE AND AUTHOR
The Cingalee	Daly's	5.3.1904	365	Musical play by J. T. Tanner; music by Lionel Monckton and Paul Rubens
A Country Girl	Daly's	18.1.1902	729	Musical play by J. T. Tanner; music by Lionel Monckton
Diplomacy (revival)	Wyndham's	26.3.1913	455	Play by B. C. Stephenson and Clement Scott from Sardou's *Dora*
The Dollar Princess	Daly's	25.9.1909	428	Musical play by Basil Hood (from the German); music by Leo Fall
The Earl and the Girl	Adelphi	10.12.1903	371	Musical comedy by Seymour Hicks; music by Ivan Caryll
Everybody's Doing It	Empire	14.2.1912	354	Revue by George Grossmith, jun., and C. H. Bovill; music by Cuthbert Clarke
Fanny's First Play	{ Little { Kingsway	19.4.1911 } 1.1.1912 }	622	'An easy play for a Little Theatre' by Bernard Shaw
The Flag Lieutenant	Playhouse	16.6.1908	381	Naval comedy by W. P. Drury and Leo Trevor
The Follies (third run in regular theatre)	Apollo	1.12.1908	571	Musical entertainment devised by H. G. Pélissier
The Follies (fourth run)	Apollo	30.8.1910	521	Musical entertainment

PLAY	THEATRE	DATE	PERFORM-ANCES	TYPE AND AUTHOR
The Girl from Kay's	Apollo	15.11.1902	432	Musical play by Owen Hall; music by Cecil Cook
The Girl in the Taxi	Lyric	5.9.1912	385	Musical play by Frederick Fenn and Arthur Wimperis (from the French); music by Jean Gilbert
The Glad Eye	Globe	4.11.1912	493	Farcical comedy by José G. Levy, from the French
The Great Adventure	Kingsway	25.3.1913	673	Comedy by Arnold Bennett
His House in Order	St James's	1.2.1906	430	Comedy by A. W. Pinero
Hullo! Ragtime	London Hippodrome	23.12.1912	451	Revue by Max Pemberton and Albert P. De Courville
Hullo! Tango	London Hippodrome	23.12.1913	485	Revue by Max Pemberton and Albert P. De Courville
Lady Frederick	Court Garrick Criterion Haymarket	26.10.1907 10.3.1908 27.4.1908 1.8.1908	422	Comedy by W. Somerset Maugham
Lady Madcap	Prince of Wales	17.12.1904	354	Musical play by Paul Rubens and Lieut. Col. N. Newnham-Davis; music by Paul Rubens
The Little Michus	Daly's	29.4.1905	401	Musical play by Henry Hamilton (from the French); music by André Messager.

PLAY	THEATRE	DATE	PERFORM-ANCES	TYPE AND AUTHOR
The Marriage Market	Day's	17.5.1913	423	Musical play adapted by Gladys Unger (from the German); music by Victor Jacobi
The Messenger Boy	Gaiety	3.2.1900	429	Musical play by J. T. Tanner and A. Murray; music by Ivan Caryll and Lionel Monckton
Mice and Men	Lyric	27.1.1902	361	Play by Madeleine Lucette Ryley
Milestones	Royalty	5.3.1912	607	Play by Arnold Bennett and Edward Knoblock
Miss Hook of Holland	Prince of Wales	31.1.1907	462	Musical play by Paul Rubens and Austen Hurgon; music by Paul Rubens
Mr Wu	Strand	27.11.1913	403	Anglo-Chinese play by Harry M. Vernon and Harold Owen
Monsieur Beaucaire	Comedy	25.10.1902	430	Romantic comedy by Booth Tarkington and Mrs E. G. Sutherland
The Orchid	Gaiety	26.10.1903	559	Musical play by J. T. Tanner; music by Ivan Caryll and Lionel Monckton
Our Miss Gibbs	Gaiety	23.1.1909	636	Musical comedy by 'Cryptos'; constructed by J. T. Tanner; music by Ivan Caryll and Lionel Monckton

PLAY	THEATRE	DATE	PERFORM-ANCES	TYPE AND AUTHOR
The Passing Show	Palace	20.4.1914	351	Revue by Arthur Wimperis and P. L. Flers; music by Herman Finck
Potash and Perlmutter	Queen's	14.4.1914	665	Comedy by Montague Glass and Charles Klein
The Quaker Girl	Adelphi	5.11.1910	536	Musical play by J. T. Tanner; music by Lionel Monckton
Quality Street	Vaudeville	17.9.1901	459	Comedy by J. M. Barrie
Raffles	Comedy	12.5.1906	351	Play by Eugene W. Presbrey and E. W. Hornung
The Second in Command	Haymarket	27.11.1900	378	Comedy by Robert Marshall
The Spring Chicken	Gaiety	30.5.1905	401	Musical play by George Grossmith, jun., from the French; music by Ivan Caryll, Lionel Monckton
The Toreador	Gaiety	17.6.1901	675	Musical play by J. T. Tanner and Harry Nicholls; music by Ivan Caryll and Lionel Monckton
Véronique	Apollo	18.5.1904	495	Comic opera by A. Vanloo and G. Duval; version by Henry Hamilton; music by André Messager

159

PLAY	THEATRE	DATE	PERFORM-ANCES	TYPE AND AUTHOR
The Walls of Jericho	Garrick	31.10.1904	423	Play by Alfred Sutro
What Every Woman Knows	Duke of York's	3.9.1908	384	Comedy by J. M. Barrie
When Knights Were Bold	Wyndham's	29.1.1907	579	Farce by Charles Marlowe (Harriet Jay)
Within the Law	Haymarket	24.5.1913	427	Play by Bayard Veiller; adapted by Frederick Fenn and Arthur Wimperis

IV

In this list musical comedy dominates. No one cherished it more than the Edwardians did in its lamb-frisking youth: of all entertainments, music-hall excepted, the most popular and undemanding. Already in 1900 these shows—you could have called them nothing else—were purposeful formula-pieces, romantically or comically irrational among their expensively irrational settings. Through the years, served by a specialised group of librettists and composers, they depended on a glitter of 'personality' playing: the postcard-smiles of Marie Studholme or Gertie Millar, the generous broad comedy of Edmund Payne or Connie Ediss (her last home, in a Surrey village, was a flat over a bank, called 'Connie's Cot'),[20] the interpolated numbers in a comfortably flexible fabric, and the girls who, as someone said, were often married from the stage door. These were ephemeral delights, minor shooting stars that rushed across the Edwardian evening and were gone, but because they belonged to a serener age and to a theatre where unhappiness was never allowed to conquer, they are remembered with a wistful sentimentality. Several of their tunes survive. The musical comedies themselves, except for such an iridescent bubble, Viennese-blown, as *The Merry Widow*,[21] have melted into the darkness.

Playgoers in 1900 were still coming away from Daly's, humming the airs of *San Toy* (1899),[22] 'Rhoda and her Pagoda' and 'Chinese Soldier Man'. Down at the old Gaiety in the Strand, Rosie Boote (later the Marchioness of Headfort) was singing 'Maisie' in *The Messenger Boy*:

> Maisie is a daisy,
> Maisie is a dear,
> For the boys are mad about her,
> And they can't get on without her,
> And they all cry 'Whoops!' when Maisie's getting near.

The public could not get on without the Savoy sequence of Gilbert and Sullivan; but these operas were minor classics and in a mood and method far from the carefully irresponsible musical comedies that set the town talking. Some are remembered like bright exhalations in the evening; only connoisseurs can get them in their right order and know how to place all those Girls: *A Country Girl, The Earl and the Girl, The Girl Behind the Counter*,[23] *The Quaker Girl, The Sunshine Girl*[24] (in which Connie Ediss sang 'Pop me on the boat to Brighton'), *The Girl from Kay's, The Girl in the Taxi*. If the girl was none of these, or a dollar princess, a Balkan princess, a merry widow, a beauty of Bath, or the catch of the season, she could be someone elaborately rural from a European land that looked like a travel poster and had a bunch of low comedians and a blaze of national costume. Never were palaces more palatial, snows whiter, seas bluer, suns hotter, wines more potent, than in Daly's and the Gaiety—'the shimmer of Gaiety silk against the lustre of Daly's velvet'[25]—at the meridian of the great George Edwardes who controlled both houses (the Gaiety and its girls moved to the Aldwych-Strand corner in 1903); at the Prince of Wales's in Coventry Street, under Frank Curzon; and at various theatres in Shaftesbury Avenue, under Robert Courtneidge.

Edwardians would recite in a jubilant litany the names of Marie Studholme of the silver-encrusted postcards, Ada Reeve, 161

Evie Greene, Phyllis and Zena Dare, Gertie Millar, Lily Elsie (the merry widow), Florence Smithson (who sang 'The Pipes of Pan' in *The Arcadians*); the improvising George Graves, G. P. Huntley, Huntley Wright, W. H. Berry (master of hand-properties), Joseph Coyne, Robert Michaelis, Lauri de Frece, Edmund Payne (loved low comedian with the lisping voice), or George Grossmith, junior, the young man of the period ('Archie, Archie, of the upper ten'). It is the kind of random catalogue that for me recalls the sifting of a vast pile of *Play Pictorials* in confusion on a Cornish attic floor. Names of the characters in *Our Miss Gibbs* (1909) speak for the period: The Hon. Hugh Pierrepoint, an amateur criminal; the Earl of St Ives; Slithers, a professional crook; Mr Toplady, manager of Garrods; Timothy Gibbs, Mary's Yorkshire cousin; Lady Elizabeth Thanet; the Duchess of Minster; Mrs Farquharson (an impecunious woman of fashion); Miss Gibbs; colleens of Irish village at the White City; girls at the Stores; Dudes. It was in the setting of the White City at night that Gertie Millar, as a pierrot, sang 'Moonstruck': 'I'm such a silly when the moon comes out / I hardly seem to know what I'm about.'

Though there have been efforts to resurrect them, the musical comedies were for an age, not for all time, and that age was brief. The libretti seem now to be uniformly naïve, mainly because so much is left unwritten. It was for a popular comedian—such a man as the avuncular George Graves with his *Merry Widow* anecdotes of Hetty the Hen—to add to the night his own resourceful charade-humour. Good enough for the moment; but the stage has bubbles as the water has, and these were of them:

> For we've all of us a mania
> To trot through Transylvania,
> To totter in the Transylvanian rain:
> So pick up your umbrella,
> Ev'ry girl and ev'ry fella,
> And travel by the Transylvanian train.

Revues, just arriving then, were even flimsier mayflies (flimsy or not, they would be dangerous competitors to the music-hall). Such titles as *Hullo! Ragtime* (1912), led by the strenuous Ethel

Levey—Rupert Brooke saw it ten times[26]—and *Hullo! Tango* (1913) are period exhibits; but the only shows laurelled now in theatre memory are the various editions of the Pélissier Follies. Pedants will say that, with its skull-caps and ruffles, the *Follies* was simply a pierrot night in a West End theatre, a more exciting ancestor of *The Co-optimists*. Whatever it was, it had—thanks to the ebullience of H. G. Pélissier and his cast—a swift, topical sting, especially in its Potted Plays, comic distillations of the West End stage. These caused even so grave a critic as C. E. Montague, on one of his rare visits to London from Manchester, to forswear all other exercises and go to the *Follies* twice.

V

The *Follies* had potted pantomime as well. Pantomime is an acquired taste—visitors from abroad seldom acquire it—but nothing except musical comedy and music-hall has bred more rapturous reminiscence. Once it was a point of honour among autobiographers to describe a first Christmas visit to Drury Lane. In discussing pantomime it helps little to probe the ocean-deeps of history; to be erudite about the Saturnalia, or, for that matter, to analyse the *commedia dell'arte* from which Clown and Pantaloon, Harlequin and Columbine derived. Roughly, this form of spectacular revel, long ruled by Harlequin, had developed in the late Victorian theatre to a bulging Christmas cracker. Throughout the country it was a hallowed routine in dozens of Theatres Royal, Grands, and Hippodromes; and when the music-hall was in early riot its performers were recruited to pantomime to do their usual acts. Buried somewhere there had to be a nursery story; it was an excuse for the title (even if Crusoe's island had never been so fully peopled) and for the names of certain characters. Tradition hardening, a Principal Boy had to be a girl, the Dame a man; a Transformation Scene was essential. Little had changed by the Edwardian period. It remained a holiday gallimaufry, a music-hall in disguise, a spectacle for parents as much as their children. It was all a rout of Dames and Demon Kings, Cats and Brokers' Men, Babes and Barons (advertisement in trade paper: 'Wanted

Singing Baron. Experienced. Good Feed'), grotesques slish-sloshing in paperhangers' paste, chorus-songs about food, sentimental balladry, schoolroom scenes or haunted bedrooms. Roaring men would fall down and keep on falling; sometimes they could be funny when upright. Children might have been puzzled at a choice between Perrault and Panto. But it was Christmas; anything could go, even panto-rhyme. One drops into it naturally, recalling the flash and flare (and the corps-de-ballet), the sizzling stuff of a Christmas rally, where reason totters and the comic rules, Twankey triumphant at a feast of fools.

Down the Edwardian years children were taught to take pantomime as it came: a soprano Principal Boy, an excessively aproned Dame, Brokers' Men floundering in whitewash, and Demon and Good Fairy addressing each other, venomously or tepidly, from opposite sides of the stage. For two reactions to pantomime I quote a pair of small boys. Taffy (Sir Arthur Quiller-Couch, 'Q' when young) came up to Plymouth for his first theatre night, a late Victorian *Jack the Giant-Killer*. In his disguised autobiography, *The Ship of Stars*,[27] 'Q' recorded a child's astonishment at 'the new and unimagined world, stretching deeper and deeper as the scenes were lifted; a world in which solid walls crumbled and forests melted, and loveliness broke through the ruins, unfolding like a rose'. Taffy was a Romantic; but there was also the boy Jeremy in a book by Hugh Walpole[28] (autobiography as well), who watched *Aladdin* from the gallery at Polchester': 'In the middle of the scene was an old woman, her hat tumbling off her head, her shabby skirt dragging large boots, and a red nose. . . . She had, this old woman, a number of bales of cloth under her arm, and she tried to carry them all, but one slipped and then another, and then another; she bent to pick them up and her hat fell off; she turned for her hat, and all the bales tumbled together. Jeremy began to laugh—everyone laughed . . . He turned round and exclaimed convulsively, "Why, she's a man!"'

So she was; she always is. At Drury Lane she would have been played by Dan Leno whom a poet would apostrophise—long after his death—as 'all in little, peerless droll, / An impudent purgation of the soul'.[29] Leno ('the King's Jester'), small, impish, urgent, with high, arched eyebrows, was in partnership with Herbert Campbell, big, lethargic, cheerfully extrovert. They were the lords of Boxing Night and after. When, just before the turn of the century, Arthur Collins had taken over as manager from the late Sir Augustus Harris, there was less professional pageantry than in the Augustan age and not so much of the final harlequinade. Collins was a man for the wilder humours. Though one is inclined to suspect rhapsodies about this or the other eccentric comedian—their qualities can fade on paper—it seems plain that Campbell and Leno were exceptional. They both died in 1904; *Blue Beard, Mother Goose,* and *Humpty Dumpty,* not that the names matter much, had been among their immediate successes. Max Beerbohm wrote of Leno's voice and manner: 'Half croak, half chirp. . . . That general air of physical fatigue overcome by spiritual energy, of faintness undeterrible from the pursuit: the humble man or woman, preplexed but undaunted in the struggle for life.'[30]

Drury Lane was always the prime Christmas adventure; the Lyceum began its broadly popular sequence in 1907. But every inner and outer suburb and every provincial town had its own sparkle of pantomime as necessary as the Christmas-card. Intermittently, Edwardian children had other Christmas plays: from 1904 *Peter Pan* was the only one that kept on a sustained progress. There were such productions as *Bluebell in Fairyland* (1901), with Ellaline Terriss, though it would be many years, and after our period, before this 'musical dream-play' had any full Christmas authority; *Pinkie and the Fairies,* with Graham Robertson's strangely moving lyrics, which Tree staged for two years in 1908–9; and, from 1911, the patriotic and moral *Where the Rainbow Ends* which would have a long annual life. In 1909 Maeterlinck's *The Blue Bird (L'oiseau bleu)* was more specialised: an allegory of the search by a woodcutter's children, Tyltyl and Mytyl, for the blue bird of happiness: not all of the watchers troubled about an inner meaning. A farce, *When Knights Were Bold* (1907) had no inner meaning at all; a house-party that had been praising the good old times too extravagantly was dumped back into the year 1196 with obvious alarming consequences. Fortunate on three counts as a farce (originally with James Welch), as a costume-play, and—not the first intention— 165 something for the children, it was turned after our period into a Christmas-holiday piece.

VI

Drury Lane was the London temple of pantomime. In effect, we can say now, its autumn melodramas were pantomimes as well, complex manoeuvres charted affectionately by Brian Dobbs in his book on the Lane.[31] Thus *The Price of Peace* (1900) included the Chamber of the House of Commons, a steam yacht in collision, and Westminster Abbey; *The Great Millionaire* (1901) Guildhall, the Carlton Hotel, and a fine car crash; *Ben-Hur* (in the spring of 1902) a chariot race and a Roman galley; *The Flood Tide* (1903) Kempton Park paddock, and a flood; *The Bondman* (1906) Etna in eruption, and real cows milked on the stage; *The Sins of Society* (1907), the sinking of a troopship; *The Marriage of Mayfair* (1908), an avalanche; *The Whip* (1909, 1910), a train smash, the Chamber of Horrors, and the race for the Two Thousand Guineas; *Sealed Orders* (1913), Chelsea Flower Show and an airship brought down by a gun. The adventuress who causes the train smash in *The Whip* speaks a magnificent Edwardian line: 'Never mind, they were only third-class passengers—something is always happening to people of that kind.' These were the gilded melodramas of mixed disasters. Their actors, falling from balloons, clinging to flood-swept house-tops, or crashing from any handy vehicle, had to be men of steel and amiably survived.

A great deal, too, was happening on less conspicuous stages, little room for spectacle but plenty for emotion. Though I have not read the text, the characters' names speak loudly in Nita Rae's *A Mother's Salvation* (Theatre Royal, Wednesbury, and Theatre Royal, Stratford, E., 1908): Leslie Mervyne, I am fairly sure, was the hero; the villain would be Reuben Smith; Joe Turntail and Billy Bumpkin would be comic relief, Little Paul the sentiment, and Daisy Delaval an adventuress. I see no particular trouble in Frederick Melville's *Married to the Wrong Man* (Elephant and Castle, 1908): Jack Gladwin, Jasper Skinner, Bertie Swanker, Dolly Fritter, and Ruth. But Jack Denton's romantic military drama, *A Queen for a Wife* (Royal, Stratford, 1912) does baffle me a little: Teddy Spanner and Evangeline Hopkins are the comics; but what do we do with Prince Hugfried of Menekhrinia, King Sergius, Paulus Damoski, Elissa Menovitch, the Princess Allitza, and the Veiled Woman? It was a good year (1912) for provincial melodrama: *The Mormon and His Wives, The Mormon and the Maid, One Life, One Love* (in this a personage named the Rev. Nobel Pryce), *Pathfinders; or, Builders of Empire, The Collier's Lass, By Right of Sword*, and *Foiled by a Woman*: everything much larger than life, Virtue milk-white, Vice a fiery scarlet. I wonder yet about a piece further back, *As Your Hair Grows Whiter* (Opera House, St Helen's, 1907): its cast, untouched by the Theatre of Ideas, contained a Maniac, a Drunken Pauper, Jake, and Nurse Von Grip. That sort of thing has gone with Thebes the golden. From central London the titles of the Lyceum melodramas, Drury Lane's junior rival (and a sad drop from Irving) are now merely labels: *The Monk and the Woman, The Sins of London, The Fighting Chance*.

The cast—uncommonly bizarre—of *A Queen for a Wife* is from the blank on the map left by the fall of a confederation of inner-Balkan states, a private empire that belonged by right to the Edwardian stage. Shaw had been mocking Sergius Saranoff—who elsewhere would have been taken seriously—at least half-a-dozen years before the new century opened; but for once the Shavian mockery had little effect. For another twenty years the romantics ruled. There is no blank in memory. We can see in the mind that cartographer's puzzle, emerald and cobalt, crimson lake and azure and elaborately hachured, the sub-Balkans of the Edwardian theatre: thrones, princedoms, powers, pine-forests and crag-piled castles. There was always a rebellion of some kind. It kept the army busy; it kept the people cheerful; and for high-level plotting it was invaluable. Ruritania, 'Anthony Hope's' invention, was at the centre of the inner kingdoms, mountainous and shaggy-pelted, inhabited—the royal families apart—by devious Prime Ministers, designing Barons, and here and there, for the look of the thing, a peasant. In the midnight ballrooms more candles burned to the square inch than anywhere else in Europe. No heroes were more like Lewis Waller, no villains craftier, no 167 uniforms so sumptuous. The stage would seem curiously bare when an iron curtain slid down upon Styria and Kraja, Kravonia, Carpathia, Cadonia, Novia, Croabia, a hundred others crammed on the chequer-board, huddling together like birds in a storm. It was there that the Captain of Hussars, in a cherry-coloured cloak, would defy the Colonel of Cuirassiers, thigh-booted, silver-spurred. It was there, at the twelfth hour, that Princess Marietta would save her lover from execution by disguising herself as a prison chaplain. It was there that a Grand Duke and a Cadonian Count would fight with sabres, or King Siegfried, shot in the forehead, would collapse on the steps of his throne.

Though all of this expired with the first world war, some of the plays did linger in the lesser stock companies. It was a high moment, I remember, when Captain Rellsberg, uniformed in blue-sashed scarlet by a colour-blind War Office, faced Baron Nelkau on the stage of a seaport gaff, crying: 'Duty, first watchword of a soldier, must sway an officer of the Crimson Guards more than the dictates of his heart.' At this the leading lady, five feet tall with a despairing seagull-voice and her eyes rimmed in lamp-black, fainted clean away. It would be all right in the end. One could rely on these Ruritanians even when their world was dead.

VII

All of this was melodrama and the Edwardians were devoted to it. Gerald du Maurier did not call his masterpiece of the moment 'a thick-ear play' until a première at Wyndham's in 1921;[32] but it would have been reasonably accurate, since the beginning of the century, for such events as *Sherlock Holmes*, *Raffles*,[33] *The House of Temperley*, *Alias Jimmy Valentine*,[34] and *Within the Law*. Not wholly accurate because, *Temperley* apart—it was Conan Doyle's Regency boxing drama in the mood of his novel, *Rodney Stone*—the violence, as often as not, was implied. What Americans called the 'crook play' was coming in: often elementary stuff from a stage that was still growing up, but keeping, for Johnny Tarleton's approval, a pleasure in forthright narrative. Rarely spoken about now, these plays, English and American, do belong to the mosaic of the Edwardian theatre; and one or two of them may have renewed life as period pieces. *Sherlock Holmes* certainly had in a Royal Shakespeare revival during 1974. Ascribed to the actor-dramatist, William Gillette, and Conan Doyle, it was less Doyle's than Gillette's: he even provided a final romantic two minutes as implausible as the scene for the Duke and Isabella in another play. Produced in New York (1899), brought to London in 1901 and revived again four years later, it is lucky in a central figure to fortify any plot. Holmes was about again in Doyle's own and more compact melodrama, *The Speckled Band* (Adelphi, 1910), with its snake on the bellrope: 'Curious fad to ventilate one room into another.' But the original *Sherlock Holmes*, with plenty of curious fads, is a strongly-carpentered, actable affair that, in performance, can survive even Professor Moriarty's order: 'Notify the Lascar that I may require the gas chamber at Stepney, the one that looks over the river.' When the Royal Shakespeare Company resurrected it, some had clearly come in the hope of a wild night; audience-guyed melodrama in the vein of *Lady Audley's Secret*. Yet, ten minutes after curtain-rise, the house was still.

We have had no means of testing other, and shelved, melodramas, though I can affirm that, when twenty or thirty years old, they made their appropriate points. Gerald du Maurier acted in three of them: *Raffles* (1906), with its amateur cricketer-cracksman, a figure not highly regarded at Lord's; *Arsène Lupin* (1909),[35] about a French crook who was also a Duke; and *Alias Jimmy Valentine* (1910), in which Valentine was a safe-blower from Sing-Sing. Conscientious and stilted, all had been constructed with an eye for a single big scene. Du Maurier, using the unflurried naturalism that would perplex his imitators, could command the stage with a half-turn of his head. Basically, it was Charles Hawtrey's style, but du Maurier could get it to work in the tenser situation-drama and it became entirely his own, every swift under-statement, every mannerism. George Alexander, at the St James's, preferred a more solidly-made play; usually at his theatre one heard somewhere an echo of Pinero. Behind A. E. W. Mason's *The Witness for the Defence* 169

(1911) is the jingle and rattle of a hansom. The title sounds like court drama (butterflies to be broken on the wheel), but the only trial is between first scene and second. In the remainder of the play we are with a woman-with-a-past who has been acquitted of murder (bullying husband, shot by a rook-rifle in Rajputana), and because of it is suffering in an English village 'the treatment of a leper'. This is an authoritative survival from the Theatre Theatrical; upper lips are stiff, and the barrister, Alexander's part, smokes nothing but an ancient briar.

If I were to take one melodrama from the Edwardian pack, the ancient briars, it would be neither Ruritanian, crooked, nor sub-Pinerotic. It would be Joseph Comyns Carr's version of Stevenson's fable of dualism, Dr Jekyll and Mr Hyde,[36] and not merely because it was among the earliest plays I met in repertory during the 1920s, 'by arrangement with the executors of H. B. Irving'. As played by Irving it must have been a shivering excitement. The danger is to make Jekyll unnaturally flamboyant, Hyde too much of an arachnid. But Hyde is animal, man-monkey; Jekyll must live in dignified restraint. Dignity and horror are close neighbours here in a London that, for all the formalities, the lawyers and doctors and senatorial butlers, is a haunted place, a world where Jekyll is most dreadfully attended. Carr warmed the Stevensonian Jekyll; he added, too, a blind wife, a part Dorothea Baird acted finely. H. B. Irving, who could turn the screw more surely than any of his contemporaries, was never more chilling than in what his son has called 'the physical change from the tall austere Jekyll to the dwarfish creature that was the shell of unmitigated evil'.[37] Beside this, other melodramas of the time must disperse like that powder added to the few minims of red tincture in Hyde's graduated glass. Quickly, we move from the play-room.

Notes

1. *Dramatic Criticism*, Vol. IV, 1902–1903 (1904).
2. Adapted from a play by Maurice Hennequin and Albin Valabrèque. Avenue, 8 April 1902.
3. By J. Dudley Morgan. Wyndham's, 12 April 1902.
4. By Mrs G. C. Ashton Johnson. Wyndham's, 4 July 1902.
5. By Frank Stayton. Avenue, 18 October 1902.

6. By Malcolm Watson and Murray Carson. Adelphi, 23 October 1902.
7. By Frank Stayton. Farcical musical drama; Prince of Wales's, 30 April, 1902.
8. Cyril Maude: *The Haymarket Theatre* (1903).
9. By Isaac Henderson. Wyndham's, 10 October 1901.
10. By Madeleine Lucette Ryley. Criterion, 24 March 1903.
11. By Cosmo Gordon-Lennox from the French. Haymarket, 6 December 1905.
12. Allardyce Nicoll: *English Drama, 1900–1930* (Cambridge, 1973).
13. By Paul Kester. Waldorf. 13 May 1907.
14. By Baroness Orczy and Montague Barstow. New, 5 January 1905.
15. Romantic comedy by Booth Tarkington and Mrs E. G. Sutherland. Comedy Theatre, 25 October 1902.
16. *The Saturday Review*, 5 September 1908. Reprinted in *Around Theatres* (1953 edition), p. 516.
17. Sir Johnston Forbes-Robertson: *A Player Under Three Reigns* (1925), p. 152.
18. Richard Findlater: *Banned!* (1967), p. 120.
19. *The Secret Woman* (1912), Act II.
20. Dean A. V. Baillie: *My First Eighty Years* (1951), p. 120.
21. Adapted from the Viennese; music by Franz Lehar. Daly's, 8 June 1907.
22. By Edward Morton; music by Sidney Jones. Daly's, 21 October 1899.
23. By Leedham Bantock and Arthur Anderson; music by Edward Talbot; Wyndham's, 21 October, 1906.
24. By Paul Rubens and Cecil Raleigh; music by Rubens. Gaiety, 24 February 1912.
25. W. Macqueen Pope: *Carriages at Eleven* (1947), p. 101.
26. Christopher Hassall: *Rupert Brooke* (1964). The company included the American Ragtime Octet and Ethel Levey, 'a woman of barbarous vigour', said Brooke, 'with cropped hair under wagging osprey, hobble skirt, and a bracelet on her ankle'.
27. 'Q' (Sir Arthur Quiller-Couch): *The Ship of Stars* (1899). Duchy Edition (1928), p. 94.
28. Hugh Walpole: 'Jeremy' in *The Jeremy Stories* (1941 edition), pp. 80–1.
29. John Drinkwater: 'Prologue to a Royal Night of Variety, May 1934', in *Collected Poems of John Drinkwater*, Vol. III, 1923–1937 (1937), p. 300.
30. *Saturday Review*, 5 November 1904. *Around Theatres* (1953 edition), p. 349. 'To the last, long after illness had sapped his powers of actual expression and invention, the power of his personality was unchanged and irresistible.'
31. Brian Dobbs: *Three Centuries of the Theatre Royal: 1663–1971* (1972), p. 171.
32. *Bulldog Drummond*.
33. By Eugene W. Presbrey and E. W. Hornung. Comedy Theatre. 12 May, 1906.
34. By Paul Armstrong. Comedy Theatre, 29 March 1910.
35. By Francis de Croisset and Maurice Leblanc. Duke of York's, 30 August 1909; transferred to the Globe, 13 December.
36. Queen's, 29 January 1910.
37. Laurence Irving: *The Precarious Crust* (1971), p. 159.

CHAPTER SIX

Closing the Door

I

All had seemed reasonably well with the house in the warm early summer of 1914. Most of the rooms were actively occupied. In the Theatre Theatrical various basic principles were unchanged. One was the use of the lie, or the mild evasion, as the root of a comedy: something that Henry Arthur Jones had marked once when he used as an epigraph Sir Henry Sidney's letter to his son Philip: 'Above all things, tell no untruth; no, not in trifles; the custom of it is naughty.'[1] Another theme was what Captain Hawtree, in Robertson's play long before, had called 'the inexorable law of caste'.[2] He went on:

The social law, so becoming and so good, that commands like to mate with like, and forbids a giraffe to fall in love with a squirrel. . . . All those marriages of people with common people are all very well in novels and in plays on the stage, because the real people don't exist, and have no relatives who do exist, and no connections, and so no harm's done, and it's rather interesting to look at; but in real life with real relations, and real mothers, and so forth, its absolute bosh. It's worse—it's utter social and personal annihilation and damnation.

Shaw would claim, on the whole rightly, that 'an armoury against despair and dullness' still spoke for the Theatre of Ideas and its preoccupation with social problems, though few camp-followers had a tithe of his intellectual agility or his gift for the irrepressible *boutade*. He faced calmly the dislike of Sydney Grundy who in the spring of 1914 had uttered a sad and heavy pamphlet-attack[3] on the drama of ideas, roused by John Palmer's book, *The Future of the Theatre*: 'Will Mr Shaw leave any mark whatever, or will his footprints be obliterated from the sands? . . . His star is on the wane; his candle only gutters in its socket; his beauty is *passée*, his wheezes are chestnuts, his sleight-of-hand transparent, his humours rheum.'[4] And so on. Grundy might protest too much; but it was clear that the Theatre of Ideas would not be put down.

A visitor from 1900 would have seen many of the old names on the 1914 playbills, though not Grundy's. No fresh Pinero since his one-acters, *The Widow of Wasdale Head* and *Playgoers*; but there were already rumours of an autumn revival of *His House in Order* at the St James's; Alexander's Hilary to relate, 'in a tone which compels attention', the tragical narrative of Henri and Adolphe,[5] and Irene Vanbrugh to time Nina's third-act exit, as firm as Eliza Doolittle's, if less pungent. No Jones; yet that autumn H. B. Irving, an actor as ready, in the old professional manner, to challenge comparison as to innovate, would be showing what he could do with Wilfred Denver in the apparently deathless *Silver King*. (He had already played the part at an all-star matinee.) At His Majesty's, where the year had begun fashionably in the East, with a revival of *The Darling of the Gods*, Shaw was apparently poised between play-room and study in a 'farcical play'—not his description—*Pygmalion*; Mrs Patrick Campbell was fluting adjectivally, and Sir Herbert Tree receiving the full force of Eliza's slippers. Stephen Phillips's fading name, an echo of echoes now, had appeared once more on a programme—a weary *Armageddon* for Martin-Harvey in the following year would be the last.[6] This time it was *The Sin of David*, put on by the unwavering H. B. Irving at the Savoy. Phillips had published it ten years earlier. Before then he said to William Archer:[7] 'The subject that perhaps attracts me most—an intensely dramatic story—is banned by our sapient censorship.'

173

ARCHER: And what is that?

PHILLIPS. The story of David, Uriah, and Bathsheba . . . I suppose I should have to do as Massinger did with the story of Herod—make the characters medieval Italians or something of that sort, and so lose all the colour and character of the theme. No, I shall not do that. . . .

But he went on to a much less pictorial time and place: the Fenland in the English Civil War. It would not have pleased an anonymous writer in *The Poetry Review* two years earlier, who said sourly:[8] 'Any poet who really gets into the hands of the actor-managers may be expected to share the sad fate of Mr Stephen Phillips. That the writer of *Paolo and Francesca* should eventually fall to *Pietro of Siena* may well serve as a caution to aspiring 'dramatic poets.' In the same issue Lascelles Abercombie, himself later a dramatic poet, murmured hopefully:[9] 'Can a play written in poetry deal conveniently with contemporary life? Well, why not. . . . The practical criticism of modern life is no work for poetry; but, apart from that, I see no reason whatever why poetry should not be used for contemporary drama—as it is used in that great play, *Brand*. . . .'

If the stage had nothing of this kind in the first part of 1914, much else had happened according to plan. The romantics were unaware of disaster ahead. A modishly described 'revusical comedy' by Paul Rubens, *After the Girl*, ran at the Gaiety between February and May. A 'musical farcical comedy', *The Cinema Star*,[10] from the German and nodding to the youngest (and, to theatre-men, tiresome) art, appeared to be established at the Shaftesbury. H. V. Esmond, acting himself with his wife Eva Moore, had a comedy called *The Dangerous Age* (characters including the Marquis of Mardon and Sir Egbert Englefield). Alexander, back with Wilde, no longer a smudge on the St James's posters, was the epigrammatic Lord Goring in *An Ideal Husband*: it was the piece Henry James had seen at the Haymarket on that dreadful evening in January 1895 before he walked over to the St James's to take the booing for *Guy Domville*. Somerset Maugham, calculated man of the world, was represented by his strong-arm, Canadian-settler play, *The Land of Promise* ('The shack at Prentice, Manitoba . . . has an untidy, comfortless, bedraggled air'). A new musical by the German authors and composer of *The Cinema Star*, entitled *Mam'selle Tralala*, ran for three months at the Lyric. Israel Zangwill, a dramatist of highly embarrassing fervour, supplied *The Melting Pot* in which a young Jewish musician, composer of a symbolic symphony, falls in love with the daughter of a persecuting Russian and marries her. Esme Percy, for a few performances, played Hamlet (Gertrude, the young actress Edith Evans) in a Poel version of the Second Quarto at the Little Theatre: this was designed to emphasise the King,[11] shown as a 'pale and neat' man still in his thirties.

Much else. The golden fairies were prickly in Barker's flute-and-hautbois revival of *A Midsummer Night's Dream*. The Lyceum put on a melodrama, *You Made Me Love You*.[12] Three plays that would live for a while, for various reasons, began their runs: Edward Knoblock's episodic *My Lady's Dress*, with its detailed skirmish through the places and periods, and its three sections, 'The Material', 'The Trimming', 'The Making'; *A Pair of Silk Stockings*, amiable light comedy by the actor-dramatist Cyril Harcourt (real name, Cyril Wotsley Perkins), much happier at the Criterion than he had been at the Court; and the zestful American-Jewish *Potash and Perlmutter* (its vogue recognised by a music-hall sketch about a Mr Borax and Mr Baking Powder).[13] On a different matter E. A. Baughan—the 'Vaughan' of *Fanny's First Play*—was able to write: 'The production of Tchehov's *Uncle Vanya* [by the Stage Society], although by no means well done, was quite an event and converted many of us from our indifference to this strange Russian dramatist.'[14] There was also a stirring at a shabby old theatre-cum-social centre, massively forthright at a Waterloo Road corner. Lilian Baylis, who governed the place with a brusque single-mindedness, had been staging opera. Presently she would gamble on Shakespeare. The grimy old horseshoe among the jellied-eel stalls and the cheap cafes would turn during her lifetime into one of the most famous theatres in Britain.

Out of London the usual London plays travelled round the red-brick and terra-cotta theatres with their copper domes, crimson and green plush, cherubs and allegorical figures, curtained boxes, gilt mirrors, flock wallpapers, decorative 175 plaster-work and severely undecorative dressing-rooms. The repertory theatres were in cry (though only Granville Barker had kept experimenting in London). Manchester, which had a London season as well, did work by Pinero, Shaw, and Galsworthy, and an affectionate Jewish comedy, *Consequences*, by the young dramatist, H. F. Rubinstein. Liverpool had Wilde, Masefield, Jones, Robertson, and Pinero; Birmingham—potentially best of all as it would be during Barry Jackson's life—Euripides, Shakespeare, Shaw, Molière, Hankin. Lesser stock companies were on their toes, ready with plots enough to please Johnny Tarleton: *Good-bye, Sweetheart, Good-bye*; *The Girl Who Wronged Her Husband* (Miss Dolly Dene as Little Irene); *The Great White Silence; or, Heroes of the Antarctic*, with a character called Captain Robert Falcon; *A Mill-Girl's Secret; or, A Lad and His Lass*; and *The Woman of Death* (Amos Dubbin, Augustus FitzGibson, Sergeant Chumpler, and Flame Desborough). Most things, then, as usual: early summer concert-parties round the coast; music-halls volleying and thundering, though bothered now by the growth of revue and a steady cinema-flicker in Bijou, Elite, or Jewel, Picturedromes or Gem.

Down at Stratford-upon-Avon that spring there had been a marking-time festival, under Patrick Kirwan and not especially important. In the summer Frank Benson and his Bensonians returned from their North American tour. They had wanted to see Quebec and an extra 'date' was arranged that allowed a few more days in Canada; if they had left at once their boat would have been the *Empress of Ireland*. Laurence Irving and his much-loved wife Mabel Hackney, who had been on a three months' tour of thirty Canadian towns with *Typhoon* and *The Unwritten Law*, had also changed plans so that they could sail before their company in the *Empress of Ireland* from Montreal. Soon after midnight on 29 May, in the sheeted fog of the Gulf of St Lawrence, a Norwegian collier rammed the great liner which sank with the loss of more than a thousand lives, the Irvings among them to the intense sorrow of the profession.

II

Laurence Irving and his elder brother, H. B., were two of the Edwardian theatre's most redoubtable talents. H. B. Irving was a romantic with a progressively hypnotic authority. One recognised in him the feeling about which Gordon Craig wrote to Ellen Terry during the first world war: 'I am going to try to bring back mystery about all concerning the theatre; it used to be one of its greatest attractions and was so right.'[15] Laurence Irving had a scorching flash of genius. Besides his Iago (to Tree's Othello), his Raskolnikov in *The Unwritten Law* (his own version of *Crime and Punishment*), and his Takeramo in *Typhoon*, he offered one of the prizes of the period in Ibsen's *The Pretenders* at the Haymarket.[16] He appeared as Earl Skule, the man who would be king, without knowing a king's duties, in the 'church that stands as yet unconsecrated', medieval Norway. Skule, much of Macbeth in him, covets and gains the crown, only to fail and fall but, at the last, to hear the words of his sister Sigrid, and to 'go forth, go into the great church to take the crown of life'. Irving walked in from the Middle Ages; William Haviland, an actor forgotten now, transformed the diabolical deathbed of Bishop Nicholas. Though *The Pretenders* ran for only thirty-five performances, its memory endures.

During the years since the greatest Irving died, the English stage had been strongly garrisoned: by Tree, even if his fantasies could outrun his judgment; Alexander, kindly mould of form; Forbes-Robertson, prematurely a potent, grave, and reverend signior; Charles Wyndham, the veteran high comedian whose second wife, the actress Mary Moore, was the widow of the dramatist James Albery; Lewis Waller and Martin Harvey, romantics both, Harvey the more intellectual, Waller given to the kind of play John Drinkwater called, in another context, ginger in the mouth but a trifle deficient in grey matter. Matheson Lang was younger, powerful and picturesque; Arthur Bourchier worked too laboriously; Cyril Maude slipped across the generations (*Grumpy*, *The Flag Lieutenant*) with an ease that concealed the hard labour; and Charles Hawtrey and Gerald du   177

Maurier gave no idea that there was labour of any sort. All of these were actor-managers. Many other names belonged to the London fabric: Irene Vanbrugh, responsive to any drawing-room; her more emotional sister, Violet, married to Arthur Bourchier; Marie Tempest, whose comedy seemed to be wrought in metal; Ethel Irving, whom Pinero in 1912 described as 'the best English actress';[17] such players as Lillah McCarthy (goddess of the Theatre of Ideas); Mrs Patrick Campbell, now a kind of Brocken-spectre in the swirl of legend; Lena Ashwell, Marie Löhr, Nancy Price; Henry Ainley, who needed a Granville Barker's direction to fortify his rare voice and leonine aspect; Dennis Eadie, Norman McKinnel, Edmund Gwenn. We have already called the roll of musical comedy, a medium Daisy Ashford might have been thinking of when she wrote in *The Young Visiters*: 'You could hardly moove in the gay throng. Dukes were as nought as there were a good lot of princes and Arch Dukes as it was a very superier levie indeed. . . .'[18]

One major name is missing: Ellen Terry, who did very little in the theatre after 1908. She lives on in a tranquil glow. We know of her gaiety, gentleness, and dignity; but some of the detail of her performance has been lost in a nebulous dazzle; critics would speak of her in a shower of affectionate abstract terms. Today those who never saw her can summon her best by imagining a nonpareil of Beatrice's in the scene from *Much Ado About Nothing* (II. i. 331–41):

DON PEDRO: To be merry best becomes you, for out a' question, you were born in a merry hour.
BEATRICE: No, sure, my lord, my mother cried, but then there was a star danc'd, and under that was I born. Cousins, God give you joy!
LEONATO: Niece, will you look to those things I told you of.
BEATRICE: I cry you mercy, uncle. By your Grace's pardon. *Exit.*
DON PEDRO: By my troth, a pleasant-spirited lady. . . .

III

Most Edwardians—though some would have haughtily denied it—would have known at least the principal names of the music-
178 hall. An aggressively popular entertainment, it was always hoping

to be accepted above its station: witness the complication of jealousies at a Royal Command Performance in July 1912. Why was one artist out, another in? What had happened to Marie Lloyd? *The Times*[19] described the occasion as 'a new and signal honour . . . an honour, too, which the art has thoroughly earned by its steady progress from obscurity (not unmixed with obscenity) in "caves" and "cellars" to general favour as an indispensable form of harmless amusement housed in sumptuous palaces'. No theatrical form was so elaborately discussed. Essayists liked to choose some competent broad comedian or entertainer and glorify him, or her, in a thousand words or so. The young lions of the Edwardian *Manchester Guardian* used to exercise themselves at the local halls and expend a good deal of decorative writing on nothing in particular. Obviously there were expert performers. They lived in a world self-consciously Bohemian where they were either praised extravagantly or ignored by the people they were eager to impress. It is the extravagance that lingers, and it is not easy now to assess these legends.

We do realise that George Robey was an authoritative comedian of richly mannered relish, who in later life could drive at Falstaff; that 'Harry Tate,' from the man with the swivelling moustache, became a catch-phrase for comic chaos; that Vesta Tilley was an elegant male impersonator ('The Piccadilly Johnny with the Little Glass Eye'); that Eugene Stratton sang Leslie Stuart's coon melodies with an enchanting grace; and that such diverse figures as Harry Lauder, with his simple Scottish tunes ('Roamin' in the Gloamin'), G. H. Chirgwin (one-string fiddle; white diamond over right eye), Wilkie Bard, Harry Champion (with the voice of an inebriated buzz-saw), and Albert Chevalier (knocking 'em in the Old Kent Road), all stood, in their several ways, for the spirit of the halls. Possibly the most contentious figure was Marie Lloyd (1870–1922), whose real name was Matilda Wood, and who would be treated either as a raucous genius in her low-comedy songs or as the figure Arnold Bennett noted in his journal for 2 January 1910 after visiting the Tivoli: 'I couldn't see the legendary cleverness of the vulgarity of Marie Lloyd. . . . All her songs were variations on the same theme of sexual naughtiness. No censor would ever pass them, and 179 especially he wouldn't pass her winks and her silences.'[20] Marie Lloyd was thought to be too broad for the Royal Command. Her private life has been thoroughly explored. She has been at the centre of at least two biographical musicals. To write of her now as Bennett did would be blasphemy. What she and her music-hall colleagues did superbly was at once to capture their audiences. They had a mesmeric popular appeal; it seemed, wrongly, to be as simple as flicking on an electric-light switch. Most of the material, if it is analysed now (and no one wants to do this for long) is dire. Audiences did not mind. They wanted the personality, broad, compelling, often bizarre; the chorus song; good fellowship. Here the Edwardian music-hall and its artists never failed them.

Still, by 1914 the halls were in danger. They were imperilled by the sudden growth of revue. The cinema, once thought of as a minor turn, the bioscope, was encroaching. It had been mocked, but in 1914 the laughs were fewer. Not many would have committed themselves as a writer on Variety had done late in 1909: 'The opposition of skating-rinks and electric theatres has been felt keenly in certain quarters, but the rivalry of these forms of amusement to the variety theatre is hardly likely to be permanent and the dawn of 1910 brings with it the prospect of more settled conditions.'[21] In 1910 the cinema had even raided Stratford-upon-Avon. Frank Benson and his company made four brief films for the Co-operative Cinematograph Company, acting them upon the stage of the Shakespeare Memorial Theatre. Eleanor Elder, a Bensonian, remembered *Julius Caesar* in an undated section of her diary:[22]

We have done *Caesar*, a most trying performance, although the actual scenes ran for about two-and-a-half minutes each. We rehearse everything before we play it. Weird sights we are, too—eyelashes and lips made up, and a little rouge. Awful blinding mauve light flickered at us all the time. The flying, hurried way we got through it was quite funny; and the language too ('Give your cue and get off!) Cassius exclaimed: 'Good gracious, hullo!' When egged on to murder Caesar, Brutus made his exit, saying: 'I can't do it, you beasts.'

Towards the end of 1913 a writer insisted, with worried 180 dogmatism, speaking for the theatre at large as well as for the music-hall: 'The drama can never be affected by the popularity or otherwise of the kinematograph, for the simple reason that it has no more to do, as a counter attraction, with the living and spoken drama, than has a glove-fight at the National Sporting Club, or a Cup tie football match at that draughty, over-grown greenhouse known as the Crystal Palace. It seems rather late in the day to have to repeat the evident truth that the drama can have no enemy but the one that comes from within, and that so long as it is true to itself, and produces the right kind of play, all the picture palaces in the world can have no effect upon box-office receipts.'[23] That was whistling rather loudly. Already the Theatre of Ideas had challenged the Theatre Theatrical just as the sharp, bright radiance of electricity had challenged the more romantic glow of the old gas limes on a storytellers' stage of illusion and make-believe. Now the theatre of spectacle had to face the kinema-men who claimed to perform marvels merely by turning a handle. (Other means also: 1914 was the year of D. W. Griffith's vast film with a title that could have been taken as symbolic: *The Birth of a Nation.*)

IV

Early in August 1914 'comfort, content, delight, / The ages' slow-bought gain' vanished in a few hours, and what we call the Edwardian theatre with it. One day it would be something to look back upon much as J. B. Priestley's characters, who are living in it, do in *Eden End* from their country depths. 'Daly's,' says one of them, 'lights, and everybody in the stalls dressed, stunning girls, the band playing—and then Gertie Millar—and—oh—everything.'[24] Wistfulness would take over; outlines would be blurred.

At first in those summer weeks of 1914, playgoers had no time to reflect. They may have noticed that a Ruritanian romantic drama, *Queen at Seventeen*, faded quietly after only eight performances at the Princes: all at once there was no more room for General von Hapsburg, Princess Maritza, and Eugene von Tarlitz. A thriving musical comedy would be withdrawn because its authors were German. At His Majesty's, *Pygmalion* finished, 181

Tree hastily revived Louis N. Parker's 'patriotic spectacular play', *Drake*; all the stir of the Elizabethan adventurers, Tree himself as Sir Francis, and St Andrew's Church at Plymouth brought down conveniently to the Barbican water-front. Through the autumn the war plays arrived (*England Expects*; *The Dynasts* in sudden glory; *The Man Who Stayed at Home*); with a surge of desperate revivals (nothing, anywhere, for long). Slowly, watchers had to realise that a door was closed for ever, a garden deserted, music lost. No one moved in the drawing-room; no one from below stairs answered the bell. It was the doom of the great Edwardian house. One day another door would open; but that would be far off, in a world dimly as yet beyond the gulf.

Notes

1. *The Liars* (1897).
2. T. W. Robertson: *Caste* (1867), Act I.
3. *The Play of the Future* by Sydney Grundy, A Playwright of the Past. A Glance at 'The Future of the Theatre' by John Palmer, sometime Scholar of Balliol (1914).
4. *Ibid.*, p. 16. Grundy said (pp. 38–9): 'My generation has been attacked, my period ridiculed, my cult held up to obloquy; and when I am attacked, I defend myself. A cuttle-fish may do that. I am not ashamed of my generation; I justify the past; I indict the present. It would not have been possible without us; it has entered into our labours; where we sowed, it reaps; and it is undoing our life's work. It is living on the capital it has inherited. *It is alienating the public.* By the next generation the work of the last will have to be done all over again. The clock has been put back. On a foundation well and truly laid, this generation, in its short-sighted haste and self-sufficient pride, has reared a gimcrack skyscraper, which shakes and shivers like a house of cards; and the rain is already descending, and the floods are rising, and the winds beating; and great will be the fall of it.'
5. *His House In Order* (1906), p. 100.
6. *Armageddon*, Phillips's last play (1 June 1915; New Theatre) contained the lines for the spirit of Joan of Arc (p. 86):

> Nations at times, as men, may nobler stand,
> And finer in refusal than in act.
> Have I not seen the very stars in Heaven.
> Flash altogether at some splendid 'No'?

7. *Real Conversations*: Recorded by William Archer (1904), p. 82.

8. *The Poetry Review*, No. 3, March 1912, p. 132.
9. *Ibid.*, p. 117.
10. Musical farcical comedy from the German of Georg Okonkowski and Julius Freund; music by Jean Gilbert. Shaftesbury, 4 June 1914.
11. He was acted by Desmond Brannigan.
12. Play in four acts and ten scenes by Percy Gordon Holmes.
13. Tottenham Palace, 18 May 1914.
14. *Stage Year Book 1915*, p. 7.
15. Quoted by Marguerite Steen in her fine *A Pride of Terrys* (1962), p. 272.
16. Translated by William Archer. Haymarket, 13 February 1913.
17. *The Collected Letters of Sir Arthur Pinero*, ed. by J. P. Wearing (Minnesota, 1974), p. 247.
18. Daisy Ashford: *The Young Visiters; or, Mr Salteena's Plan* (1919), p. 56.
19. 1 July 1912.
20. *The Journals of Arnold Bennett, 1896–1910* (1932), p. 349: 2 Jan., 1910.
21. *The Stage Year Book 1910*, 'The Variety Year', p. 36.
22. Quoted in *Benson and the Bensonians* (Trewin); 1960), p. 176.
23. *The Stage Year Book 1914*. 'My Lady Kinema', by Arthur Coles Armstrong, p. 36.
24. *Eden End* (1934), Act I, p. 4.

Index

Theatres named are in London unless otherwise stated. The lists on pages 75, 92, 95, and 155–60 are not indexed.

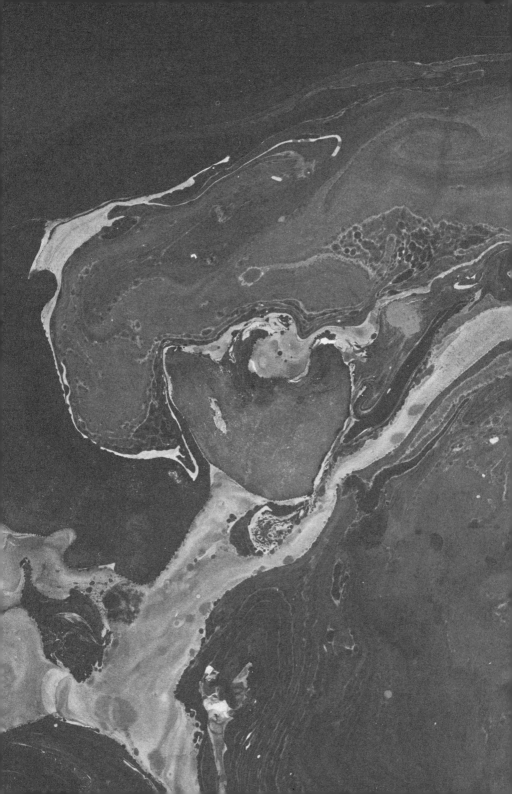